New Plays from the Abbey Theatre

Volume Two, 1996–1998

Sanford Sternlicht, *Series Editor*

New Plays
from the
ABBEY
THEATRE

VOLUME TWO 1996–1998

Michael Harding
Thomas Kilroy
Alex Johnston
Marina Carr

Edited and with an Introduction by
Judy Friel *and*
Sanford Sternlicht

 Syracuse University Press

Copyright © 2001 by Syracuse University Press
Syracuse, New York 13244–5160
All Rights Reserved

First Edition 2001
01 02 03 04 05 06   6 5 4 3 2 1

The Library of Congress has cataloged volume 1 as follows:

Library of Congress Cataloging-in-Publication Data
New plays from the Abbey Theatre, 1993–1995 / Michael Harding . . . [et.
al] ; edited and with an introduction by Christopher Fitz-Simon and
Sanford Sternlicht. — 1st ed.
        p.   cm. — (Irish studies)
Contents: Hubert Murray's widow / Michael Harding — Sheep's milk
on the boil / Tom Mac Intyre — Asylum! Asylum! / Donal O'Kelly —
The duty master / Neil Donnelly — A little like paradise / Niall Williams.
ISBN 0-8156-2699-1 (alk. paper). — ISBN 0-8156-0345-2 (pbk. : alk. paper)
1. English drama — Irish authors. 2. English drama — 20th century.
3. Ireland — Drama. I. Harding, Michael P., 1953–   . II. Fitz-
Simon, Christopher. III. Sternlicht, Sanford V. IV. Series: Irish
studies (Syracuse, N.Y.)
PR8869.N48   1996
822'.914080415—dc20   95-53289

ISBN 0-8156-2928-1 (cl.); 0-8156-0723-7 (pbk.)

Contents

Judy Friel was born in Derry in the north of Ireland and educated in Trinity College, Dublin. She is the literary manager of Ireland's National Theatre.

Sanford Sternlicht is a professor of English at Syracuse University. He is the author of a number of books, most recently *C. S. Forester and the Hornblower Saga* (1999) and *A Reader's Guide to Modern Irish Drama* (1998), both published by Syracuse University Press.

Illustrations

Introduction

The Abbey Theatre, Dublin

New Plays from the Abbey Theatre, 1993–1995, includes plays by Michael Harding, Tom Mac Intyre, Donal O'Kelly, Neil Donnelly, and Niall Williams. Here in Volume Two, *New Plays from the Abbey Theatre, 1996–1998,* it is a particular pleasure to add the names of Thomas Kilroy (who accepted the appointment of National Theatre Writer in Association in 1998), Marina Carr, Alex Johnston, and again, Michael Harding. The Abbey Theatre now also collaborates with a number of Irish and British publishers on a new single-edition programme playscript series, the Abbey Theatre New Playscript Series. This fine development was largely inspired by the success of the anthology series, coedited by Dr Sanford Sternlicht and published, of course, by the prestigious Syracuse University Press.

To look at the two volumes together and the years 1993–1998 is, inevitably, to look at the National Theatre of Ireland under the artistic directorship of Patrick Mason. On his appointment in 1994, Mason inherited an institution demoralised by the financial and artistic crises of the preceding years, and he set it on a determined course of change and sustained achievement.

He moved quickly to ask two major questions of the Abbey Theatre and to reintroduce those questions into the national cultural and political discourse. First, he looked back to the writers W. B. Yeats, Lady Gregory, and J. M. Synge who founded the Abbey Theatre, and asked what significance their pioneering ideas for an Irish National Theatre might have for Irish, and indeed international, audiences today. Second, he questioned the Abbey's title as the National Theatre of Ireland and, again, what that might mean as the century closed.

His response to these questions was to forge an artistic policy that was, in many ways, Yeatsian. The business of the National Theatre was, as he often quoted Yeats, "to bring to the stage the deeper thoughts and emotions of Ireland." Simultaneously—and this point was critical—he insisted that if the plays produced by the National Theatre did express or engage with a shared Irish experience or consciousness, nevertheless the originality of the theatre resides with one individual: the playwright.

His assertion that the Abbey's primary responsibility is to its playwrights marked a revitalizing and seamless return to what was most potent and controversial in the vision of the theatre's founders. More important, this reassurance was of great value to the numerous playwrights he both directed and produced, particularly during years that were often characterised by an antiliterary and anti-intellectual orthodoxy in quarters of the Irish media and indeed the arts themselves.

The playwrights produced during these years were often oppositional and uneasy forces in contemporary Irish culture: for some of them, the Abbey Theatre was more safe house than home. Yet the best of them, and again I would like to salute Thomas Kilroy, Marina Carr, Alex Johnston, and Michael Harding, would also instinctively understand J. M. Synge when he wrote, "In Ireland, for a few years more, we have a popular imagination that is fiery, and magnificent, and tender; so that those of us who wish to write start with a chance that is not given to writers in places where the springtime of the local life has been forgotten, and the harvest is a memory only, and the straw has been turned into bricks" (preface to *The Playboy of the Western World,* 21 Jan. 1907).

Judy Friel
Dublin

The Plays and the Playwrights

Four plays selected by the editors from the 1996–1998 seasons illustrate the amazing variety of Irish drama today as well as the brilliance of Irish playwrights, both seasoned veterans and those beginning to build reputations on the stages of the world's premier national theater, the Abbey. The plays are Michael Harding's *Sour Grapes,* Thomas Kilroy's *Secret Fall of Constance Wilde,* Alex Johnston's *Melonfarmer,* and Marina Carr's *By the Bog of Cats.*

.   .   .

Sour Grapes is Michael Harding's fifth play with the Abbey. *Strawboys* was produced in 1988, *Una Pooka* in 1990, and *Misogynist* in 1992. *Hubert Murray's Widow,* a political thriller laced with black humor and set near the border with Northern Ireland, was produced in 1993. *Misogynist* was also critically acclaimed at the 1992 Edinburgh Festival.

In recognition of his talent as a fiction writer, Harding in 1989 was short-listed for the *Irish Times's* Aer Lingus Literature Prize and the Hughes Irish Fiction Award. In 1990 Harding was awarded the Stewart Parker Award, named after one of the finest Northern Ireland dramatists of modern times. Harding was born in 1953 and lives in Carrick on Shannon, County Leitrim. He is a former Catholic priest.

Sour Grapes opened on the Abbey's Peacock stage on 9 April 1997. The play expresses the author's anger and disillusion with both the hierarchy and the general priesthood of the contemporary Roman Catholic Church in Ireland. Harding explores some of the taboos of seminary and priestly life: pedophilia and homosexuality. Harding's vision of lewd, drunken, worldly, ambitious clergy with foul mouths is shocking. The world of the play is all male, and seven of the eight men are priests, bachelors stuffed with power. They are perhaps the seven deadly sins. Surely at least individually they are prideful, lusting, covetous, gluttonous, and angry.

In the play, a new bishop, Bishop Lynam, who has come from academic life, is accused of sexually abusing one of his former seminarians, Peter, a delicate, deeply religious, saintly, sandle-wearing, mentally unstable young man. The investigation is handled very badly by the priest, Father Rehill, who is doggedly determined to find out what really happened. The process proves to be mostly at the expense of the victim. It drives Peter from abuse to suicide, and no priest in the drama is without culpability in the destruction of the youth.

Harding is very skilled at creating the milieus of the rectory and the seminary. His characters are so lifelike, so human, so believable that the drama has the ring of nonfiction. The audience is stunned into asking themselves these questions: Who may be trusted with the care of the souls, as well as the bodies, of the young? Is celibacy so unnatural as to be destructive? Does sexual torment lead inevitably to a crisis of faith? *Sour Grapes* is as current as today's newspaper.

. . .

Thomas Kilroy is one of Ireland's most distinguished writers. He has also found time to be a university lecturer and a highly regarded academic critic. He was born in Callan in County Killkenny in 1934. Kilroy was educated at University College Dublin. In the world of letters he has proved to be not only a major playwright but also a successful novelist. *The Big Chapel* (1971) received the *Guardian* Fiction Prize and the Heinemann Award for Fiction, as well as being short-listed for the Booker Prize.

Of Kilroy's many produced plays to date, the best known are *The Death and Resurrection of Mr. Roche* (1969), a character study of a middle-aged Dublin bachelor, and *Talbot's Box* (1979), a macabre drama about a religious mystic who is made "the workers' saint," and who is exploited by unprincipled manipulators. Kilroy is especially considerate of, and concerned for, working-class and lower-middle-class people who are lonely and suppressed and who feel themselves to be outside of the system.

Kilroy has also written an outstanding Irish history play, *The O'Neill* (1969), about the sixteenth-century Irish soldier and hero Hugh O'Neill, the Earl of Tyrone, who sojourned briefly in the court of Queen Elizabeth I, and who, for a while, was her most successful Irish antagonist. More recent plays include *Double Cross* (1986) and *The Madam MacAdam Travelling Theatre* (1991).

The Secret Fall of Constance Wilde opened in the Abbey Theatre on 8 October 1997. It is an historical drama, a Greek tragedy with masked attendants as a chorus, and a Yeatsian Noh play with puppets and Kabuki effects. A three-hander about a love triangle, it is a haunting drama.

Constance Wilde was Oscar Wilde's wife and the mother of his two sons. When they were married in London in 1884 the wedding was one of the most fashionable and talked about social events of the year. She was twenty-six, beautiful, highly educated, and wealthy; he was twenty-eight and already a celebrity. The marriage, which at first was happy and close, changed with the birth of the second son. Wilde seems to have lost interest in heterosexual love.

In a few years Wilde, who had begun frequenting male prostitutes, then referred to as "rent boys," met the beautiful but unstable would-be poet Lord Alfred Douglas, nicknamed Bosie, and they became lovers. In 1895, just after his brilliant success with *The Importance of Being Earnest,* Wilde in the second of two trials was convicted of sodomy and sentenced to two years in prison at hard labor.

Early in that fateful year for the Wilde family, just before the theatrical triumph and the two trials, when Constance already knew of the relationship between Oscar and Bosie, she suffered a mysterious fall down a flight of stairs when alone in her Chelsea house. She severely injured her spine. Was it an accident? Attempted suicide? Self-punishment? An attempt to expiate feelings of guilt over some perceived flaw or wrongful act? Had her father, a man once arrested for indecent exposure, abused her? Regardless, she was partially and permanently disabled, and the accident hastened her death in 1898, two years before Oscar's. She was only forty years old at the end of her life.

Constance's fall symbolically foretold the tragic fall of the artist at the hands of the philistine establishment that also led to the destruction of her family and her early death. Thus, the tragedy of Oscar Wilde was also a woman's tragedy. She lost her home, she and her children were sometimes engulfed by mobs, and she changed their name from Wilde to Holland. She visited Oscar in prison and settled money on him. But she denied his access to the children. Fathers were not to be trusted. Indeed, the play opens and closes with Oscar begging his wife to let him see the children.

In *The Secret Fall of Constance Wilde,* Constance is retrieved from literary history and a minor role in Oscar's story. Kilroy dramatizes her tale of imperfect human nature in a series of confessions concerning her relationship with her husband and, vicariously but inevitably, with his lover. She reveals the deepest, darkest secrets of her unhappy, possibly abused childhood as a means of purgation, and in the end she realizes that the man she married is the man he is, and what does that say about herself? Kilroy brilliantly explores gender roles, sexual ambiguities, and familial discourse—all clearly reflecting on our own time. Kilroy has written a woman's worst nightmare.

The woman's tragedy is private and quiet; the man's is loud and public. Oscar is Christlike, sacrificed for and by the philistines. The kiss of betrayal is Bosie's. Douglas is given his due as Kilroy portrays him as selfish, manipulative, and very cruel. Did Oscar, the man of continual self-invention intent on center-stage martyrdom in the theater of the world, ever really answer Constance's question in the play: "But what about the cost to others?"?

The Secret Fall of Constance Wilde is sure to be performed again and again in the years to come, and to have a long life as a literary text. It is an example of Irish dramatic writing at its best, and it is another great achievement for Thomas Kilroy.

.   .   .

Alex Johnston's play, *Melonfarmer,* opened on the Abbey's Peacock stage on 15 October 1997. The author is the grandson of the Sean O'Casey-era playwright Denis Johnston. Alex Johnston was born in 1970, son of an Irish father and an English mother who took him to live in Ireland in 1973.

Melonfarmer (the title is a euphemistic slurring of a curse) is Johnston's first with Ireland's National Theatre. Johnston's mission as a writer is to write with irreverent humor about the contemporary Dublin scene and the lives of young Irishwomen and Irishmen trying to adjust to the confusing social patterns of the new, less religious, sexually liberated, urban Ireland. In this regard Johnston has spoken of "a certain naïveté in the younger me, regarding the whole distinction between art and life."

Melonfarmer is an iconoclastic work. The traditional well-made play of nineteenth- and early-twentieth-century bourgeois drama and the constrictions of classical drama are not for Johnston, who has stated: "I couldn't understand the convention of unity of time and place—how often in life does anything get sorted out in one location and within a couple of hours?"

The interlocking lives of a varied group of eight morally adrift young Dublin women and men, all of whom are groping to make human contact with others, are presented episodically and fragmentarily in this comedy-drama. Thus, the subject of *Melonfarmer* is the difficulty of human communication in the mad pace and pinball-bumper contacts of urban society. The point-of-view character is Sean Spence, a would-be entertainer in his late twenties who weaves his way through a Nighttown that is both funny and foreboding. His descent is into drunkenness and depression.

Johnston is very skilled at quick characterization and funny dialogue. He has a good ear and a sharp eye. Revealing and provocative conversations are almost like phone calls. Vignette situations are hilarious, and the total effect is a satiric, slice-of-life representation of the twenty-somethings social zeitgeist in Dublin, a weird, sometimes threatening terra incognita for most members of the typical audience for professional theater: middle-class people in middle age.

Yet we can readily believe Johnston's men and women. There is angst but not existentialism. They are unburdened with deep philosophical symbols. There is little self-pity or soul-searching; they just get on with living as best they can, which is not so well.

In its irreverence for traditional social values and dramatic theory, *Melonfarmer* plays as if it may bring a new and missing generation to the theater. That is a good thing and a necessary denouement. So, hurrah for drink, drugs, and rock and roll! Not to mention masturbation, lesbian love, and of course straight sex. *Melonfarmer* is Dostoyevsky-like, notes from the Dublin underground, a playground where grown children are waiting for they know not what.

. . .

Marina Carr, born in 1964 and brought up in County Offaly, is Ireland's leading woman playwright. She has had a meteoric early career. She is thirty-seven years old at this writing. Her plays have had successful runs in Dublin at the Abbey, London at the Royal Court, and in New Jersey at the McCarter Theater, beginning with *Low in the Dark* (1989), and continuing with *The Deer's Surrender* (1990), *This Love Thing* (1991), *Ullalo* (1991), the smash Abbey hit *The Mai* (1994), and *Portia Couglan* (1996).

Marina Carr is a dramatist who writes passionately about passions. Naturally, women are at the center of the drama, whether they are active or passive in the patriarchal society in which they endure, sometimes survive, but seldom triumph. As is frequently the case in

Carr's dramas, men are almost incidental. Frank McGuinness has said of Carr's work: "I love her plays for the light they cast on darkness." The darkness illuminated may be the primitive cruelty and archetypal vengefulness, also the potential in relations between women and men.

By the Bog of Cats opened at the Abbey on 7 October 1998. The play was Carr's first production on the Abbey's main stage. It is an intense, profound, and poetic tragedy of brutal Irish rural midlands life in which money and land outweigh all other values. As in a Brian Friel or a Martin McDonagh play, the local priest is troubled and totally ineffective. The barbarism of the people is archetypal. The terrain is fiercely hostile. The pervasive bog symbolizes the pull of the prehistoric past on the trapped present. Ultimately, however, the subject of the play is death.

Living beside the peat bog is Hester Swane, a woman in her forties, once a caravan traveler, who has an illegitimate daughter, seven-year-old Josie. The father, Carthage Kilbride, ten years younger than Hester, is about to marry a wealthy woman ten years younger than he is. They plan to take Josie away from her mother. Hester is desperate to prevent the marriage because she still loves, wants, and feels bound to Carthage. Most of all, she does not want to lose her child. Furthermore, she is simply not a woman equipped for submission.

Carr has studied Greek tragedy, for the drama contains prophecy from a bird, as well as from a visitor from the spirit world named Ghost Fancier, and more prophecy from a Teiresias-like Catwoman, blind, unwashed, and a devourer of mice. Because classical tragedy requires that the audience knows from the beginning what is the fate of the protagonist and the nature and extent of the catastrophe, the Ghost Fancier, the angel of death, informs Hester and us of her impending doom. But most classical of all is that Hester is an Irish peasant Medea, an outsider, a sexual threat, a savage revenger. Her frustration, anger, and hatred lead her to madness as well as death. The young bride's big, mean farmer father is like Creon in *Antigone,* proud, powerful, and controlling but unable to alter fate. A house is burned, animals are brutally sacrificed, and human blood pours out onto the bog. The tragic foreboding and foreshadowing are so thick that one could cut them with a fish knife, and in the play there is terrible cutting with such a knife. Of course, the events of the play take place within a day, conforming with the central unity of time.

Carr, perhaps intuitively, conflates melodramatic Jacobean tragedy, that bloody theater of cruelty, with the Aristotelian. *By the Bog of Cats* evokes the horrific wonderment of Cyril Tourneur's *Revenger's Tragedy* (1606).

Unlike classical Greek tragedy, but like Jacobean tragedy, *By the Bog of Cats* has humor. It comes in the form of two female characters who would seem at home in a Beckett play: the Catwoman and Mrs. Kilbride, Carthage's mother, the meanest grandmother in creation, who wears a wedding dress to her son's wedding in commemoration of her incestuous feelings for the man who slept in her bed when he was a boy. And the disastrous wedding celebration scene is deliriously funny, a father-of-the bride's nightmare. The comedy, of course, provides extension of, and relief from, the tension and suspense of the tragic plot.

The politics of *By the Bog of Cats* are about gender and sex. The current sword dancers of Belfast, Dublin, and Westminster might just as well be tripping in Timbuktu for all their effect on Bogland: ancient, timeless, rural midlands Ireland, where women may be as violent in their self-interest as any feline, and where they endure a purgatory that will lead not to salvation but damnation.

Like all great tragedy, *By the Bog of Cats* exists on the cosmic and the human levels simultaneously. Forces are at work that are beyond human understanding. Good is absent. Compassion is nonexistent. Love is primitively possessive, whether it is sexual or maternal. As Eric Bentley states, the ultimate vision of the tragic world is "an unmitigated horror." Because of its fearful symmetry and torrential power, *By the Bog of Cats* may be one of the most significant plays ever written by an Irish dramatist.

· · ·

As the twenty-first century makes its entrance from the wings, the world continues to watch with fascination and admiration the growth and development of a theater tradition begun at the start of the twentieth century by William Butler Yeats, Lady Augusta Gregory, and John Millington Synge in a tiny theater in a building on Lower Abbey Street that had once served as Dublin's morgue. Irish playwrights today are international stars, and their plays command attention and inspire brilliant productions in New York and London as well as Dublin. Australian, Canadian, and New Zealand productions are frequent. The plays are read and performed on the European continent and in Asian and African countries too. The future is bright for Irish dramatists as they continue to produce their inspired, profound, and socially committed contributions to world theater.

Sanford Sternlicht
Syracuse

The Plays

Michael Harding.
Courtesy Amelia Stein.

Sour Grapes

MICHAEL HARDING

1997

Original Cast

Pat Laffan	Clive Geraghty
Shane Hagan	Barry Barnes
Tom Murphy	Andrew Bennett
Frank Laverty	Terry Byrne
Director: Brian Brady	

Characters

CANON ADAM BAILEY

BISHOP LYNAM

PETER

FATHER REHILL

CIARAN

DERMOT

NIGEL

MR. HANRATTY

The play is set in Ireland in the recent past.

ACT I

The stage allows for a number of playing areas, all simply represented, with perhaps a single prop or stick of furniture for each place and each having an isolated pool of light. Upstage: some gothic arches. The cloisters of a seminary.

A large door. The space is a cloistered area. Cool and grey. Dominated by fish-bowl on a plinth, slightly upstage, slightly stage left. All the scenes are played against the persistent backdrop of the cloisters.

Scene 1

The Canon is alone.

CANON. I know you're out there . . . God . . . you and your angelic associates. And your young lad. And your communion of saints, martyrs and virgins . . . Like a great shoal of fish . . . and you see the sad little bunch of frightened men we call the clergy. Up to their necks in the shit. Why don't you do something? Intelligent life force me arse . . . a goldfish could run the universe better than you. We have finally reached the moment, when the bishops . . . the bishops are being accused of tampering with children. *(Laughs.)* Imagine. A bishop. Playing with the little boys. And they have the gall to come to me . . . to help them with their inquiries. Me. The fools.

Scene 2

Lynam, in Episcopal soutane and trappings, walking in the cloister, pursued by Peter.

PETER. Father . . . Father . . . please.

BISHOP. I am no longer Father Lynam. I am no longer a professor in this college.

PETER. My Lord Bishop . . .

BISHOP. That's better. Now what do you want? What do you want? Someone could see us.

PETER. I just wanted to congratulate you.

BISHOP. Now listen, Peter. You were a student and I was a teacher. That was different. You understand?

PETER. No.

BISHOP. We had a friendship. I may have been a bit . . . informal . . . with you. But not anymore. It's finished. I'm a bishop. Now get away from me. *(Smiles.)* As they used to say—get behind me.

Canon observes this and laughs.

CANON. What's this? My new bishop. Well well, and how is the hat fitting, sir?

BISHOP. Don't mock me, Canon Bailey. This is not a parish pantomime. This is a seminary.

CANON. Of course sir. And I'm a parish pump ignoramus. Well go on. Go on. *(Gestures him to move.)* Go on!

BISHOP. Go on what?

CANON. Let's see you walk. I've always heard that seminary men who became bishops walk like turkey cocks. I'm sure we could find out now.

BISHOP. Canon. I am your superior now. And the Church has its rules. So kindly observe them.

CANON. Like fasting from meat on Good Friday. And what does the seminary serve its professors instead? Let me guess. Fresh salmon. Yeah. Who's the boy?

BISHOP. I haven't a notion. I'm not expected to know every bloody student in the college. Am I?

He walks off, huffed, observed by the Canon for any resemblance to a turkey cock.

CANON. He's in a bad mood.

PETER. Hello, Canon Bailey. It's nice to see you again.

CANON. Who are you? Ohhhhhh Peter. Peter. Peter. Peter. Little Peter. Ahhhh. So this is where you are. And it's only like yesterday I gave you first Holy Communion. It is nice to see you.

PETER. How is everyone at home, Canon?

CANON. Everyone at home is very well, Peter. And very happy. Listen! Mind yourself up here! They're a bad lot up here! Don't ever forget that.

Fade.

Scene 3

Rehill grooming his hair at mirror in his room while someone knocks on the door.

REHILL. Come in.

Peter enters.

You know why I have sent for you?
    PETER. Yes, Father.
    REHILL. I am the dean here in the seminary. I am the keeper of good order.
    PETER. Yes, Father.
    REHILL. What age are you, Peter?
    PETER. Sixteen, Father.
    REHILL. Mmmmmmmm. You come here to the seminary . . . and then . . . before a year is up, you claim that this . . . professor, this priest, interfered with you. Sexually.
    PETER. Yes, Father.
    REHILL. Well, Peter. I want you to be assured. I want you to rest assured. We are looking into it.
    PETER. But Father.
    REHILL. *(Having put on a stylish raincoat.)* That will be all, Peter. Thank you.

He vanishes.

Peter alone becomes distressed and speaks in whispers.

    PETER. Dear God. Dear Jesus. I felt I had a vocation. Thought being a priest would be cozy. Spiritually cozy. Like a new car. With soft upholstery and bucket seats. A winter's night lashing against the windscreen. And inside, I'm gliding, dry and silent, in a capsule of buttons and green lights.

Rehill in a separate space, sneering.

    REHILL. And where would you go?
    PETER. Home. From the seminary to the west. In a new car. From here to the heart of Ireland.
    REHILL. You'd hate Ireland. Miserable little towns in the dark, with wet and empty streets, closed down cinemas, and streetlamps illuminating the litter of late-night chip shops.
    PETER. Is that you, Jesus?

REHILL. The countryside dripping wet ditches, and puddles of flooding water encroaching from the flooded fields. The misery of it. And past all the country and western lounge bars of the universe, where thick peasants go for refuge. No. You wouldn't like that at all.

PETER. But a priest floats through it all behind the windscreen of a good car. The engine purring. The heater blowing dry air. And the radio blasting night music from the BBC.

REHILL. Oh, yes. Floating through it all in blissful ignorance. The cockiness of it. Never bothering to read the road maps and going helter-skelter in the wrong direction. If priests got mileage expenses they would have bankrupt the Church years ago.

PETER. (*Kneeling.*) Oh, most Blessed Mother of Christ. Can I tell you a secret? What if . . . I love men. What if . . . I knew it even as a little boy. But the priest told me it was evil. And I trusted him. And then he broke his own rules. And touched me. Most pure virgin, hear my prayer. I need you. This Church confuses me.

REHILL. (*Entering Peter's space.*) Forgive me, Peter. I heard a voice, I thought there was someone with you in here. Is there anyone with you in here?

PETER. I was praying.

REHILL. Yes. That's obvious.

PETER. I need to pray, Father. I'm frightened. I feel bad.

REHILL. Well you have made very serious allegations, my boy. Against a member of our staff. Bad enough. But this member of staff has this very day been appointed a bishop. Now how does that make you feel? Thing is. How are we to be sure you haven't some ulterior motive? Are you a sexual pervert perhaps? I must search your room. Must see your diaries. Must examine your pyjamas. Do you pray enough? Do you pray too much? We must investigate everything. Come here, boy.

He has opened Peter's laundry bag, which the boy had been holding, and tosses everything on the floor. He has now discovered a flashy fishnet vest.

What is this, for example? Is it a vest or a lobster net? What is the meaning of something like this?

PETER. No. No. No. No. No. No.

Peter rushes away frightened. Fade.

Scene 4

Canon Bailey in his old armchair. A globe of water on the plinth now high-lighted. Upstage, at door, stands Rehill.

CANON. You're late. You said on the phone—teatime. It's almost midnight.

REHILL. I took the wrong turn after Kinnegad. Went over fifty miles in the wrong direction before I realised it.

CANON. So you're stupid. Well, there you are. I was wondering who they would send.

REHILL. If it's too late, Canon, I could return some other evening.

CANON. No no no. Don't be ridiculous. The Grand Inquisitor can hardly be expected to pander to the feelings of an old parish priest who wants to get to bed.

REHILL. I'm not an inquisitor, Canon.

CANON. No? Are you not? But it has come to this.

REHILL. To what?

CANON. You. Here. Me. And it's not just an ordinary priest they've got for the dock this time. Is it? No. Not even a little Christian brother. Or a nun. No. This time they've got the big fish. A bishop in the dock.

REHILL. There's nobody in the dock. Yet.

CANON. They've got what they wanted.

REHILL. Who?

CANON. How could you lose your way? All those enormous road signs. European money of course. You know that.

REHILL. Sorry?

CANON. The road, Father. The road. It's practically a motorway from here to Dublin now. An eegid could find their way.

REHILL. Look, Canon. These allegations against the bishop. They're extremely grave. We're . . .

CANON. Roads for Europeans.

REHILL . . . obliged to examine them. The boy in question . . . is being . . .

CANON. BMWs. Lancias.

REHILL . . . monitored. Anyone whom he may have confided in is now being questioned.

CANON. Mitsubishis.

REHILL. That means you. So you will oblige me with your coop-eration.

CANON. How long have you been dean in the seminary now, Father?

REHILL. Almost four years. Why?

CANON. Oh just wondering. The way you talk. Sort of odd. Like a civil servant. Or someone on the wireless. Very educated. Or groomed or something. Very . . . nice.

REHILL. Canon, do you consider sexual abuse to be a serious mat-ter?

CANON. Put a tune to it and I'll sing it. Of course I do.

REHILL. And does it bother you that so many of our brother priests have been shown to be criminal in this matter?

CANON. You're talking like the wireless again.

REHILL. The boy told us he confided in you. Said you were the one we should be talking to. For the truth.

CANON. He's not a boy. He's a young man.

REHILL. Sixteen.

CANON. Nonsense. He's much older. Must be eighteen now.

REHILL. And he was sixteen when he first made the allegation.

CANON. Ahhhhhhhh. So he was in the seminary at the time this is supposed to have happened. Well there you are.

REHILL. There you are, where?

CANON. Why couldn't you have investigated it then? And not now? Before they made him a bishop? That was silly. Why couldn't you have nipped it in the bud? If you seminary people were doing your jobs right . . . I mean . . . I'm sorry . . . but this has nothing to do with me.

REHILL. I don't have a lot of questions, Canon. His allegations may be corroborated by things he confided in you. Or indeed you may know something more, that would let the bishop off the hook. Do you?

CANON. They're out there you know. Make no mistake about it. At the other end of that motorway. And when they bring him down, they'll be on the telly for weeks. Cackling and chattering. Glee writ-ten all over their faces. That's what this is really about. Isn't it? But of course, they don't have to bring down the bishop do they? Because we are going to do that for them.

REHILL. Who are 'They,' Canon?

CANON. You know damn well who. With their fancy hairdos, and their padded shoulder pads and their high heel shoes.

Fade.

Scene 5

Rehill prays alone. As he does so, Peter appears to him, barefooted and slightly altered in appearance.

PETER. Wrong about me, weren't you?

REHILL. I couldn't imagine it. Not here. His hands on your body. Couldn't see it. You had to be making it up.

PETER. Go down to my hometown, I said. Ask the old canon. He'll tell you what happened. But all you did was poke your nose in my underwear. And now I'm just a ghost. To haunt you for the rest of your life.

REHILL. I remember you describing it to me. One night in winter you said. No moon. Snow on the ground. Not a sound in the night. The dry texture of his old withered tongue on the nape of your neck. Not possible I thought. Not in my seminary. Not in my church. No one here could . . . could not happen. I delayed. And in the meantime they made him a bishop. Oh Jesus Christ.

PETER. You did nothing. Because you were brooding. You were looking at me in that sleazy way priests have of looking. In your own funny little way. You were jealous.

REHILL. You were always a ghost, Peter.

Peter vanishes.

Peter. You were always a phantom.

Fade.

Scene 6

Canon pointing at the gold fishbowl.

CANON. See this thing? Used to keep it in the bathroom. Found it helped. When I couldn't sleep. Talk to the goldfish. You see?

REHILL. But it's empty.

CANON. Yes, I know. I know it's empty. Now. He's dead. I talk now to a dead goldfish. My absent friend. And in his absence, he is ever present.

REHILL. The metaphysical poets.

CANON. Good. You're following me. Alright. I'll tell you. Here's what I know. He was from this parish. Peter was his name. No interest in football. None whatsoever. And dangerously good looking. An artistic type. But I must admit . . . devotional as a child.

REHILL. Actually, we know all that.

CANON. He'd have the church ablaze with penny candles underneath the statue of the Blessed Mother. I was always terrified he'd burn the place down. Always wore a miraculous medal. That sort of thing—but that's all I know. And that's all I'm ever going to say about the boy. So what does the bishop say?

REHILL. I'm afraid I can't tell you that.

CANON. Young lads today. Don't take enough exercise. Lie through their teeth. Stick their pricks up the water spout if it would fit. Am I right?

REHILL. Why did you become a priest, Canon?

CANON. I wanted to say Mass.

REHILL. We all wanted to say Mass.

CANON. But it's the truth.

REHILL. It's an evasive answer.

CANON. I wanted to say Mass. Alright? That was all. To offer the holy sacrifice at the dressing table in my mother's room, with a ladies' lace handkerchief and a jewelry box. Isn't that good enough?

REHILL. No.

CANON. Wouldn't get me into the seminary nowadays would it?

REHILL. A nod in the direction of God wouldn't go astray.

CANON. Sentimental.

REHILL. Pardon?

CANON. Nods in the direction of the Divinity.

REHILL. And they told me you had a soft spot somewhere, if I could find it.

CANON. All that tenderness for God. Young curates parading their affection for the Almighty, on the altars, as if God was their best mate. Sentimental.

REHILL. I see.

CANON. I doubt it. You'll find no soft spots here, Father.

REHILL. Not even for your brother priests?

CANON. I feel nothing for my brother priests.

REHILL. Why is that?

CANON. No reason.

REHILL. Most of them think you're a bollix.

CANON. When I was ordained, Father Rehill, we didn't join a club for friendship. I was ordained to offer a lifetime of service to the Church. A lifetime of loyalty.

REHILL. I see.

CANON. You don't. You see that bowl?

REHILL. Yes.

CANON. It's empty.

REHILL. There's water in it.

CANON. I mean, there's no fish in it. Alright?

REHILL. Alright.

CANON. They taught us at the seminary that there is a difference between Love, and Justice.

REHILL. Go on.

CANON. In Love, I give the fish what belongs to me. But in strict Justice, I only give the fish what belongs to the fish. So what do you make of that?

REHILL. Nowadays the Church stresses Love.

CANON. As the be all and end all.

REHILL. Your generation are out of date. You were taught to rely too much on justice alone.

CANON. To revere Justice. And why?

REHILL. Because doing justice to one's fellow man is safer than tampering with the woolly concept of love.

CANON. You amaze me, Father.

REHILL. Thank you.

CANON. It wasn't a compliment. Look. I fed the fish. My food. See? So that was an act of love. Yes?

REHILL. If you say so.

CANON. I do. And one day I stopped. No more food. It was my food. According to moral theology, I did no injustice to the fish. Correct?

REHILL. Get to the point.

CANON. I had no obligation to feed him since it was my food. So I watched him starve to death. Ha. Ha. Now what do you make of that?

REHILL. You've gone off fish.

CANON. Have you any notion in your head just how long it takes a goldfish to die? He got dizzy in the end. Bumped against the glass a lot. Old Mogodon Eyes I'd call him. I put him beside my bed, with my digital clock alongside, so I could see him hovering over the dark. It was nice in bed, to know he was there. Sometimes I would wake up and wonder . . . is there a God, in the dark? And then I would say . . . no. No. Just a fish. I found that strangely comforting.

Fade.

Scene 7

Peter watching Rehill.

PETER. Don't forget, Rehill. You never did anything to help. Remember. When I first went to you.

Peter moves into the memory. He becomes ill. Vomiting. Rehill assists him.

Ohhhhhh . . . ahhhhhhhh . . . dirty fucking bastard.

REHILL. Alright. Alright. Take it easy.

PETER. The dirty fucking bastard. I remember the ornaments. On the mantelpiece. A brass elephant god from India dancing on its hind legs. A little statue of Saint Patrick. Glossy green.

REHILL. Who was it, Peter? You must tell me.

PETER. Oh no. I name someone, and you would say don't be ridiculous. And you'd say I've no proof. And then where would I be? I'd be the one in trouble.

REHILL. Was it the professor?

PETER. It was a shadow. Like God or Christ behind me. Promising me. Promising me everything.

REHILL. You cried wolf before.

PETER. 'Get me a glass of water from the bathroom,' he said. And I went and then I saw him in the mirror behind me. Taking the water. Wiping his lips on his shirtsleeve. I dream of him now. Shouting. Choking me. Like an animal feeding. Like a God. Jesus help me. Jesus protect me. Jesus have mercy on me . . . ahhhhh.

REHILL. Peter. Who are you accusing?

PETER. No. Get away. You did nothing.

REHILL. You tell me a different story every time.

PETER. I'm confused.

REHILL. Was it a member of staff? Was it your friend? The professor? The one they say will be the next bishop?

PETER. No. No it wasn't. I'm afraid.

REHILL. Just tell me, Peter. Was it him?

PETER. Ask the canon. Ask Canon Bailey. He knows. I'm not accusing anyone. I'm just saying, you ask the canon. Ask him. He knows.

REHILL. I can't walk into some canon down the country and ask him, like excuse me, but could you give us a bit of juice on the bishop, Canon?

PETER. *(Releasing himself from the memory.)* You see? You did nothing. All the time, when I was trying to tell you. Until it was too late. And you wouldn't ask the canon anything because you were terrified of him.

Fade.

Scene 8

Return to scene of Rehill and the Canon's discourse.

CANON. You're the dean, aren't you?

REHILL. As well you know. But it's me came to ask the questions, if you don't mind.

CANON. Nobody comes to ask me questions,

REHILL. I came for your help.

CANON. That's better.

REHILL. And as it's not forthcoming, I think I'll go. We can arrange another meeting in the city. At your convenience.

CANON. Never go to Dublin. Too much crime. The car wouldn't be safe on the street.

REHILL. Then at the seminary perhaps.

CANON. Haven't set foot in that place since I was ordained.

REHILL. Fine. Then forget it. It's for you to decide. Maybe you are being loyal to the bishop. Or maybe you are just protecting him. Good night.

CANON. Tell me, Father. The men you're turning out of the seminary these days: are you proud of them?

REHILL. I'll let myself out. I think it's still raining.

CANON. They're soft. They wouldn't have got next or near the altar in my time.

REHILL. I think we've heard all that. Your generation found it difficult to show their feelings. The emotional vocabulary of senior parish priests in the country is not very nuanced, is it?

CANON. Oh we're getting tetchy are we? Well, shite to you too Father. Shite. There. I can show my feelings quite well thank you very much.

REHILL. I was speaking in general.

CANON. You were speaking as if you were in a group therapy session.

REHILL. How would you know?

CANON. Our generation were soldiers of Christ. This crowd is more like a rash on the Mystical Body.

REHILL. You're making a point, Father?

CANON. Yes. I am.

REHILL. What is it?

CANON. I'm on your side.

REHILL. Not exactly as obvious as daylight.

CANON. Priests were different in my time. The Church was different. And bishops were very very different. Better men. Oh yes. I remember one old fellow. From Cork he was. If you only saw the way he genuflected before the tabernacle. If you only saw him, even in his eighties. Well. The back as straight as a young ash plant. You see?

REHILL. Yes. I think so.

CANON. They were different. Not schooled in the same universe as some of these younger modern bishops. That's the point. Do I make myself clear? I am trying to help.

REHILL. I understand. Forgive me. I know this can't be easy for you.

Peter enters.

PETER. You couldn't just ask him a straight question could you?

REHILL. I was trying to coax him.

PETER. Rehill. This thing before your eyes is the last remnant of the blackthorn-stick clergy. This is the parish tyrant who accepts God, reluctantly, as his equal. And you're afraid to upset his feelings?

REHILL. No, wait a bit. Just wait a bit. There was something very strange about you, Peter. Just look at yourself. Too much flamboyance in your attire. Too much individuality. I used to think, so what are you trying to do? Draw attention to yourself? And remember that evening I caught you grooming yourself?

PETER. You had no right to walk into my room.

Peter turns into his room. Rehill follows, sniffing the air.

REHILL. Oh dear, oh dear, Peter, all these perfumes, and deodorants, and aftershave lotions. Goodness. Just what does it all mean, Peter? That's what I ask myself.

PETER. I'm leaving the seminary Father.

REHILL. Good. All for the best. May I ask why?

PETER. I don't have a vocation. I'm going. I think I have personal problems. I need to work them out. Good-bye. *(He leaves.)*

REHILL. Good-bye.

Fade.

Scene 9

Canon staring at Ciaran, who is dressed in an apron over clerical suit, and working the ground with a dustpan and brush.

CANON. How long are you ordained now, Ciaran?

CIARAN. Two months, Canon.

CANON. And you're sure you did the right thing?

CIARAN. I hope so, Canon. Am I doing something wrong?

CANON. I've been watching you say Mass. You move around the altar like you were presenting a cookery programme on the TV.

Ciaran returns to industrious work.

Now stop that, Ciaran. It's just that, you see, my crowd was the bare-floorboards generation. Football jerseys. Whiskey and poker on a Friday night. Your lot are all carpets, compact discs. Woks. Pastas. Aerosols and aprons. Dustpans and vases of aquilegia. I said stop that. You're getting on my nerves.

CIARAN. I don't want mice in here. I had mice once in the seminary. I lived with them all over the place. In the wardrobe. Under the bed. In the clothes. I know what it's like.

CANON. Ciaran. You are a mouse. Gimmie that thing. *(He swipes the brush and pan.)* What is this? Mouse shite? Here. *(He flings it across the room.)* What's the point in sweeping up mouse shite? Think about it. You're walking round after a mouse, cleaning up its shit. When you ought to be out in the parish, visiting the sick people and the old people. You ought to be visiting the hospital. Or what do they train yous for in the seminary nowadays? I just don't know.

CIARAN. This is intolerable. I'm a grown man. I'm twenty-six. You have no right to call me a mouse. Or to throw that in my face. I'm not to be bullied. You were told that. You are not to bully me. *(He exits.)*

CANON. Ciaran. Ciaran.

Fade.

Scene 10

Rehill walks to where the Canon is standing.

REHILL. I understand that your curate made a complaint against you.

CANON. You're barking up the wrong tree, Rehill. My curate complained about everything.

REHILL. But he went to the bishop about you.

CANON. He went to the bishop about everything. If the altar boys had snots in their noses, or if they didn't polish their shoes he went to the bishop. Always running with tales. Pure eegid.

Fade.

Scene 11

The Bishop at his desk on the telephone. Ciaran sheepishly at the door. The Bishop waves him to come in as he continues his telephone call.

BISHOP. No. No, it's out of the question. Your newspaper wouldn't dare publish allegations against me. Sorry? Oh well, as I said to your colleague earlier, it's not for the bishop to speculate on what might or might not come before the courts. *(Aside.)* Arsehole. *(To phone.)* No. I said . . . it's a goal. Yes. I'm watching the match. Pardon? Yes I know it was yesterday. Did you never hear of a video? And the same to you. Good-bye. *(Finishes with telephone.)* Fucking journalists. Oh, excuse me, Ciaran. What can I do for you?

CIARAN. I'm very depressed, my lord. I just can't go on with that awful parish priest you sent me to. He frightens me. It's affecting my mind.

BISHOP. Ciaran. This month you are unhappy with your parish priest. Last month it was the landscape. You're pestering me.

CIARAN. But the place is a wilderness. I didn't know rural Ireland was so remote. And the people . . . they're utterly . . . uncouth.

BISHOP. You're going through a rough patch, Ciaran. Happens to the best of us. A bit of stormy weather, as we used to say. You'll get over it. Now let yourself out.

CIARAN. He's a bully, my lord. He shouts in his sleep. You can hear him all over the house. He murdered the goldfish. My lord, I'm really, really, really, terribly depressed.

BISHOP. Well get tablets or something. No. Talk to a priest. Yes. That's what you do. Have a little chat with your priest. You must know lots of them. But don't bother me. I'm the bishop. I have monumental depressions. My depressions are of such proportions that your entire life assumes, for me, the magnitude of . . . mouse shite.

He laughs. Ciaran cries.

Just a joke. Oh Ciaran . . . get out . . . please.

CIARAN. Yes Bishop. I'm sorry for taking up your time. I'm sure this little chat will be of great help. Thank you.

BISHOP. No problem. After all that's what I'm here for.

Fade.

Scene 12

Return to scene of Rehill and the Canon's discourse.

CANON. And you have no right to go asking that young jackass anything about me. I'm not under investigation here.

REHILL. But they say the new bishop despises you.

CANON. Do they?

REHILL. You pester him.

CANON. I do not.

REHILL. You barged into his house one afternoon, when you thought he was away. He found you snooping in his office.

CANON. *(Moving into the Bishop's office.)* I was looking for marriage documents. He was always forgetting to send things in the post. *(Searches the desk.)* They must be here somewhere.

BISHOP. Can I help you?

CANON. Oh. It's you. I thought you were in Dublin.

BISHOP. Get out of my office.

CANON. Goodness, Bishop. You look pale.

BISHOP. I'm marking your card, my boy.

CANON. And you've got puffy lips. You're not well, Bishop. I can tell.

BISHOP. Have you entirely lost the run of yourself, Bailey? What are you looking for?

CANON. Prenuptial forms. The blue ones. Look. I'm sorry, son. It doesn't work.

BISHOP. What doesn't work?

CANON. Seeing you in that fancy hat and bellyband. Doesn't have any effect.

BISHOP. You are a parish priest who owes me obedience, respect, and loyalty. Is that crystal clear?

CANON. Well I can give you loyalty, my lord. And even obedience. But I draw the line at respect.

BISHOP. I'm going to the bathroom. Just be gone from here, when I come down again.

CANON. *(After the Bishop's departure.)* I'm warning you, Bishop. Puffy lips. Not a good sign.

REHILL. Father Ciaran says you bullied everyone. Teachers. Altar boys. The parish council. The ladies' football team.

CANON. Don't give me Father Ciaran as an authority on human psychology. That bastard was warped in the cradle. Look. His mother died when he was seven. Alright. He said I bullied him. But what does he do? He gets moved to the other end of the parish, where he has a house all to himself. And what's the first thing he does? He invites his father for a weekend. You'll rue the day you let your father inside that door I said to him. If it's independence you're looking for. Oh yes, the father came alright. But he hasn't left since. *(Laughs.)*

Fade.

Scene 13

Ciaran sleeping under a duvet centre stage. The Canon's voiceover whispering in his ear.

CANON. Ciaran. Ciaran. Ciaran. You're sleeping very deeply, Ciaran. Wake up. There's a mouse running riot on your pillow and he's dropping his turds all over your face. Ciaran. Ciaran. Ciaran.

The voice of the Canon is replaced by that of the father.

FATHER. Ciaran. Ciaran. Ciaran.

CIARAN. What? What is it?

FATHER. There's someone on the phone. I think it's the hospital.

CIARAN. Yes, Da. It's probably a sick call Da, if it's the hospital.

FATHER. I think it might be the hospital. But I didn't like to waken you.

CIARAN. Did they say it's the hospital?

FATHER. They did. But I said it was very late in the night to be phoning.

CIARAN. Then it's the hospital. Tell them I'm coming.

FATHER. Oh, I can't do that son.

CIARAN. Why not?

FATHER. Well it's morning, son. They phoned about five hours ago.

CIARAN. *(Shouts.)* Jesus.

Fade.

Scene 14

CANON. Don't try to interrogate me, Father. It's not what you came for. Oh, you think you can come down here and look down your nose at the simple old parish priest with his bottle of whiskey. That, Father, is truly the pot calling the kettle black—when I think of the reports we get about the seminary. The drinking and carousing of Ireland's future priests. I believe that in Senior House now, things are so hectic, that the younger students have renamed the building . . . Farmhouse. Why is that, Father? Eh? Why? An inordinate interest in horse racing have they? Eh?

REHILL. It's all lies. There is absolutely nothing wrong with the seminary. Nothing. It is a peaceful, prayerful place. It is an oasis of quietude and serenity in a turbulent world. And the young priests of tomorrow are steady men. Whose gaze is firmly on the other world of higher things. Their feet are firmly on the stepping-stones that lead to the distant shore.

Fade.

Scene 15

Cloisters of the seminary. Nighttime. Dermot chasing Ciaran with thurible swinging. Both dressed in black trousers, coloured jumpers and anoraks.

DERMOT. Yahoo. Yahoo.

CIARAN. Stop it.

DERMOT. Yahoo. Come on me boy. Circle them wagons and git

them thar wimmen under covers boys. Before ah comes and takes them offa ya.

He catches Ciaran and wrestles him to the ground, and affects raping him.

CIARAN. (*Upset.*) Get off me. For fuck sake. You silly bastard.

DERMOT. It's just a bit of fun, Ciaran.

CIARAN. What if the dean heard us? Or came round the corner?

DERMOT. We're senior students. We're finished all our exams. We're going to be ordained in a few weeks. If he did come round the corner I'd tell him to fuck off. We can do what we like now. Catch us with women! He couldn't touch us. We're being ordained.

CIARAN. (*Brushing himself down.*) I'm going to bed.

DERMOT. Ciaran . . . we agreed. Down to the village for a few pints.

Nigel enters, with coat, scarf and umbrella.

NIGEL. Are we all set then?

CIARAN. I'm not going. I don't feel like it. Good night. (*He exits.*)

DERMOT. He's a right prick.

NIGEL. No, Dermot. He's just nervous.

DERMOT. What has he to be nervous of?

NIGEL. Ordination.

DERMOT. Well, that's really ridiculous. I mean, who ever heard of someone being nervous of ordination? It's only a ceremony. Nobody is going to bite him.

NIGEL. Your confidence in Our Lord Jesus Christ is breathtaking, Dermot. Ordination doesn't take a feather out of you, does it?

DERMOT. I'm definite about things, Nigel. I have faith. I see the truth. I don't have worries. If I should walk in the valley of death, no evil would I fear. The Lord is my shepherd.

NIGEL. Yes. Ciaran reads too much Albert Camus. Too much Hegel. And Heidegger. Makes him iffy.

DERMOT. The correct attitude to ordination is to go to the church, let the bishop do the talking, go to the hotel, offer your little speech and thank your mother. And then get scuttered drunk.

Nigel is staring at him in amazement.

NIGEL. Well done, Dermot. You're a man of almost undiluted courage. You never have to think twice about anything. In fact, you never even have to think even once about anything. It's truly remarkable.

DERMOT. Are you making fun of me Nigel?

NIGEL. But Ciaran is a cripple in comparison. Crippled with doubts. You ever notice him in the refectory? Never eats his fries. No sausage. Or rasher. Never. Doubts their nutritional value. You see? Iffy. And a danger to himself. So come on.

Nigel about to leave.

DERMOT. Nigel?

NIGEL. Yes?

DERMOT. Who is Albert Camus?

NIGEL. Albert Camus is a neurological infection against which God has completely immunised you.

Fade.

Scene 16

Canon alone in an isolated pool of light.

CANON. Oh yes. Well I must admit, I do remember, yes, the bishop . . . I must admit, he did, know the boy. Ohhhh yes. It was in Lourdes. They met at Lourdes. He wasn't a bishop then. Just on the edge of it. It was a diocesan pilgrimage. Went out from Knock Airport. All the young girls in wheelchairs. Well of course, we, the other priests, we let the big shot from the seminary lead the troops. On the plane he led the rosary after the flight lunch, and he stood at the front of the bus from the airport into Lourdes itself. Were you ever in Lourdes, Father? Of course you were. The cream-walled houses, with salmon-coloured roofing. The wooden shutters. The warm steamy rain. I was in Hotel Florida. A mustard building. On the street below young people from all over the world, in plastic raincoats and plastic hats. I went down to the grotto. I couldn't sleep.

Pat Laffan in *Sour Grapes*.
Courtesy Amelia Stein.

He moves to the grotto where the Bishop, in a black clerical suit, is seated on the bench. The shed of tall candles dripping and flickering.

You could almost see him praying—Mother of God, I'll do anything you like—only please, please, make me the next bishop of my diocese.

He joins the Bishop on the bench. They say nothing. For a moment they are absorbed in the silence.

BISHOP. You know, they say, the pope, when he can't sleep at night, he goes across from his apartment to Saint Peter's and he goes all the way up into the dome with a pair of binoculars. And just sits. For hours. He can see the entire city, north, south, east and west, from that dome. Funny isn't it. What people do when they can't sleep.

CANON. There's rumours that you're going to be the next bishop.

BISHOP. I certainly hope not. I hope and pray. Not. Not. Not me Lord.

CANON. What would you be afraid of?

BISHOP. Oh it's not a question of fear. No. But I'm not the ambitious type. I'll be happy if I end up a simple parish priest, like you.

CANON. A question of—may this chalice pass you by, eh?

BISHOP. Something like that.

CANON. You should spend less time canvassing.

BISHOP. What?

CANON. You know. After Mass this morning. The way you went round shaking hands with every priest in the diocese. You looked like a politician.

BISHOP. Can I tell you something, Adam?

CANON. Certainly.

BISHOP. Mary. See? Here. Our Blessed Mother. Unlimited compassion. Here. Under her protection. Adam. Whatever sins we are afflicted with, we can leave them here. And ask forgiveness.

Peter, in raincoat, soaked, enters, and kneels on tarmac with great piety. Blesses himself and prays. Both men watch him for a while.

CANON. Ambition is not the biggest sin that comes to mind. *(He rises.)* I'm going to bed. Good night. I'll pray for you. Pray for all of us.

He goes. Then the light fades on the Bishop and the boy.

Scene 17

The cloisters of the seminary. The door opens and Dermot enters furtively. Late at night. Nigel follows slowly, carefully. They are returning from the night in the pub.

In the distance there is a faint scream. A disturbed dream perhaps.

DERMOT. Scary place this, at night.

NIGEL. Dermot, you're not afraid of ghosts are you?

DERMOT. Afraid of the friggin dean. Here. Let's go into the chapel and get up on the pulpit and give an old sermon. Just for practise.

Another scream.

NIGEL. Shhhhhhh.

DERMOT. What was that?

NIGEL. Be quiet.

They both look down the cloister into the darkness. Suddenly Peter comes running across their path, muttering and distressed, and bumps into Dermot.

Dermot and Nigel are startled.

Peter vanishes with the speed of a rabbit.

Dermot and Nigel watch after him.

I'm going to do it, Dermot. I'm going to spill the beans on Professor Lynam.

DERMOT. Nigel, you're not suggesting . . .

NIGEL. He's a bit too friendly with that young fella. Do those phones work? *(Indicating phone on the wall.)*

DERMOT. Of course they work. Nigel. Lynam is not worth it.

NIGEL. And what about the young fella? All I'm going to do is phone the dean. When he picks up the phone I'll tell him what I know.

DERMOT. Which is nothing. And how do you know the dean is in bed?

NIGEL. I saw the light in his room as we crossed the square.

DERMOT. You can't handle the fact that he didn't give you first class honours, can you?

NIGEL. What? Do you think I would do something like this out of jealousy?

DERMOT. Yeah. Revenge. It had occurred to me.

NIGEL. And how long has that little nugget of twisted logic been up your arse Dermot? How long?

DERMOT. Ah fuck off. You haven't the slightest bit of proof. Good night. *(He exits.)*

Scene 18

Return to scene of Rehill and the Canon's discourse.

CANON. I'm seventy-one, Father Rehill. All this sex—children— priests—it's difficult for our generation. You know I had a soft spot once, for a young woman. I was just ordained. She taught in the school. She asked me to go the whole way with her, as we used to say in those days. I cut her off. Hurt her terribly. She wrote me a letter, calling me a reptile. Still have the letter somewhere. Eventually I had to get her removed from the school. The only way. And now? You see? What's happened to the Church over these last few years? Amazing. But it makes me regret soooo much.

REHILL. Should you have left the priesthood back then? Married her?

CANON. No Father. Probably not. Probably I should have left her at the school, and enjoyed it. Like they all do now. But you see I was loyal. Loyal to the Letter of the Law. I'm utterly crushed and disillusioned when I hear about all this . . . *(whispers)* abuse.

Peter appears in white shirt and hovers close to Rehill. Only Rehill sees him.

REHILL. Canon, whatever agony we may have to go through, it will pass. The TV and the newspapers may come for a day to our door. Or a week. But they'll go again. And we can continue, as we were. As brother priests.

CANON. Of course we can't. This is different.

REHILL. We have been found out.

CANON. Yes.

REHILL. So we too are sinners.

CANON. Who are you talking about?

REHILL. Us. The clergy.

CANON. *(Laughs.)* You know it was us was trying for centuries to eradicate sex. Like it was TB in cattle or something.

REHILL. We may have been wrong about that. After all, with Galileo, we were wrong about the universe.

CANON. I've started wearing polo neck jumpers. When I'm in public. I'm ashamed.

PETER. I'm losing my patience with you, Rehill. This is getting us nowhere.

REHILL. Will you please give him a chance? Can't you see what this is doing to him?

PETER. I'm the one that suffered, Rehill. I'm the one shivered with fear at the sound of a footstep so that for months, the piss ran down the legs of my trousers. I'm the one ended up with belly cramps so severe I couldn't hold down food. Don't tell me what it's doing to him.

REHILL. Get out of here. Just get out. I'm sick of you. And your selfishness.

PETER. You're all the same, aren't you? You still haven't a clue about the people yous fuck up. You just never ever listen.

REHILL. No, sorry, you're the one couldn't forgive. And that was your downfall. You're the one just wanted vengeance. Consumed by the desire to get someone. Anyone. For everything that was ever wrong with you.

PETER. Getting annoyed again, Father Rehill? So what's your problem?

CANON. Christ of Almighty. When you think of all the nuns and brothers. The generations of sacrifice. Did they look for anything? Bungalows or central heating? No.

REHILL. It's not quite that black and white, Canon.

CANON. It is. They just hate us Rehill, hate. Do you understand? Priests. Christ. God. It's all the same.

REHILL. May I be less formal? May I call you Adam?

CANON. They're out there you know.

REHILL. Adam. We are brother priests. We share at the table of the Last Supper. And because of that single fact, we must support each other. Your burden is my burden.

CANON. They're plotting and conniving.

REHILL. We feel cheated. We feel as if they had stolen our most precious jewel.

CANON. There's battalions of them, legions. All lined up against the Church. And 99 percent of them is women.

REHILL. Okay. Okay. Sometimes . . . it can seem like that.

CANON. You agree?

REHILL. No. Not exactly. But you're hurting. And whatever you feel, it's valid. Let go of your anger, Adam. Get rid of it.

CANON. Get a fucking grip on yourself, Father Rehill. You're blathering. My mother died when I was ten. I was reared in institutions. Do you hear me blaming anyone? I'm probably alcoholic. But I do my job. There are hundreds of people out there who have let me down. But do I complain? No. So now my own church lets me down. And you tell me to let go of my anger. To get rid of it. Just like that. You see we quenched any little tenderness we might have felt for women. Because we were told to. We crucified ourselves for this 'church,' only to be told at the end of our lives that the goalposts have changed, and that we should all be in fucking therapy.

REHILL. Alright, Bailey. I'll tell you. I'll tell you something for nothing. You're full of shit. And you want to make my job difficult. Fine. We'll play it the hard way. But I will win. Remember that. I will win.

Fade.

Scene 19

The grotto. Bishop still on bench staring at Peter, who kneels. Canon staggers back.

CANON. Here. Shouldn't you be getting back to your hotel? It's cold out here.

The boy leaves. Both men watch him leave.

Do you sit out here all night?

BISHOP. No.

CANON. She doesn't communicate with you or anything like that? No? Is there something you're not telling us?

BISHOP. I was at a funeral last week. An old friend.

CANON. Yes. I know. Father Reilly. Very sad. Did away with himself didn't he?

BISHOP. Walked into the lake. Clutching his briefcase.

CANON. And no one saw him?

BISHOP. It's not something you do when people are watching is it? Kill yourself.

CANON. So how do you know he was clutching his briefcase? Ha ha.

BISHOP. His dead hand was still locked around the handle when they dragged him out, three days later. He was a good man. He would have made a fine bishop.

They remain in place for next scene.

Fade.

Scene 20

Dermot drunk comes downstage and faces audience. He is wearing a chasuble very casually over his shoulders.

DERMOT. Well, I just can't wait to be ordained. Can't wait to get into one of these things. (*Peers out into the audience.*) Nigel. Nigel. You know what your problem is? You don't let go enough. You're tight arsed. You see, I'm a mixer. I'm the priest of the next century. I was out there at a party tonight. All lay students. Women. Yes. No problem. And I'm in the kitchen, right? Beer. Whiskey. No problem. And there's this one, feminist. Goes round in a pink Toyota Corolla if you don't mind and she's blathering to everyone about women priests for fuck sake. Was only doing it to get at me. I know that. So what do I do? Nigel. I say what do I do? I turns to her and I says, Come here Miss. Why do you go round in a pink Toyota says I. Is it to make a point or something? And do you know, Nigel, she fairly lost the head. I mean, she was going to have my blood on the walls there, I can tell you. You, she says. Ye little fucking cleric. I can't stand yis, says she. Yis are thinking of girls when yous are saying Mass, and thinking of Mass when yous are wanking. You're incomplete before God and incomplete before the world. Yis are half men. But you see what I mean, Nigel? I mix. Talk to them. That's the only way. Talk to them Nigel. Nigel. Is that you Nigel?

Rehill enters.
Ahhhhhhh. Father Rehill.

REHILL. I won't ask you what this desecration is about at this hour of night. Just go to my office immediately and wait for me there.

DERMOT. Yes, Father.

Fade.

Scene 21

Nigel lifts telephone. Dials number. We hear it ring out. Canon appears alone.

CANON. I was a boy. I knelt at her bed until they came with the coffin and took her away. When the funeral was over I came back, closed the door, found one of her old lace handkerchiefs and a little silver jewelry box. And I pretended to say Mass. Odd, isn't it, how we can pick up a vocation?

REHILL. There have been allegations. Which implicate the bishop. They're not new. Now, we know that the young boy in question confided in you over the years. We need you to tell us.

Peter appears in a separate space and suddenly screams. Rehill goes to him.

PETER. He surprised me. I can't remember. I don't know. I'm not sure. I forget. I'm not certain. It was the bathroom. It was in the bath. He undressed me. He made me undress. He took a shower. I took a shower. He sponged me down. My body was cold. He put the water on. I was in the bed. I was lonely. I trusted him. I went to him for help. I didn't believe it was happening. I was naked and he was kissing me. Help me please. Help me. Who is going to help me?

Phone ringing out.

It answers. We hear Rehill's voiceover as we see Nigel on the other end.

REHILL. Hello. Father Dean speaking.

Fade Nigel on phone.

Fade everything but Canon.

CANON. I have worshiped a dead fish that hovers over the darkness. A huge dead fish that waits for us all. And he hath spoken unto me, this fish, and he hath said— *(Sings.)*
The inchy winchy spider climbed up the waterspout
Down came the rain, and washed the spider out. *(Laughs.)*
But behold. I did not listen to him. For I was fox-trotting. On the *Titanic.* That's what it felt like. For years. Saying Mass. Like fox-trotting on the *Titanic. (Laughs.) (Sings.)*
Oh the inchy winchy spider climbed up the waterspout
Down came the rain and washed the spider out
Up came the sun and dried up all the rain
And the inchy winchy spider climbed up the spout again.

Up music, as the Canon dances.

END OF ACT I

ACT II

Scene 1

Rehill is in the seminary. He is arranging papers in a folder. The Bishop enters. He watches Rehill for a moment without speaking. The Bishop is furious.

BISHOP. You wanted to see me?

REHILL. I'm just sorting copies of some transcripts—previous witnesses—for the Board of Inquiry. It's all got very legal now, Bishop. Hasn't it?

BISHOP. Get on with it, Rehill. I'm busy.

REHILL. You do appreciate the gravity of this inquiry, Bishop? Don't you?

BISHOP. Completely. And I hope you do as well. For when this is over, your career here in the seminary is going to look like shite on a slate.

REHILL. The boy was totally mad, Bishop. You ought to have kept away from him.

BISHOP. Look I took him under my wing. He was having difficul-
ties. It happens.

REHILL. You took him, 'under your wing.'

BISHOP. Grow up, Rehill.

REHILL. You were a professor here in this college. You had your
responsibilities to act at all times professionally and never, never ever,
become intimate with young seminarians.

BISHOP. We weren't intimate. Whatever that is supposed to
imply.

REHILL. Of all the boys you could have approached. You had to
choose . . .

BISHOP. You're not listening. I did not approach him.

REHILL. You had to choose the one single fruitcake in the entire
seminary. You had to choose someone by the way who was underage
for Christ's sake. And mad. Mad. Mad. Mad. Off his trolley. Why
Bishop Lynam? Professor Lynam. Why? He wasn't playing with a full
deck.

BISHOP. Then what the hell are you questioning me for? Get him
a psychiatrist.

REHILL. Jesus. Bishop. Isn't that the point? Are you that stupid
that you don't see? Wasn't it obvious to you, when you were display-
ing all your fatherly affection to this 'child,' wasn't it obvious that
sooner or later, he would be sitting on a therapist's couch somewhere,
blabbering it all out? Now. Won't that be interesting?

Fade.

Scene 2

*Peter in isolated light. Barefooted and in soutane. A bunch of flowers in his
hands. He looks up and out towards the Virgin Mary.*

PETER. Look what I've got. I pinched them. From the infirmary.
Hope the nuns don't mind. They're for you, for your feast. For today.
The Assumption of Mary into Heaven.I honour thee above all others.
On this day. When thou were taken up into the clouds. *(He kneels.)*
Beyond this, my locked door, there is a corridor. Echoing with foot-
steps. And outside my window, there, is the tall spire. The wind bat-
ters the crows about the spire. But I am safe here. Blessed Mother. I

honour the day when thy body was enfolded in white fluffy clouds and the sun shone on thy face as you rose into the sky. I can still see thee. As if rising from the Altar of the Great Chapel. And I see thee now above the spire. I see thee over the rooftops, among the crows. Mother. Queen of Heaven. Come to me. Come visit thy servant in this room. Now.

Fade.

Scene 3

Continuing from where Rehill and the Bishop left off.

BISHOP. Father Rehill. The world is full of closet faggots. The church is full of embryo faggots. Tiny little unborn urgings that we are prohibited from letting loose because they are considered as sexual disorders. Instead it all gets sublimated into flip-flop sandals, cardigans, and wristwatches worn back to front. And. Occasionally. Peculiar devotions to the Virgin Mary. You don't need a psychiatrist to tell you that.

REHILL. Would you like to hear what his therapist suggests?

BISHOP. I'd love to.

REHILL. It says here that . . . he has a fascination with purity and innocence which he identifies with the female, Mother of God, and so on. He also displays deep self-loathing. He is by nature homosexual. And would most likely have developed a normal and healthy self-image as such, were it not for the probability that he was . . . wait for it . . . sexually abused sometime in his teenage years. An incident perhaps about which he is as yet unable to talk, due to the repressive nature of his Catholic faith. What do you think of that?

BISHOP. Fascinating. Psychobabble. Jungian Freudian horseshit. Let me give you the view from the summit. He believes in the Assumption of the Virgin Mary. We all do. Mary got old. Got fed up being wheelbarrowed round the streets of Ephesus by Saint Paul. She was bored. She had no alternative. One afternoon she dozes off to sleep. A fog comes in the window. Envelops her. And carries her off. Nothing could be more natural. And we all believe it. Tell that to his therapist.

REHILL. He identifies with the Mother of God because she found peace at the end of her pain. The boy is in pain. According to his therapist there is a danger he would seek a similar resolution to his pain.

BISHOP. What? That he'll float out the window? Spare me your flirtations with psychiatry Father.

REHILL. Okay. Did I mention that he has been providing very vivid, dare I say, colourful, accounts of his liaison with you?

BISHOP. Oh?

The light fades slightly. Both men remain still.

Scene 4

Peter downstage alone, separate from Rehill and the Bishop.

PETER. He would wait for me in the cloisters. In the shadows. After evening prayer.

Bishop moves to him.

BISHOP. Peter.

PETER. Who's that?

BISHOP. We can't talk here. Someone might see us. But come up to my room tonight. After solemn silence. Tell no one.

PETER. We would sit on his sofa.

Bishop arranges himself on a seat. Peter joins him. Sitting on the floor. A physical relaxed closeness between them.

Listening to Handel. Looking out the window onto the square. The Virginia creeper. The roses. And at night the lights in the other windows around the square.

BISHOP. What you say, to a ride, in my car? (*Laughs.*)

PETER. Yes.

BISHOP. An aeroplane perhaps.

PETER. Oh yes.

BISHOP. Paris. London. Cardiff. (*He takes from his pocket tickets to a rugby match.*)

PETER. In Paris he wore perfume and oil in his hair. And everywhere we went he kept his arm around me. And on the plane back to Dublin he was cold and he told me to say I was his nephew.

BISHOP. For God's sake, I took him to a rugby match once. That's all.

PETER. I didn't know it was wrong. Until one morning at the altar, I saw Our Lady. She appeared. Hovering over the tabernacle. In her shining white dress, and gazing into my eyes. And I felt ashamed. And I knew I would have nothing to do with him.

Fade.

Scene 5

Leaving Peter, the Bishop reengages with Rehill, who continues his investigation.

BISHOP. So some creep of a therapist is going to make something of that are they?

REHILL. That's the world we live in, Bishop.

BISHOP. Don't talk to me about the world we live in. I know all about it. Shall I tell you something? I went to a chemist this morning. Right? Why? Ask me why.

REHILL. Why?

BISHOP. For a particular type of mouthwash. I happen to have a mouth ulcer. I would not have gone to the chemist for any old mouthwash. I could have bought any old mouthwash in a supermarket. I have a sore mouth. I wanted something serious.

REHILL. I'm not entirely understanding your line of thought Bishop.

BISHOP. I have a preference. I pay for it. I am entitled to my choice.

REHILL. If you don't feel well enough to continue this meeting, we can always take a break and resume after tea.

BISHOP. Listen to me. Three hundred years ago the pope could keep a concubine in the cellar and a chaplain in the attic and receive services from both in his bedroom. That's the sort of world he was living in. So what do you say to that?

REHILL. And did the popes of ancient days have mouth ulcers? Is that the point you're coming to? Or did they not? I'm afraid you're losing me.

BISHOP. You're not listening. I went to a chemist because I wanted one particular brand.

REHILL. You've made that point.

BISHOP. And what does she say to me? They're all the same. Well fine, Miss. Let's not be fussy. Yeah? Relax! Don't get yourself in a twist over something as trivial as mouthwash. That's what she was saying to me. That's what she meant.

REHILL. Your oral hygiene is remarkable my lord. But what, may I ask, has it to do with this inquiry?

BISHOP. People tell me not to be neurotic about my teeth. Fine. I'm telling you and your fucking inquiry not to go getting yourselves all neurotic and high and mighty about a few tickets to a rugby match, or the fact that I took him to France. I was a member of staff. He was a student. It was normal. Right? To use your own words—it's the kind of world we live in.

REHILL. Is that the only place you ever took him on a trip?

BISHOP. Of course.

REHILL. He's also mentioned Cardiff. London. Armagh. Bantry. Inniscrone. In fact . . . all over the place.

BISHOP. Okay. Okay. I took him a few other places. I was friendly. But don't think some little therapist is going to pin anything on me.

REHILL. No one has to pin anything on you. The boy is pressing charges.

BISHOP. Yeah?

REHILL. He's taking us to court. You see we had to expel him. He was unsuitable for the priesthood, and . . . he has decided to go to solicitors.

BISHOP. You expelled him. Are you a complete fucking eegid?

REHILL. Sorry?

BISHOP. You know what you are? A mandarin, a church 'official.' You don't believe Mary was assumed into heaven. You probably don't believe Christ rose from the grave either. But your job in life is to maintain an image. Do you know who your Christ is? Your Christ is a dead cadaver that rots and stinks and smells. But you keep him in a glass case, with aerosols and golden vestments. And hope that if the audience is kept far enough away when you wheel it about, then no one will notice.

REHILL. The boy claims that you threw tantrums. Went into rages and kept him in such fear that he was prepared to submit to your sexual cravings.

BISHOP. Utter horseshit.

REHILL. Says you threw him out of a hotel room one night in Galway. Threw him out onto the corridor. Stark naked. He had to go down to reception with a potted plant between his legs.

BISHOP. Mother of Jesus.

REHILL. I understand there was evidence from other witnesses.

BISHOP. Look, Father Rehill, all these documents, evidence, therapist's reports, all of it. Why don't you get them all, and put them in the fire? Give the boy a few pounds. Set him up for life. But please. We have more important things to do. You have more important things to do with your life. Please. It's not true.

Fade.

Scene 6

Peter enters a space in underwear and socks.

PETER. I was wearing a miraculous medal. I liked the image of Our Lady around my neck for protection. And one night he saw me wearing it. I was coming out of the bathroom, and he just went into this terrible rage.

BISHOP. Sweet Christ what is this?

PETER. It's a miraculous medal.

BISHOP. Right. That's enough. Here. Take your clothes. Here. Go on. Get them on. And out. Get out of this room, now.

He flings things at Peter.

PETER. But why?

BISHOP. Don't you see? It's over. Our friendship is finished. I never want to see you again. I never want to hear anything more about you. Okay?

PETER. It's only a medal. Look, I'll throw it away if you really want me to. What am I doing wrong?

BISHOP. What are you doing wrong! You're sick! Do you know!

Sick! You need to sort yourself out lad. You know what I'm talking about? Good. Come on, out, out, out, out, out. Get out of here.

Throws him out.

REHILL. You're denying the incident.

BISHOP. No. I'm not.

REHILL. You flung him out. Naked. Onto a corridor in a public hotel. What more do we need?

BISHOP. Oh you need a whole heck of a lot more. Listen to yourself. He was naked. Right? That's the point. I was at a meeting downstairs. Right? I have this student with me for the weekend. Bit of a break for him. Twin beds mind. I come up after a few drinks. Tired. Only to find him at the bathroom door. Undressed. Undressed. And in a manner and pose that left no doubt as to his intentions. So I threw him out. I only hope you would have done the same.

REHILL. Mmmmmmmmmm.

BISHOP. So think again, Rehill. Think again. If you're trying to stitch me up with this.

REHILL. Perhaps. Unless there were other nights. Hundreds of nights. Or hundreds of other boys. Were there? Bishop? Other boys?

BISHOP. Ask me arse.

Fade.

Scene 7

A garden seat outdoors at Ciaran's curacy. Ciaran is chasing cattle with a stick.

CIARAN. Go on. Hup. Outa that. G'way. Get out of here.

He has successfully chased them back through the gap and secured it. He flings the stick after them in a final gesture of rage.

Dirty smelly filthy beasts. Get out of my sight.

He slumps onto seat and suddenly realises where he has put his foot.

Ahhhh. Jesus! Bloody fucking cow shite.

Ciaran's father appears, very upset and excited.

FATHER. Ciaran. Ciaran. Ciaran. Where are you!

CIARAN. No. This is too much. It's just too much. This is terrible.

FATHER. Ciaran.

CIARAN. What?

FATHER. What are you doing out here? It's going to rain.

CIARAN. I'm chasing cows, Da.

FATHER. And what are you doing that for?

CIARAN. Because it's my job, Da. It's what I was ordained for.

FATHER. Oh now, Ciaran. There's no need for that kind of sarcasm to your father. *(He turns to go.)*

CIARAN. Dad.

FATHER. What now?

CIARAN. What did you want?

FATHER. Want?

CIARAN. You came out screaming. You must have wanted something.

FATHER. Oh yes. It's the parish priest. The canon. He's been in a car crash.

CIARAN. You're joking.

FATHER. One of the nurses rang. I told her you were busy.

CIARAN. A car crash. He's not dead by any stroke of luck?

FATHER. It happened this morning, she said. On his way to Mass. Ran over two little girls on their way to school. They're in comas. The canon has fractured ribs. And his head is all bruised. And his car is ruined.

CIARAN. Jesus. I better see how he is. See how the little girls are. See their parents. Sympathize. Jesus, the fool. Why couldn't he just hit a tree and kill himself?

FATHER. Where are you going?

CIARAN. To the hospital.

FATHER. Excuse me. I have your dinner ready. I'm not a skivvy you know. There's people at the door all morning. I had to sign a dozen Mass cards in your name, and the women from the yoga class phoned to say make sure and announce that the classes are beginning on Tuesday night, and now, I have your dinner in the oven and you tell me you're going off somewhere.

CIARAN. Did you not hear what you said? The canon has had a car crash. There are children on their deathbeds.

FATHER. No one said they were dying.

CIARAN. I have to go. I must go. I'm his curate. This is an emergency.

FATHER. And you've been sitting here waiting for an emergency since you were ordained. Look. I told you, I was talking to the nurse on the phone and I said, tell the canon that Father Ciaran is having his lunch and that he'll be in to visit the patients later in the afternoon.

CIARAN. Oh Christ of Almighty.

FATHER. Ciaran. I can't run the house on my own if you keep taking this attitude.

CIARAN. No one asked you to run it.

FATHER. By God, if your mother was alive to hear you talk like that. I only came to put up the pelmets for the curtains. Tidy the rosebushes. A new priest, you expect him to have standards. At the very least to have curtains. What are people to think if you don't have curtains? But I know when I'm not wanted. I can go home in the morning.

CIARAN. Nobody is asking you to go home. Now shut up before I . . . (He *slumps onto garden seat, crying.*)

FATHER. Is there something the matter, son? You're upsetting yourself.

CIARAN. I was promised, Dad. Once I was ordained. I could finish my studies. Just get ordained, they said. And everything will fall into place.

FATHER. And so it has. You're here.

CIARAN. Ciaran, the bishop said. What do you have in mind? So I told him. I says, the previous bishop just before he retired, he said I could finish my studies. My Ph.D. Is that a fact? he says. Is that a fact? Sure you'll have plenty of time to finish your studies where I'm sending you.

FATHER. And wasn't he right? Can't you do all the studying you want here, up in your room?

CIARAN. I didn't spend eight years of college studying philosophy just to mind cows in the arsehole of nowhere.

FATHER. No. You spent eight years studying to be a priest. So you'll do what you're told. Now come in for your dinner. *(He exits.)*

Fade.

Scene 8

A coffin on a trolley is wheeled in by Nigel in clerical suit with purple stole round his neck and a prayer book in his hand. He prays over the body. Dermot sneaks up behind him. They talk in whispers.

DERMOT. There you are.

NIGEL. Shhh. The parents are outside. She died a few hours ago.

DERMOT. Oh I see. I was passing these two nurses and I says, 'How's the girls?' And they said—'One of them's dead.' And I says 'What?' And they says Father Nigel is out in the morgue with her now. I mean I was just saying how's the girls, like, to the nurses. I mean, how's the girls. I didn't know anybody was dead.

NIGEL. Dermot. Shut up. I'm nearly finished.

He solemnly anoints body with oil and pockets the small silver vessel for oil. Closes the book. Closes the coffin. Turns decidedly to Dermot.

So, what sort of trouble are you in now?

DERMOT. Well you see there's this hotel right? Just outside town. You can have a quiet drink without meeting people from the parish.

NIGEL. The Glen View. I know it.

DERMOT. Yeah. Well anyway. It's owned by this amazing woman.

NIGEL. Jasmine Mulcready.

DERMOT. You know her!

NIGEL. Pink trouser suit, matches the pink curtains. Blonde hair. Eyelids in blue and gold. Not a spring chicken.

DERMOT. No. Well anyway. Last Saturday I had a wedding, right? Got scuttered drunk and she gives me the key to a room and insists I sleep it off.

NIGEL. Wouldn't dream of letting you drive home under the influence.

DERMOT. Precisely.

NIGEL. Go on.

DERMOT. Well this is . . . I mean you'll not believe . . . anyway. About an hour after I fell asleep . . .

NIGEL. Yes?

DERMOT. I woke up.

NIGEL. Go on.

DERMOT. That's it. That's it. Isn't that amazing? I stayed in a hotel. Yeah. Overnight.

NIGEL. And you realised that Jasmine Mulcready was lying on top of you, massaging your testicles.

DERMOT. Jesus Christ, Nigel! How did you know that?

NIGEL. Ah well. There lies a story. But how did you get rid of her? (*Pause.*) Dermot. How did you get rid of her? (*Pause.*) Oh, Dermot. Oh, no.

DERMOT. Frig it, Nigel, she said she had a diploma in massage. Said I was very tense.

NIGEL. Dermot. How long are you ordained now?

DERMOT. Three months.

NIGEL. I see. So you have discovered at last that life can be more erotic than the damp football jerseys on a wet Saturday had led you to believe. Wonderful. You've reached puberty. Enjoy it.

DERMOT. But she's old enough to be my mother.

NIGEL. Oh, is she. Well, go elsewhere. You've lots of little pools you can dip into. The choir girls. The football girls. The youth club girls. Don't feel you're obliged to stick with Jasmine Mulcready. Just stay away from the altar boys. Please.

DERMOT. But I can't.

NIGEL. Can't what?

DERMOT. Get away from Jasmine Mulcready.

NIGEL. Why not?

DERMOT. She's a Eucharist minister in the parish. I see her every morning at Mass. And she looks at me very intimately. Kneeling at the altar rails with her tongue out. I'm telling you. That! Every morning at eight o'clock! Can be extremely upsetting. I can't pray Nigel!

NIGEL. Dermot. I was in New York this summer. Long Island. Saint Thomas' parish. When the Mass was over one morning, there was a chalice, half full of consecrated wine left over. What will I do with this? I asked the young priest. Meaning—shall I consume the sacred contents or shall you? I'll take it, he said, and he lifted it from my hands, and walked casually across the vestry and poured it down the sink. I knew one thing from that moment. We're fucked. Oh, we may still cling to a sense of moral order. Or an absurd degree of sexual hygiene. But between you and me and the pope: we've lost it. No faith. So don't blame Jasmine Mulcready. It's not her is stopping you pray. Excuse me. Must leave this one at the altar of repose. *(He wheels coffin off.)*

DERMOT. Jesus Nigel! If only we could figure out what you're talking about half the time.

Fade.

Scene 9

The Canon, half dressed, with bruised head, enters very distressed.

CANON. Ciaran. Ciaran. Ciaran. Where is that pup?

CIARAN. I'm coming. *(Enters with Canon's jacket.)* Now. I just took the creases out of it with the iron.

CANON. I'll be late. Hurry.

CIARAN. Stop fussing. Sister Ita said she wouldn't be here till ten.

CANON. You can't be late for the seminary, you know. Punctuality. That's the game in the seminary.

CIARAN. You won't be late. *(Helping Canon with jacket.)*

CANON. Did you tell your daddy? About this evening?

CIARAN. I told him you were going to the seminary, on business, and that the bishop was driving you home. To my house. That we would need a light supper left out. For his lordship.

CANON. God your daddy is a great man. The way he can manage. So what did he say? Can he get the supper?

CIARAN. What would he say? He said fine. Look. You keep your mind on the inquiry. And don't worry.

CANON. You know I never had a father. Always missed him. He went away to sea. Did I never tell you that?

CIARAN. No. You never did.

CANON. Well that's what we used to say. Truth was he joined the British army and went to India. Must have liked it out there.

CIARAN. Do you need your stick?

CANON. No.

CIARAN. Now, when the bishop brings you back to my house, this place will be sparkling. The fires will be lit. The food will be on the white tablecloths. Don't worry.

CANON. I saw them. The girls. Just for a second. The little girls with their schoolbags. Just for an instant. Woke up. They were in front of the car. Looking straight at me. It was like a silent film some-how. And then the noise. Their little bodies crunching underneath the wheels.

CIARAN. Canon. That's enough. You promised. No more about the accident. Now you're to concentrate on the inquiry. And let me look at you. No sloppiness there, Canon! They'll take one look at you in the seminary and they'll say . . . well there is a man that didn't go to seed. There's the kind of man the seminary could be proud of. After all these years. I'll get your coat. (*He moves to go.*)

CANON. Ciaran.

CIARAN. Yes?

CANON. My hat. As well. Don't forget my hat.

CIARAN. Right. (*Exits.*)

Scene 10

In the seminary. Somewhere offstage the committee is meeting. The Canon re-mains in the one position from the last scene. The Bishop enters from behind him.

BISHOP. Good morning, Canon.

CANON. Good morning, Bishop.

BISHOP. How are you?

CANON. Very good. Thank you.

BISHOP. You're here to give evidence?

CANON. Something like that. The committee is in there. (*Point-ing.*)

BISHOP. Good. Good. Must do what we can, eh?

CANON. You know I still can't see why they won't just forget the whole thing. I mean the lad wasn't right in the head. There are worse tragedies. Ask those girls. Or their parents.

BISHOP. Adam. Before you speak to this committee, ask yourself, what would Christ want you to do?

CANON. Ha. If Christ was here, he'd have a meeting with the Hierarchy, and he'd say, well lads, yous certainly made a balls of everything, didn't yis?

BISHOP. Perhaps.

CANON. I didn't accuse you of nothing, Bishop, I hope you know that.

BISHOP. Nobody is going to hold it against you, Adam. No matter what you say.

CANON. You're very cool. For a man that's gonna be hung.

BISHOP. Nobody is going to be hung, Adam. We just want the truth. Don't we?

CANON. Here, tell me. Tell me one thing. One thing before we go over the top.

BISHOP. Anything, Adam.

CANON. What's the secret of a good sermon?

BISHOP. You're teasing me.

CANON. No. No. I read those gospels there, every Sunday. You know? I don't know. The life has gone out of them. The words seem hollow.

BISHOP. And Jesus said to his disciples, be not afraid, for I am always with you. Does that seem hollow?

CANON. Yes. To be honest. It does. Clankity Clankity Clank.

BISHOP. Adam.

CANON. What?

BISHOP. Just because you're a priest doesn't mean anybody expects perfection from you.

CANON. Good. Good. Because I can tell you I haven't been entirely successful as a celibate either. I have failed too, Bishop. Oh yes. I have sinned against chastity. 1966. In Lagos. With a nun. Thought it was supposed to be warm and tender. It wasn't. It was a hollow, grueling experience.

BISHOP. They say it's how you do it, makes it warm and tender.

CANON. Is that so? Well of course, you might have more experience than me.

BISHOP. You know what your brother priests call you, Bailey? Do you know the contempt some of them have for you?

CANON. Oh, turning nasty are we? Well, I knew the boy. You know that. Of course. He came to me for confessions. Did you know that? Oh, yes. I gave him a retreat once, up the mountains. I could ruin you now, Lynam. Here. At this thing. If I said the wrong thing, about you and him.

BISHOP. You've been telling people already how shocked you are. At all these allegations. How ashamed and angry and distressed you are, about all this . . . sex.

CANON. I have.

BISHOP. And are you? That shocked! Are you really?

CANON. What are you getting at?

BISHOP. The truth Bailey. Please. It's time for a little bit of honesty.

They stare at each other. Rehill enters.

REHILL. Another five minutes. The committee is almost ready.

CANON. Do you watch much television, Father? I was just saying to Sister Ita as we were coming up. I love some of them soap operas. *Coronation Street. Eastenders.* I mean all of us have things in life we hate. But soap operas. They're a great comfort.

REHILL. I'm sure they have their merits.

CANON. For example I can't stand fish. Bus drivers. Jesuits. Women journalists. Or men who carry their babies on their chests.

REHILL. The committee is next door.

CANON. But soap operas. *Home and Away.*

REHILL. You are here to testify.

CANON. *Neighbours. Emmerdale.*

REHILL. Now, calm yourself.

CANON. I could watch them all day.

REHILL. Is there any possibility that you might shut up!

CANON. You come to detest sooo much in life. The anger as one gets older is exhausting. But I adore a winter's night with my feet to the fire and the wonder of the telly.

BISHOP. Bailey, conduct yourself.

CANON. The truth, Bishop. You wanted the truth! Yes? Well I love television soap operas. Is that the truth? Or is the truth that Jesus Christ died for us and washed away our sins, and our obligation is to stand firm for Christ? And that is why I won't be telling this committee what I might or might not know regarding these matters. I hold the priesthood of Christ in much too high esteem to 'inform' on a brother priest.

REHILL. The committee is in for a treat, Canon.

CANON. That's your opinion.

REHILL. We could impose a severe penalty. We could remove you from your parish if you persistently refuse to cooperate.

CANON. No. You can't do fuck all to me. All my dealings with the boy were under the seal of confession. I can't be forced to disclose anything. And I have just decided that I'm disclosing nothing.

BISHOP. And what if we brought his mother in here, Adam? Or a few other mothers and fathers whose children have been abused by members of the clergy? What if we brought in the police, Adam? To clear this up for once and for all. And find the truth. Would you be standing by me then, or would you tell them what you know?

CANON. But Bishop . . . you're my bishop.

BISHOP. And you're a sly bastard.

CANON. Alright, alright, bring them in. Bring in all the mothers and fathers and police you want. Yeah. You see you're weak, Bishop. You give an inch, and then another inch. Bring in all the mothers of Ireland for all I care. Let them steer the boat. Let them drive the ship. But I'm telling you this. Yis'll end up at the bottom of the ocean my friend. Go on, ye weak spineless bastard. Bring them all in and let them have their say, the fucking whores.

The speech exhausts the Canon. He is standing.

Half fade.

Scene 11

The Canon from previous position staggers across the stage to the garden seat, sits and holds his head in his hands.

DERMOT. *(Off.)* Canon. Canon Bailey.

CANON. Ahhh dear.

DERMOT. Oh, Canon. There you are. Ciaran said you were out here somewhere. Feeding the ducks eh? No. The cows? Do you like cows? Or is that a silly question?

CANON. Dermot, Dermot, Dermot, Dermot, Dermot.

DERMOT. That's me. So. Well I'm feeling great, thanks for asking. How's yourself?

CANON. Oh, now. The doctor says I'm to keep going.

DERMOT. Is the bishop here?

CANON. He went down to the church a few minutes ago. For altar breads. They should be back any minute. We're having the Mass in the dining room.

DERMOT. Great. Nice house.

CANON. Yes.

DERMOT. And all these trees. Keeps it private. Are they scotch pines now, or douglas firs, or what? I wonder.

CANON. They're Ciaran's. Everything here is Ciaran's. Except the cows.

DERMOT. Oh, right. The cows.

CANON. He hates the cows. Not that that's such a terrible thing. But it's a start. He's begun. I can see him. That tiny glimmer of contempt in his face. Beginning to hate.

DERMOT. Oh, here. I brought you something. (*He takes a bottle from his pocket and hands it to the Canon.*)

CANON. What is it?

DERMOT. Camomile and lavender lotion. It restores lost energy.

CANON. Is there alcohol in it?

DERMOT. I don't think so.

CANON. Good. Because I'm off alcohol.

DERMOT. Jesus, Canon. You don't drink it. You put it in the bath. It's relaxing.

CANON. Where did you get it?

DERMOT. Oh just a friend. Well. An amazing German woman actually. Her husband is a chef in Dublin. But she left him. Now she's staying with a performance artist in Manor Hamilton. And well. They're going through a rough patch. So I told her. Stay with me. You know? In my house. For a couple of weeks. For counseling. Yeah. I'm counseling her.

CANON. I was just thinking how intimate an accident can be. You run over somebody; you become part of each other. Have you heard anything from the hospital? The other girl made no improvement did she?

DERMOT. No, Canon. Sorry.

CANON. No. Well. Camomile and lavender you say. Yes. Well that will help. Thank you.

He exits.

Fade.

Scene 12

The Bishop enters, carrying vestments, sacred utensils for Mass, and struggling with them.

BISHOP. Nigel. Nigel. Where is that pup? Nigel. By Jesus if he thinks he's going to sit on his arse around here, when he's working for me, he has another thing coming. Look at him. In the bloody car. On the telephone again. Nigel. Come here at once. Help me with these things.
NIGEL. *(Off.)* Coming.
BISHOP. Hurry up.

Nigel arrives.

NIGEL. Sorry.
BISHOP. Well, take them, take them, don't just stand there.
NIGEL. My lord.
BISHOP. What is it?
NIGEL. I've just received a rather disturbing phone message.
BISHOP. No. Don't tell me. It's the boy again. Isn't it?
NIGEL. Yes my lord. It's the boy.
BISHOP. Mother of Christ. Is there any end to this?

Fade.

Scene 13

Mr. Hanratty, with apron on, is vacuuming the dining room. The Canon startles him.

FATHER. Oh, Canon Bailey. I didn't hear you come in.

CANON. Yes. The bishop is just gone down for altar breads. Where's Ciaran?

FATHER. He's just gone out into the garden. To fetch you. Or to check the cows.

CANON. They're a full-time job, those cows.

FATHER. Well, it's not my place Canon, but I was saying to him, wouldn't the parish not get a proper fence around the grounds? Or maybe, a groundsman?

CANON. You're full of ideas, Mr. Hanratty.

FATHER. Yes. Well I'm just finished here now, Canon. Shall I get you a cup of tea? Before I go?

CANON. No. No thank you.

FATHER. You know of course, Ciaran insisted I go. Well I have everything done. For his lordship. The cold meats are under the tea towels in the pantry and the fish is in the fridge. All he has to do is eat it.

CANON. Good.

FATHER. I mean Ciaran said yous might want some confidentiality. Not that I was going to get in the way. I mean, we're all men. I mean yous are only human like the rest of us.

CANON. That's what you think, Mr. Hanratty.

FATHER. Yes. Well excuse me. (*He exits.*)

Ciaran who has been lurking in shadow now emerges.

CIARAN. Is he gone?

CANON. Why don't you tell him?

CIARAN. Tell him what?

CANON. That you're miserable in the priesthood. That you'd be better off leaving.

CIARAN. Oh, no, Canon. That would be totally untrue. I'm not unhappy. I just need time. To get used to things. I owe it to myself. I owe it to the bishop. I can't just . . . quit.

CANON. Come here, Ciaran. Do you see that car coming up the avenue?

CIARAN. That's the bishop, Canon.

CANON. No. That's a BMW, about to be parked with impeccable precision by the bishop's secretary. The lord bishop is the ridiculous lump of lard on the backseat. And what is he lord of? Bog. Ditch. Hill. Rushes. And forestry. The people are long gone from here. It's over. The football match is long over but his lordship is still out on the pitch, throwing in the balls. You owe his lordship nothing, Ciaran.

CIARAN. And what about you? Don't you think that in a funny sort of way, you have taught me a lot? Perhaps I owe you something.

CANON. Fuck off, Ciaran. Let the dead bury the dead.

In another place the Bishop and Nigel discuss very intimately. They are carrying the utensils for Mass.

NIGEL. Apparently the idea of Our Blessed Mother's Ascension into the Clouds continued to affect his mind. After he had been expelled from the seminary. He was too ashamed to go home. Then the solicitors said he hadn't a hope of suing anyone if he was not prepared to name the culprit. He was left in a bed sit in Dublin, with an irrational desire for affection, stemming from a deep-rooted sense of self-loathing. The idea of being taken up to heaven absorbed him . . .

BISHOP. For frig sake, will you get on with it.

NIGEL. He hanged himself, my lord.

BISHOP. I see.

NIGEL. One of the residents of the flats found him. In the toilet. Hanging from the skylight.

BISHOP. So that's the end.

NIGEL. Not quite. He left a note. You're mentioned in it.

BISHOP. Go on.

NIGEL. He says he regrets having accused you in the wrong. He says you only tried to bring him different places to cheer him up. That you were a kind man, and he asks forgiveness for having told lies about you.

BISHOP. I see.

NIGEL. As far as the Gardai are concerned, this is the last of the matter. The case is closed.

BISHOP. Oh no, Nigel. Not by a long shot. No. The case hasn't even opened yet.

Fade.

Scene 14

The Canon alone.

CANON. And so we gathered. You would have enjoyed it, Rehill. The brothers of Christ. That they might remain faithful to each other. In the breaking of bread.

The Bishop enters.

BISHOP. Bailey. I want a word with you.

CANON. I'm sorry, Bishop. Do you want me to read the Gospel for you?

BISHOP. That was clever, today.

CANON. Pardon?

BISHOP. Thought you'd incriminate me by innuendo.

CANON. I'm sorry. I don't know what you're talking about.

BISHOP. As if your silence was protecting me. Very clever.

CANON. I never meant to imply such a thing. It was the seal of confession. That was all.

BISHOP. He's dead, Bailey. He hanged himself.

CANON. Christ.

BISHOP. Does that hurt?

CANON. Yes.

BISHOP. He left a note. Which you will want your solicitors to examine.

CANON. What? What note?

BISHOP. A suicide note.

CANON. Did he tell?

BISHOP. So it was you Adam, wasn't it? All along. It was you.

CANON. Yes.

BISHOP. Why?

CANON. I was lonely.

BISHOP. That boy's life was destroyed. Why? Because you were lonely. We're all lonely. You soldiered through fifty years of loneliness. Why? Why now?

CANON. It was only once.

BISHOP. When?

CANON. Years ago. Before he went to the seminary. I took him up the mountains. It was supposed to be a weekend retreat. Just him and me. We had separate sleeping bags. On a mattress in the kitchen of the cottage. I watched him for hours. His closed eyes. His sleeping mouth. He shivered once, and suddenly was upright, and unzipped, setting out for water in the pantry. It said three A.M. in digits on the clock. His sudden breaking loose from sleep, like a cormorant fighting to be above the waves, made me hope I had another chance at conversation on the mattress in the night. But afterwards he pulled the bag across his shoulders and tucked it under his chin like the walls of Troy. All night, I watched the even swell of his breathing. Just once, I leaned over and kissed his mouth. I thought he would not wake. That was my mistake. He woke.

Nigel, being the soul of discretion knocks.

    NIGEL. I'm sorry, my lord, we're about to begin.
    BISHOP. Send them in, Nigel. That's the good man.
    NIGEL. Right, my lord. I'll do that.

Exits.

The procession of all the priests enters. They are all in white albs. The Bishop remains in his soutane.

    CANON. The priests have always found consolation in the Mass. There is a bond, at the altar, between brothers.

Canon puts on his alb. Rehill appears somewhere stage left alone, watching, wearing an overcoat.

Dermot and Nigel stretch a long linen cloth to make an altar, upstage of which everyone else gathers to pray.

The bishop asked Ciaran to be the main celebrant, which was nice. I read the Gospel. It was the one about the Last Supper. 'When he said unto them, one of you will this night betray me. And shortly thereafter, Judas Iscariot left their company and withdrew into the darkness.' But none of us would ever leave that table. Maybe it's fear. Maybe it's because we believe that salvation, peace, happiness is all simply a matter of . . . access. To that table. Maybe we have just nowhere else to go. We're cornered.

The altar cloth is dropped and they all sit around on stools.

After Communion, we all sat down and each one made a special prayer.

CIARAN. *(With earnest passion.)* Help me, Lord. When I doubt. Help me, Lord. When my heart is restless.

DERMOT. Forgive me, Lord. When I sin. Forgive me, Lord. When I commit sins.

CANON. And we could always rely on Nigel, since the bishop was present, to pray like a man with an honours degree.

NIGEL. My prayer this evening is for the entire Church. That we would accomplish the redemptive energy of the suffering of the cross during this time of anxiety. In the light of the resurrection of Christ. Which we already anticipate in the fellowship of this table.

BISHOP. *(Stands.)* And I pray, too. For my priests. That they would realise that this Eucharist, this night, is their last refuge. We are like men in a boat that is lost. The storm rages about our ears. And we are afraid. But here, in this place, at this moment in time, we recognise our last and only refuge from the world.

REHILL. *(Still present and at a distance.)* And did you have a prayer?

Canon moves to Rehill.

CANON. No. No. I've always found the Mass a consolation. But when I come to think about it, I haven't actually prayed in years. After all, you don't really expect me to pray to a dead fish, do you?

REHILL. No. I suppose not.

Rehill moves to go. He has a letter in his hand.

CANON. What about you? Did you win?

REHILL. No. I didn't.

CANON. So there won't be anything further about this business?

REHILL. Not from me. I'm leaving the priesthood, Canon. In fact, I was just about to go post my resignation.

CANON. Oh. So there there won't be anymore investigations about the young lad?

REHILL. I hardly think so. He's dead. Not enough evidence to go on. And I suppose, they've got plenty of other cases coming up.

Rehill makes another move to go.

CANON. Was there anything in particular, Father, caused you to leave?

REHILL. No. Nothing in particular. Good-bye.

All the characters remain still. Peter enters and stares across the stage at no one in particular.

PETER. Father. Father. Father. Father. Father. Father.

Fade.

Curtain.

END OF PLAY

Thomas Kilroy.
Courtesy of Joe O'Shaughnessy and the Gallery Press.

The Secret Fall of Constance Wilde

THOMAS KILROY

1997

Original Cast

Jane Brennan	Robert O'Mahoney
Andrew Scott	Muirne Bloomer
Eric Lacey	Kevin Murphy
Ciara O'Callaghan	Jonathan Shankey
Jack Walsh	

Director: Patrick Mason

For Patrick Mason

Characters

Speaking Parts
CONSTANCE WILDE
OSCAR WILDE, her husband
LORD ALFRED DOUGLAS, his lover

Mute Parts
An ANDROGYNE
Six ATTENDANT PUPPETEERS, white, faceless masks, bowler hats, Victorian jackets and pants, white gloves, clappers.
The parts of DOUGLAS and the ANDROGYNE may be played by the same actor (male or female).

PART ONE

A dark stage. The attendant figures, mute, emerge out of the darkness: white, faceless masks, bowler hats, tight Victorian jackets, chequered pants, white gloves, a cross between Victorian toffs and street theatre performers, stagehands and puppeteers, dressers, waiters and Figures of Fate.

Out of the darkness four of the attendant figures roll a great white disk, a performance space like a circus ring, into place downstage under a brilliant spot.
NOTE: *The disk effect throughout may be accomplished through the use of lighting.*

At the same time the voice of Constance from the darkness crying: 'No! No! No!'

Then two other attendant figures lead Oscar and Constance into the spot, onto the disk, rather like hospital attendants with frail patients. All six attendant figures then melt back into darkness leaving Oscar and Constance on their own.

Oscar and Constance perform on the disk, circling one another. They are both at the end of their lives, he in frock coat and hat, she in a cape, both unsteady and worn, both leaning heavily on walking sticks. At first the exchange between them is rapid.

CONSTANCE. No—no—no—no—

OSCAR. *(Low.)* I must see them. Before I die. That's all. *(Outburst.)* They're my children, too, Constance! Why are you doing this to me? Why? Why?

CONSTANCE. Protection—

OSCAR. Protection! My two little boys protected from me? Is that it? Because I'm a pervert? A gaol-bird? Two years hard labour in the clink for gross indecency with male persons known and unknown—

CONSTANCE. Don't Oscar.

OSCAR. Don't Oscar! I can't touch my little boys because I'm a poof, a Marjorie, a Mary Ann. A prick lover. All you see is the invert. They can't breed. So! Let them be without children! That's it, isn't it?

CONSTANCE. Don't bully, Oscar. It makes you seem tiresome. Funny. A few years ago I wouldn't even know what you were talking about. How I've changed. Simply by living with you.

OSCAR. What exactly do you want now, Constance?

CONSTANCE. Actually, what I really want is to face myself, face my own role in this whole sorry—spectacle.

OSCAR. What are you talking about?

CONSTANCE. Evil.

OSCAR. Evil? Evil! You know, Constance, you positively drip with goodness. You drench everyone around you—drip drip—drip. Wet, wet, wet. Just like your sanctimonious relatives. Aunt Mary and Cousin Lizzie. Lizzie Busybody. You leak, Constance, drowning in that wet, deadly morality of yours!

CONSTANCE. I'm not at all like that and well you know it.

OSCAR. I'm sorry. I've no idea why I spoke like that—utterly inexcusable of me, sorry. Evil. I've had that word thrown in my face by every Tom, Dick and Harry and now, coming from you—

CONSTANCE. Do you know, you're the most self-obsessed creature—I wasn't talking about you! I was talking about myself—

OSCAR. I don't understand—

CONSTANCE. Evil! In me! Which I've never been able to face.

OSCAR. You're not evil, Constance.

CONSTANCE. *(Shakes her head.)* No, Oscar, not that, not anymore. You can never invent me again. Constance the good wife who never screamed aloud at what was being done to her and her children, the horror, the filth. What a creation you made of me! Constance, the loyal wife who kept him in cash to the bitter end, even while he betrayed her. No. I want to be restored to myself, now. Even if it's all over.

OSCAR. But you always acted out of—goodness.

CONSTANCE. Most times I acted out of rage! Rage! Deep, silent rage. You know sometimes I broke things in the house. But you weren't there to see that, were you?

OSCAR. You mustn't punish yourself like this, Constance—mustn't!

CONSTANCE. Why did you like having the good woman as your wife, Oscar? Have you ever asked yourself that? Have you? Did it make your wretched debauchery more easy? Hmm? Did it somehow—protect you?

OSCAR. We had—happiness—

CONSTANCE. I think we were imprisoned by happiness.

OSCAR. What on earth do you mean?

CONSTANCE. Do you remember in the early days? How we wouldn't leave the house for days on end? Our House Beautiful! People would ask: Where on earth have you two been for the past few days? And we would smile at one another across the room. I thought no one is as tender, as loving, as exquisite, as mysterious as this man, and he is mine! He is my prisoner in this white palace. Then one day, I remember the moment exactly, I saw your face actually change—

OSCAR. Please, Constance—

CONSTANCE. Dripping with goodness, did you say? Wet, indeed! How you turned away from me with that stylish disgust of yours! I blamed myself, of course, lying there in the darkness. Women always do. Thinking in the night. What is wrong with me? Why is he unable to look me in the face in the act of love? Why does he make me turn my back on him, on all fours, like an animal when all I want to do is look into his eyes?

OSCAR. It was not like that!

CONSTANCE. And when I conceived with Cyril I will never, never forget that look of revulsion on your face, the disgust at what my body had become. When I tried to touch you you sprang away from me as if from something rancid.

OSCAR. *(Cry.)* Oh, God of creation, what you have given us to live with! *(Shift.)* What is—mysterious is that none of this makes any difference to my love for you. Or the children. *(Discovery.)* There is so much truth in failure and destruction.

CONSTANCE. At least you've sometimes expressed the truth to me, Oscar. Even when you surround me with lies.

OSCAR. *(Heavy irony.)* The problem with *my* marriage is that my wife understands me— *(Rush.)* You went back on our agreement. You sat across from me in that filthy prison cage and you promised! Yes, Oscar, you said. Everything will be the same as before. You and I. Cyril and Vyvyan.

CONSTANCE. I've learned that nothing is ever the same as before, nothing—

OSCAR. And where did you learn that, may I ask?

CONSTANCE. From your friend Alfred Douglas.

OSCAR. *(Shocked pause.)* Bosie! What's he got to with this?

CONSTANCE. Can you really ask that? After all that has happened?

OSCAR. I have nothing more to do with him! Nothing!

CONSTANCE. Oh, really?

OSCAR. You don't believe me?

CONSTANCE. No, I don't believe you because on this one subject you are capable of endless lying. And you wonder why I must protect the children! This is ridiculous!

OSCAR. Protect. The children. *(Working it out.)* From Bosie! Bosie? Did he do something?

CONSTANCE. I see! You believe he's corrupt, too, don't you?

OSCAR. Bosie! What did he do? Did he do something to the children? Did something happen? Answer me, woman! By God, I will kill him! My own sons—what did he do?

CONSTANCE. Nothing.

OSCAR. But he tried to?

CONSTANCE. I wouldn't allow it.

OSCAR. It? You wouldn't allow it? What is this 'it'? Maybe its just something in your mind, Constance, hmm? Thinking up something monstrous about someone else—

CONSTANCE. Why did I marry you, Oscar? Why? Why?

OSCAR. *(Long pause. Brokenly.)* Because. We loved.

CONSTANCE. People keep asking me: what was it like, Constance, really like, to be married to him? Of course, they're thinking of you-know-what. It's as if they are undressing me with their eyes. Why, I answer them in my best wifely voice, it was theatre, m'dears, theatre! Theatre all the way! You know what Oscar is like! Every day a different performance. With frequent costume changes, of course. They are also wondering although they never ask: *when did she know?* All those young men and boys about the place. All those late dinners in Kettners and the Café Royal. When you consorted with sodomites and— what's that curious term? Rent boys! You didn't become someone else. You were the same person I had married. What is more, you were the same person I had wanted to marry. What does that say, Oscar? About us? About me?

OSCAR. Why did you marry me, Constance?

CONSTANCE. I fear that I may be about to find out. *(She suddenly doubles up in pain.)*

OSCAR. Constance! Are you in pain?

CONSTANCE. *(Breaking.)* I fell—

OSCAR. I know that, dear. You were alone—

CONSTANCE. Alone. In the house. I fell. Or flew. Down flights. Our House Beautiful, oh, Oscar!

OSCAR. Are you in constant pain?

CONSTANCE. There are times when I cannot walk.

OSCAR. And will they operate again?

CONSTANCE. They say there's little point. The injury—paralysis is progressive. What a word. Progressive. You used to use that word of me, Oscar. Remember? My wife is Progressive! She campaigns for Peace, the dockers, Rational Dress and Lady Sandhurst. Progressive. Paralysis. Do you really care about my pain?

OSCAR. Of course I care. Terribly. *(Pause.)* Constance. What actually happened to you? On that staircase?

CONSTANCE. Don't wish to speak about it—

OSCAR. But something happened?

CONSTANCE. —fall—

OSCAR. But something else?

CONSTANCE. —on the landing—

OSCAR. What was it, Constance?

CONSTANCE. *(Whisper. In tears.)* Unspeakable. Evil. Crouching there on the landing. Squat. Evil.

OSCAR. What did you see, Constance?

CONSTANCE. I cannot tell you!

OSCAR. Please—

CONSTANCE. No! It cannot be told. It can only be—discovered. Revealed.

OSCAR. Please confide in me, Constance! Please! Don't you see? If you did it would—save me. Talk to me, Constance! Otherwise I'm finished. Back on the streets. Alone.

CONSTANCE. But firstly, firstly it has to be—acted out. Then I will be able to face it. They're waiting for us, Oscar.

OSCAR. (Frantic.) No—no. Tell me, Constance. Please!

CONSTANCE. They're waiting for us, Oscar. Back there. In the darkness.

OSCAR. No!

CONSTANCE. Waiting to put us through our paces. One more time. To perform. This time to face it as it really was!

OSCAR. See how we've both ended up on sticks, Constance. How demeaning! Used to admire a decent cane. In the old days. But never as a mere aid to walking.

CONSTANCE. There has always been your story, Oscar, but this time there has to be mine as well! You and I. Our— marriage. Our— children.

OSCAR. *(Sadly: towards walking stick.)* When something becomes useful it ceases to be beautiful. Don't you think?

CONSTANCE. *(Shift to anxiety.)* What's the matter?

OSCAR. *(Desperate rush.)* As a family we rather frequented the Continent, did we not? Look how we've ended up! You with the children under the Italian sun and I alone on the streets of Paris. *(Pulls himself into the debonair mode, with difficulty and without complete success.)* Each country exports its scandals. When in doubt take the boat. Otherwise life would be extremely tedious for the rest of the world.

CONSTANCE. *(Now deeply concerned for him.)* What is it, Oscar?
When you go on like this I know there is something—
OSCAR. *(Disturbed.)* Simply cannot go through all this again, from
the beginning, Constance. Cannot. Cannot.
CONSTANCE. It is the only way in which I can go back.
OSCAR. —cannot—cannot—
CONSTANCE. For me, so that I may face myself.
OSCAR. For you—
CONSTANCE. For my secret journey, Oscar.
OSCAR. For you, Constance. Finita la commédia!

*Loud clapping from the darkness around them. Lights up and for the first time
we see the full stage.*

*The clapping we have heard has come from the six attendant figures who stand
waiting, equipped with clappers. All about on stands are full-sized puppets
waiting to be used: two child puppets for the Wilde children,
nightgowns/sailor suits. Puppets of several Victorian gentlemen in frock coats,
top hats; of a judge and barristers; of a gaoler and policemen.*

*A set of stairs that may become an elaborate staircase with bannisters, a court-
room dock, a railway carriage.*

*The disk is rolled back upstage by attendants where it leans against the back
wall, a gigantic moon or wafer.*

*The attendants lead Oscar and Constance to either side of the stage, downstage
and, there, facing the audience, they communicate with one another across a
distance, without looking at one another. As they speak, they are transformed
by the attendants into their youthful selves. When the canes are taken from
them they straighten up at once, alert. Wig and costume changes complete the
transformation.*

OSCAR. Must we go back so far?
CONSTANCE. We must go back to the beginning. That beautiful
November day in Dublin. Oh, Oscar, you warned me! But I wouldn't
listen—
OSCAR. You were in love.
CONSTANCE. And you, Oscar?

OSCAR. I was ecstatic.

CONSTANCE. Not quite the same thing, is it?

OSCAR. Love should always have ecstasy. Otherwise it is in danger of dwindling into friendship.

CONSTANCE. There are times when what you say appears so very—limited.

OSCAR. Good God! My language limited!

CONSTANCE. Would you have stayed with me if I were a man, Oscar? I sometimes ask myself that. Then I say to myself you're bonkers, Constance, just like him.

OSCAR. You're impossible, Constance, absolutely impossible at times, but you're also the only one to understand me, well my— feminine.

CONSTANCE. Feminine, indeed. How could you ever understand what it is to be a woman?

OSCAR. *(Attempted lift, reaching for the joke.)* Of course I understand what it is to be a woman. Have I not been kept for years by my wife? Three pounds a week with the constant threat of withdrawal of allowance. How more like a woman could one be?

CONSTANCE. *(Despite herself, she laughs.)* Oh, Oscar, really, you are impossible!

OSCAR. *(Lost.)* When it began I was living in a dream of perfection.

CONSTANCE. Nothing is perfect in this life.

OSCAR. *(Testily.)* Of course, women always know the limits of everything. Men seldom do. Hence the divorce court.

CONSTANCE. You mean women always pick up the pieces.

OSCAR. *(Annoyance.)* You must always say something basic, mustn't you, dear?

CONSTANCE. You mean real, don't you?

The costume and other changes have now been made and Oscar has been given a new, very elegant, silver-topped cane. They have turned to confront one another. The attendants draw back.

OSCAR. *(Fury.)* Real? Real! Don't speak to me of real! I abhor realism. People who call a spade a spade should be compelled to use one.

CONSTANCE. Oh, Oscar, just accept things as they are!

OSCAR. Never! Stand off! I may end up a decrepit Prospero with a

terminal infection of the inner ear but not now! Now I can still—
play!

*Constance does, indeed, stand off and becomes the 'audience' of what follows.
Oscar waves his cane as a wand, a signal to the attendants who leap to attention, acolytes in his ceremony. Music. As he speaks, a 'statue' of an Androgyne, reclining, naked, rear view, on a classical plinth, is flown in or elevated
in, a moment of white magic to Oscar's wand. The 'statue' rises, poses, naked,
arm aloft in front of the great white disk. The attendants produce a scarlet
sheet and behind this the figure is gradually dressed as Lord Alfred Douglas:
startling whites, suit, shirt, cravat and gloves.*

(A great yell.) I must have it! I will have it! Neither man nor woman
but both. Dionysus, the man-woman as Aeschylus called it,
descended as a golden boy in whites into a London drawing room.
The great wound in Nature, the wound of gender, was healed. And
Plato's divided egg united once more in a single, perfect sphere.
Hermaphroditus born of a kiss in the clear spring of Salmacis, near
Helicarnassus—
Nec duo sunt, sed forma duplex, nec femina dici
Nec puer ut possit, neutrumque et utrumque videtur.
Woman, this is our secret history, the history of the Androgyne. In
every phase of civilization there has been this dream of perfection.
Cette gracieuse chimère, rêve de l'Antiqueté! A dream, a dream, you see. It
is the dream of Leonardo's *Baptist,* of Shakespeare's sonnets, of
Balzac's *Séraphîta!* And why? Why? Why, because it is the dream of
Paradise restored, the undivided Adam, whole and intact, where
there is no man, no woman, no duality, no contrary, no grotesque
fumbling towards the Other because the Other resides within oneself. But our frightened time cannot bear such a vision. It curls away
in terror from what it sees in the mirror. And so our age puts on its
bright red uniforms and goes out to murder its own kind. It beats its
children simply to keep the male and female in place. *(The old frivol-
ity once more.)* Was it worth it, Oscar? some buffoon called to me the
other day from the other side of the street. Haven't you noticed?
There is always a buffoon on the other side of the street. Was it worth
it, Oscar? It was worth it, my friend. Worth all the cheap jokes.
Worth the humiliation in manacles before the gaping crowd on the
platform of Clapham Junction. Worth the stink of carbolic and Jeyes

Fluid in that cell, worth all the shit, my body rotting! When one sups with the gods one must pay the full price of admission.

CONSTANCE. *(Scream.)* But what about the cost to others!

It is as if she is almost about to strike him. Then they are separated by the attendants who conduct them, separately, downstage. During the following exchange Douglas poses, an 'audience' to what is going on. Apart from Douglas the rest of the stage, and the attendants, will remain in shadow. The full front of the stage becomes a brightly lit, autumnal path on Merrion Square, in Dublin.

OSCAR. *(To audience.)* And so the young lovers met in Merrion Square where light is held in a golden net. And my mother sat in the window of the first floor, Speranza, a blue shade on Helicon, dreaming her mad dreams of Ireland. Or am I imagining it all?

CONSTANCE. *(To audience.)* Everyone in Dublin was talking about him. Have you met the naughty Mr Wilde? Oh, you mustn't be caught in his company, dear. Certainly not alone. Certainly not without chaperone. I was suddenly, incredibly, excited. Don't misunderstand me. It wasn't the scent of the forbidden. One had one's books for that. It was rather as if I were meeting someone out of my most disturbing dreams, half-realized, but now here it was, the thing itself. I immediately decided I was going to marry him.

Attendants take Constance and run her into the lit space, whirling her about and she pirouettes, a young girl, a bird alighting. Oscar turns to her, comes and takes her by the arm.

CONSTANCE. Oh, how I love Dublin! I love this park, this square! I love Granmama Mary Atkinson for bringing me here so that I could meet you. I love the House Beautiful that you talk about. Will we live there, Oscar? Forever and ever?

OSCAR. *(Putting a finger on her lips.)* How brave can you be?

CONSTANCE. What a strange question!

OSCAR. I must have an answer to it.

CONSTANCE. You're frightening me, Oscar!

OSCAR. You must answer!

CONSTANCE. But what could happen?

OSCAR. That's just the point. I don't know.

CONSTANCE. (*Pause.*) Yes. My answer is yes! No matter what happens. To me. To you.

OSCAR. And now, my sweet, I will make my vow to you. You see, I believe that there is a fundamental essence within each person. Call it soul, if you will. It is what we take with us from the womb and to the grave. And it is very rare to know someone at that level. I know you in that way, Constance. I love you in that way. And that is why, no matter what happens, I will always love you. Any other loves I might ever have will be lesser because they will be contaminated by life. They will be of this world. Not you, Constance.

CONSTANCE. Why, that's the most wonderful thing anyone has ever said to me.

OSCAR. You mustn't forget it.

CONSTANCE. I shan't forget it.

OSCAR. Well, then, we may now talk of trivial things.

CONSTANCE. Such as?

OSCAR. Our blood relations for one. I was born of the union of a small, bearded goat and a walking historical monument. This accounts for the confusion of Dionysian and Apollonian elements in my makeup. Actually, I adore my mother. She is like a Celtic goddess in reduced circumstances. I despise my father.

CONSTANCE. I don't wish to speak of my father.

OSCAR. I constantly speak about my father. His behaviour is so dreadful that I feel I shall never succeed in emulating him.

CONSTANCE. (*Blurted out.*) Papa was arrested!

OSCAR. Never mind, my dear. All the best families should include at least one convicted criminal.

CONSTANCE. Don't be facetious, Oscar. Not about this!

OSCAR. Sorry. What did he do?

CONSTANCE. He tried—he tried—to corrupt the innocent.

OSCAR. Which innocent?

CONSTANCE. I don't wish to talk about it.

OSCAR. You can confide in me, Constance. There is nothing that shocks me. Nothing.

CONSTANCE. (*Surprise.*) That's actually true, isn't it!

OSCAR. Was it sexual?

CONSTANCE. How on earth did you know?

OSCAR. One always catches the unmistakable tone of silence surrounding sexuality in this great civilization of ours.

CONSTANCE. Do you think I'm a prude?

OSCAR. Certainly not!

CONSTANCE. There are things that I cannot even tell myself. Then there are great blanks, cannot remember things; sort of—blotted out. Do you think you will always be able to tell me everything about yourself, Oscar?

OSCAR. Absolutely!

CONSTANCE. (*Deep breath.*) Papa—Horace Watson Lloyd, barrister-at-law, practising at Number 11, King's Bench Walk, was found guilty of—exposing himself in the gardens of the Temple before the perambulating nursemaids. There! I thought I could never say that aloud.

OSCAR. How extraordinary! We have been drawn to one another out of a mutual interest in patricide. (*She bursts into tears and he holds her.*) Constance, dearest Constance! I understand!

CONSTANCE. (*Shaking, through tears.*) He gave me gifts—

OSCAR. (*Puzzled but going with it.*) Yes, of course, he gave you gifts. Mustn't punish yourself like this—

CONSTANCE. Oh but I must! Mother actually dumped us, you see, after Papa died. Such selfishness! Do you know, I used to think that I'd be incapable of ever loving anyone again? Until I met you.

OSCAR. The past doesn't matter! Nor, indeed, does the future. Nothing matters but the immediate, thrilling present moment. We have to savour each moment to the full. That is what is meant by salvation.

CONSTANCE. (*Drying her eyes, escape from her hurt.*) Oscar! Tell me one of your stories!

OSCAR. You mean—here? In the park?

CONSTANCE. Why not? One of your once-upon-a-time stories.

OSCAR. How odd! I really would prefer a stage, you know. Or at least a rostrum. Or even an interestingly decorated corner of a room.

CONSTANCE. Oh, Oscar!

OSCAR. I've always felt that the outdoors should be reserved for perspiration and the perpetration of scandalous relationships. Preferably with horses. (*Offhand.*) Once upon a time.

CONSTANCE. Please—

OSCAR. Once upon a time. Yes. Once upon a time (*A shift in tone, gradually surrendering to the story.*) there were three princesses. But their father, the old king, had sent them away into a cold, barbaric country. They had different mothers, you see, and the old king wanted to forget this fact so he tried to forget his daughters. But he couldn't forget. The place they had occupied in his heart became a blazing flame. His heart burned like a furnace. And, far away, the youngest princess caught a terrible fever and died. They said her small body glowed even in death. And her two older sisters, who loved dancing, danced and danced. But one night they danced too close to the open fire. When the dress of the first sister caught fire the second threw herself into her sister's fiery embrace and she, too, was engulfed. People came and threw the bodies into the snow outside but it was too late. Where they lay, a black hole burned into the snow. And back in his palace, the old king was finally free. The fire in his heart had finally burned out, you see. The end.

CONSTANCE. Why, that's a wonderful, terrible, wonderful story. How on earth did you make it up?

OSCAR. I didn't make it up. It actually happened. It is the story of my three sisters.

CONSTANCE. I'm sorry. I didn't know you had three sisters.

OSCAR. Not many people know. My youngest sister Isola did die of a fever. And the other two—Emily and Mary—died exactly as I have described it. In a fire. Dancing. They were, both, if you will allow me, illegitimate.

CONSTANCE. I see. So your father is the king?

OSCAR. Yes. (Pause.) King Billy Goat who sent his three daughters away to die. Everything I write is autobiographical. With the facts changed, of course.

CONSTANCE. I knew there was some story. People do talk.

OSCAR. That is certainly true of Dublin.

CONSTANCE. How awful for you, Oscar!

OSCAR. (Pause.) And how awful for you, Constance.

CONSTANCE. No, I don't think we should talk like this. I won't allow it. We're much too well off when you consider how most people suffer—

OSCAR. Will you be my sister?

CONSTANCE. (Fear.) Why, Oscar, we're going to marry. Aren't we?

OSCAR. Will you be my sister, Constance?

CONSTANCE. Do you mean friend?

OSCAR. *(Fierce.)* Sister! Sister!

CONSTANCE. I don't understand!

OSCAR. Yes, you do understand, Constance. You've understood everything from the very beginning. That is why you know what I mean. My sister.

CONSTANCE. *(Slowly.)* All you ever show to the world is this brilliant surface.

OSCAR. But you can see beneath it, Constance. Can't you?

CONSTANCE. I don't know, really. *(Pause.)* There are two ways of knowing, aren't there? I mean there are facts and stuff like that. But you can also know something in your heart, even without facts. I may not know all the facts about you but I know you in my heart. But do you want me to see everything about you, Oscar? Do you? I don't think you do, you know.

Oscar doesn't answer. Douglas applauds daintily and steps forward as well into the light.

Oscar and Constance stand as if dazed. The attendants perform another quick, minimal costume/wig change on them. They now become the married couple of the trial years. The white disk is rolled forward into place again as an acting space. The staircase is also rolled forward, a full stairs with bannisters. The child puppets in nightgowns are brought forward by their puppeteers. Constance, back to audience, holding a puppet by each hand, slowly climbs the stairs, the puppeteers manipulating the puppets to either side: a mother seeing her children to bed.

Oscar, away to one side, watches all this.

DOUGLAS. *(To audience.)* Of course, one should always marry. Future of the race etcetera etcetera. Marriage is—how should one put it? Yes, a duty. Most certainly a form of protection, even a sort of—invisibility, if you follow me. But I did say to him: darling, you married the wrong kind of woman. Know what I mean? I mean she knew too much. And then there were those two children. Made things frightfully complicated, the children. *(Short pause.)* Adorable things—

CONSTANCE. *(On the stairs with the puppets.)* Time for beddy-byes, you two—upsy daisy—no, dearest, Papa isn't home. Do try not to pull on Mama's arm, Cyril. You mustn't say such things, Cyril. Papa loves you, loves you both very much indeed. (*Child's game.*) Bobalink! Bobalink! Dream time! (*To self.*) Dream time—

The puppeteers let the puppets fall and Constance stands a moment with them hanging to either side from her hands. Then the puppets are quickly removed and Constance stands alone on the stairs, looking up into darkness.

DOUGLAS. (*To audience.*) Actually, I always liked Constance. From the word go. It was always so—well, bracing to talk to her. One never quite knew what she was going to say next. You'll see what I mean in a moment.

As he speaks, Constance has descended the staircase and comes downstage. She stands there, facing out into the audience. Oscar, meanwhile, has begun to circle the disk in increasing agitation. The attendants place an ornate chaise lounge on the disk. They conduct Douglas onto the disk and seat him, delicately, upon the chaise lounge, then stand in a line above the disk.

DOUGLAS. Never know why the penny romances call this kind of affair a love triangle. Do you? Far more than three angles involved, wouldn't you agree?
OSCAR. (*As if rushing through a house, yelling.*) Bosie! Are you there, Bosie!
DOUGLAS. (*To audience.*) And that's another thing! This frightful slander that's being passed about everywhere. I never interfered with those children. Never!
OSCAR. (*Finally leaping onto the disk, arms out.*) Bosie!
DOUGLAS. Oh, it's you, is it!

Oscar embraces him, kissing him passionately and Douglas returns the kisses. The six attendant figures surround them completely, a heaving black coverlet covering the chaise lounge. Constance pays no attention to this.

CONSTANCE. (*To audience.*) Sometimes he would return to our home on Tite Street to see the children but only when he believed I was out. I would open a door and find him there, the children on his knee, clasping him, this look on his face, a look at once of happiness and horror, those large white hands falling away from the children's bodies when he caught sight of me. 'Only a few moments more, dear,' he'd murmur, unable to look me in the eye—

The six attendants have risen and departed into shadow leaving a dishevelled Oscar and a less dishevelled Douglas who rearrange themselves. Constance turns towards the disk and Oscar, looking off, spots her.

OSCAR. I really should become a gymnast! *(Looks off.)* Oh, my God, she's coming here! Get rid of her, would you! I simply can't face her.

He moves off the disk and turns his back to what happens next. Constance will eventually step onto the disk and Douglas will turn to her as if she has just entered a room.

DOUGLAS. Oscar! No! Dammit! Why, Constance! This is a surprise!

CONSTANCE. May I see my husband?

DOUGLAS. I should certainly think so. Wives see their husbands all the time, do they not?

CONSTANCE. Don't you dare mock me!

DOUGLAS. I am not Oscar's keeper, you know.

CONSTANCE. I want to see him. Now, if you please.

DOUGLAS. Well, then, you must find him, mustn't you?

CONSTANCE. I don't intend to search these rooms.

DOUGLAS. I am very relieved to hear it. One is very fearful of house searches, nowadays.

CONSTANCE. Do you think I'm a fool?

DOUGLAS. Certainly not.

CONSTANCE. Merely a woman, would you say?

DOUGLAS. Do not burden me, please, with your self-doubt.

CONSTANCE. On the contrary, Lord Douglas, right now my doubts are about other people. You, for example.

DOUGLAS. Lord Douglas! My! No Alfred? No Bosie?

CONSTANCE. *(Actually curious.)* Do you really have no idea of how much scandal is attached to your name?

DOUGLAS. I don't wish to hear it. I love to hear scandal about others but scandal about myself doesn't interest me. It doesn't have the charm of novelty.

CONSTANCE. Oh Oscar has taught you well. You even speak like him. Parrotlike.

DOUGLAS. If I am his parrot, then you must be his hen.

CONSTANCE. How offensive you are! I assure you I am not his *any-thing*. That's the difference between us. Apart from the fact that I am his wife. That is another difference. *(Douglas laughs a high-pitched laugh, quickly cut off.)* Why do you laugh?

DOUGLAS. Nothing, Mrs. Wilde. Mrs. Wilde—Mrs. Wilde. I have heard that soubriquet used of others, Mrs. Wilde. *(Again the laugh, again cut short.)*

CONSTANCE. What others?

DOUGLAS. Well, if you must know, a young man named Edward Shelley. For one.

CONSTANCE. What exactly is that supposed to mean?

DOUGLAS. Oh, God! Look here. I hate this ridiculous—fencing. It brings out the very worst in one. It makes me into a horror. I hate it. Besides, I actually like you. I admire you. We could be friends. I rather think of you as a sister. *(It is now Constance's turn to laugh.)* What is it?

CONSTANCE. Nothing. I just remembered something—sister—someone said something similar to me. A long time ago. Anyway, I don't believe you.

DOUGLAS. Oh, but you must! It is the solution to everything.

CONSTANCE. What is?

DOUGLAS. One could keep things just as they are, you see. Oscar needs me. I am his inspiration. He needs you. With you he finds peace. He needs the children—

CONSTANCE. I forbid you to speak of our children! Forbid you!

DOUGLAS. Oh, dear! Look, it's wretched that you should suffer like this. There's absolutely no need of it.

CONSTANCE. I don't need your sympathy, you contemptible person!

DOUGLAS. I'll ignore that remark. What you need is a confidante. Yes! Exactly. Someone wise in the world who can talk it all through with you, explain things to you. I wish I could. But I cannot. It is all too impossibly Parisian! A wise counsellor, a go-between. Oscar will think of someone. An older woman, perhaps?

CONSTANCE. What on earth are you talking about?

DOUGLAS. Someone to help you—

CONSTANCE. Help me? How?

DOUGLAS. To explain the situation, for heaven sakes! Oscar! I! You! What is going on!

CONSTANCE. But I am perfectly aware of what is going on. As you put it.

DOUGLAS. You are!

CONSTANCE. Yes. You and Oscar are Urnings. That is the term used by the German expert on sexual behaviour, Karl Heinrich Ulrich. Are you a true Urning, Lord Douglas, or do you also consort with women? It is apparently rather difficult to tell. Oscar is a Uranodiominge, that is to say an Urning who can also live with a woman. On the other hand, the true Urning who forces himself to cohabit with a woman, simply to conceal his true nature, say, well he is called a Virilisirt. Oscar is not a Virilisirt, no, I'm pretty certain of that.

DOUGLAS. Where on earth did you get all this?

CONSTANCE. From a book. I love to surprise people by revelations from my reading. My! But you do look a sight! Shall I fetch you some smelling salts?

DOUGLAS. A book! I really must sit down. I feel quite faint.

CONSTANCE. What you have to understand is that we women are trained from birth to conceal. Otherwise, you see, men would be unable to behave as they do. This is what is known as society. There. See? I can speak like Oscar, too.

DOUGLAS. I had no idea—I thought you had come here—I thought you were trying to sniff things out. I am utterly bewildered.

CONSTANCE. Actually, I came here to talk about money.

DOUGLAS. Money! Money? Money!

CONSTANCE. Let me list it for you. My allowance comes to just under £800 a year. Oscar, with your assistance, succeeded in going through £1,340 in three months—three months! At Goring. But I don't need to explain this to you. After all, you were there, were you not?

DOUGLAS. There are, well, certain—facilities, Constance Wilde, that I am accustomed to.

CONSTANCE. Meantime, the quarterly rent is due on Tite Street and I must ask my Aunt Mary, once more, for a loan. Meantime, Oscar has taken yet another advance from Mr Alexander for yet another unwritten play. Meantime, we have put the two boys down for schools, Bedales for Cyril, Hindlesham for Vyvie, but where, pray, are the fees? Meantime, I turn my back and Oscar has whisked you off for yet another weekend in Dieppe.

DOUGLAS. You speak of me as if I were a piece of luggage at a railway station.

CONSTANCE. How apt.

DOUGLAS. I will not have it, do you hear!

CONSTANCE. And I will not have *my* money spent on *you!* You may say all of this to my husband, Lord Douglas, should he choose to make an entrance after my departure.

DOUGLAS. Just a moment—

CONSTANCE. Good day—

She leaves but takes up a position beside the circle space with her back turned.

DOUGLAS. *(Weakly.)* But I like women—I really do!

Oscar steps onto the circle space as if from another room.

OSCAR. Has she gone?

DOUGLAS. Do you love me?

Oscar's answer is a kiss, followed by more kisses, his hands caressing Douglas's body. Douglas pushes him away.

DOUGLAS. Do you mind!

OSCAR. What did she say to you?

DOUGLAS. Do you know you married a remarkable woman? Constance Holland Lloyd. Quite, quite remarkable. Yes. Do you realize that she knows everything about us?

OSCAR. Everyone knows everything about us, dear boy. Your delightful father has seen to that, going about town with his lurid, filthy messages to everyone who will listen. I only wish we could live up to his obscene imagination.

DOUGLAS. I don't wish to speak of my monstrous father. I want to talk about your wife.

OSCAR. Not now, dear.

DOUGLAS. But you constantly talk about her. Constance this, Constance that. I find it extremely tiresome.

OSCAR. I beg your pardon!

DOUGLAS. Yes—letting her worm her way in—poking herself in

the way women always do with that whine of theirs. She brings you to heel. Here, doggy! And you trot along, on the leash! Why, Oscar? Why? Away from her you are utterly different. One thing in the country, another thing in town.

OSCAR. No, I am not!

DOUGLAS. Yes, you are! But you hate to face it. Double-faced, that's what you are. You hate them, women. You hate their smell. Mulierism. That's your word. Have you forgotten? I could never be a mulierist again, you said, tossing your locks. They are swallowing me up, you said, all those shes, sucking one in, slits, tweaks, disgusting but no, no, Jesus Oscar must keep up pretence! That bitch!

Oscar hits him. It is a shocking blow but even as the blow is struck Oscar is ready to pull back again, to take Douglas in his arms again.

OSCAR. Don't you dare speak of her like that! Ever!

DOUGLAS. Forgive me, forgive me.

OSCAR. You know nothing about her! Nothing!

DOUGLAS. Why am I like this? Why—why?

OSCAR. I tell you there are times that I return to that house and I am a piece of human wreckage. She says nothing, simply looks at me. She sits quietly in a window, reading perhaps, perhaps sketching, allowing me to play with the children on the carpet. All the mad, frantic pursuit of flesh dies down in me. That room in my house has such perfect poise, such stillness, that I have a brief, momentary illusion of the state of grace. That is what she means to me! That is what my children mean to me!

DOUGLAS. I am a monster. My blood is monstrous. Look at my father! Savagery. I am going to kill myself. It is the only way out.

OSCAR. Do you know, it's rather as if one had stepped into a cool interior on canvas. Vermeer, perhaps.

DOUGLAS. But for you I would have killed myself already. You know that. You are the only one who finds something—worthwhile in me. The only one! A reason to live. Then I do this. To her. Whom I like. I actually do like her! Like something pouring out of me, abscess, pus. I'm diseased, cannot stop. I try, oh, I try. Only with you can I see some semblance of humanity when I look in the mirror.

Oscar holds him in a deep embrace when he has ended. Then Douglas breaks away, fully restored, as if nothing unusual has happened.

DOUGLAS. What's that story about her father, then?

OSCAR. Which story?

DOUGLAS. Was he queer? Her father?

OSCAR. Her father? Nonsense. Whoever said such a thing?

DOUGLAS. There's gossip.

OSCAR. Oh, it's gossip, is it?

DOUGLAS. Don't blame me, dearie. I'm only repeating what is said behind curtains. By the way, she also asked me to tell you something.

OSCAR. What?

DOUGLAS. She said to say you were broke.

Oscar laughs, a wild laugh of despair, and then stops short. Both he and Douglas stand, drained, not looking at one another. The attendants applaud with their clappers. They remove the two men from the circle where they stand, heads averted.

First, the mobile staircase is put in place on the circular space. Constance has been dressed in a peignoir, her hair hangs loose about her and she carries a bottle. She is conducted forward, drunk, staggering slightly as she wanders through her house.

CONSTANCE. *(Drinking.)* One last sip, Constance, just one, teeny tiny one and then beddy-byes. There! What is it about an empty house? So—skeletal. *(Drinks in the words.)* Shell. Hollow. *(Sudden briskness.)* Send the children away to school, Constance. Much better for them, Constance, what with—you know? Much better for you, Constance, do something with yourself. *(Each beat.)* Remarkable, truly remarkable, how advice, of people, always, seems to—flatter those people themselves. Smart girl, Constance! Plucky girl, Constance! But how do you manage it? Pluck! People close to him want to kill themselves. Douglas said that. Should know, he should.

The society hostess. As she speaks, chair, desk, dining room table come flying by as if she were conducting a surreal auction, the attendants as auctioneer's help.

Yes, m'dears, that is Mr Wilde's chair over there, does all his great work on it, well, some of it. Used to, anyway. Used to belong to Mr Carlyle, chair that is, don't touch, please, thank you! And here is the white dining room with its famous white furniture specially made by

Mr Godwin, old Godwino, a concerto in ivory, Mr Wilde's phrase. Mr Wilde's phrasing. A phrase for everything, Mr Wilde. *(Down.)* Except failure. *(Up.)* Oh, and do let me show you the ceiling of the drawing room. Just upstairs. *(The 'ceiling' appears above her head like a canopy, peacock feathers floating down.)* Painted by Mr Whistler, no less. Notice in particular the two gold dragons with inlaid real peacock's feathers. Real! Real! What a load of rubbish it all is! *(Very carefully places bottle at her feet.)* Funny thing, now, the way people go on as if it were the flesh when it wasn't the flesh at all. You see, if it were the flesh the flesh is satisfied and he was never, never, never satisfied. How do I know? Oh, I know! You see there was something in nature that he could never accept. Maybe that's why he could write such splendid comedy?

The attendants suddenly seize her and she screams. They drag her to the staircase and she struggles against them as they push her up the steps to the landing.

No! Please! Don't! I can't go up there! I can't. Can't do it. Not on my own! Please! Where is Oscar? Where is Oscar?

She is now on the landing, crouched, facing the audience, drinking. The attendants retreat to the foot of the steps where they raise their white gloved hands to receive her.

Nothing there. Empty house. Skeletal. No sound. Nothing. Safe. Constance safe. No-one-to-harm-her. See! Empty! Then I flew. Became untouchable, you see. I saw before me this—open—expanse— blue, so blue in all the whiteness of our house, House Beautiful. I saw blue and began to fly.

Music. She launches herself into the air and is held in the upraised hands of the attendants. They turn her body slowly in the air, a choreographed tumble, and she screams. Over and over until they bring her slowly down on the floor, still screaming, at the foot of the stairs. The attendants stand aside as she lies on her back in great pain. She turns with difficulty and begins to crawl off. The attendants follow her and only when she reaches the edge of the circle do they react. They first applaud with their clappers, then lift and drag her off.

(Crawling.) Help me. Someone. Please!

Music. The staircase is removed from the white circle by the attendants.

Two elegant chairs are placed side by side on the white space. Oscar and Constance are re-dressed by the attendants, minimal costume changes, perhaps a hat and cane to him, a shawl to her.

Douglas, meanwhile, has come forward to address the audience.

DOUGLAS. Actually I was the only one of the three who had the slightest control over my fate. With this one exception. The whole thing made me more vile than I actually am. As you've seen just now. Not a bad chap usually. Really. The other thing is that I needed more than he was prepared to give. I cry out to him: Look at me! Look at me! I am human! A kind of glaze comes over his eyes. He presses money into my hands. I drink too much. I gamble like a madman. I lose. He presses more money into my hands. On and on! I am driven by this twin demon of idolatry and neglect. I have never been so attended on, never so lonely in my life. I exaggerate, of course, but you get my drift. And then I find that he is still slipping back to that house on Tite Street. To her. What on earth is he up to? He says it's to see the children. But every time he returns to me he is sunken in this black depression. What is she saying to him? Is she feeding him some dreadful woman lies? I must find out! Yes, I must!

He steps aside, off the white disk, standing with his back to what happens. Constance is led on, walking with a slight limp, and is seated in one of the chairs. Oscar steps up onto the white disk behind her. It is as if he has just entered the room behind her and she looks up.

OSCAR. I didn't wake them. Fast asleep! So beautiful! I simply stood in the doorway and peeped in. Cyril had all his navy arrayed by the bedside, flags aloft. While Vyvie was clutching old Snow Bear for dear life. Dear life! I am sorry about your accident, Constance. You must call on me at once when something like this happens.

CONSTANCE. You know, I actually did cry out for you. On that stairs. Where were you, Oscar? In St James's Place? Brighton, maybe? Perhaps in the Hôtel des Deux Mondes? Or some other Parisian hideout? Perhaps I could have sent a wire to Algiers? That's a possibility, now. *(Pause.)* I want a divorce.

OSCAR. Divorce! Is that why you invited me here?

CONSTANCE. No, as a matter of fact. There's something else I need to tell you. But this sort of—popped out.

OSCAR. Popped out! Popped out! Divorce! And that, I take it, is my cue to ask the inevitable, melodramatic question: is there someone else?

CONSTANCE. There may be.

OSCAR. How suitably inconclusive. Who is it?

CONSTANCE. Arthur.

OSCAR. Do you mean Arthur Humphreys of Hatchard's bookshop? How thrilling. You and he have been arranging to publish my aphorisms while playing hanky-panky among the bookshelves.

CONSTANCE. Why, Oscar, you're jealous!

OSCAR. Certainly not! Indeed, I am pleased that someone has been in attendance on you. I am pleased for you. Besides, what is marriage without adultery? Look at the French! Every Frenchman of note has been cuckolded by wife or mistress: Villon, Molière, Louis XIV, Napoléon, Victor Hugo, Musset, Balzac. And why? Why, because the French really love women, that's why. Englishmen don't. That is why adultery is such a scandalous novelty in this country. I intend to set up a movement for the propagation of adultery. It will do wonders for the freedom of women. *(Pause.)* My one reservation is your choice of partner. Arthur Humphreys is a walking slim volume of third-rate verse who happens to wear spectacles.

CONSTANCE. But it's not your choice, is it?

OSCAR. Obviously not.

CONSTANCE. Anyway. It's over now. It didn't mean very much. Except attention. And I've never needed that, particularly.

OSCAR. But divorce, Constance? Why divorce!

CONSTANCE. It would merely define what is already there.

OSCAR. No! We still have something, Constance!

CONSTANCE. What? What do we have?

OSCAR. *(Floundering.)* The children—

CONSTANCE. We three waited all day Christmas Day in this house for you. The boys were desolate. In the end I said you were—ill and couldn't come.

OSCAR. I was rehearsing.

CONSTANCE. Rehearsing! Rehearsing! On Christmas Day!

OSCAR. I'm afraid it's the truth. Such is theatre!

CONSTANCE. Actually, this is not why I asked you to come here. I have something else to tell you. I did have a visitor. On Boxing Day. Charles Brookfield.

OSCAR. Brookfield? The actor? The one who plays Phipps in my play?

CONSTANCE. Yes, that's the one.

OSCAR. *(Nervously.)* Not to complain, I hope.

CONSTANCE. He sat where you are sitting now. I'm sorry to have to tell you this, Mrs Wilde—

OSCAR. He's been devilishly difficult in rehearsal, Brookfield—

CONSTANCE. I knew what was coming, then. But it was the details! The details! Did he speak for an hour? I even asked questions. You know how my curiosity always gets the better of me. Even when I think I'm going to vomit.

OSCAR. *(Now very nervous.)* He hates me, Brookfield.

CONSTANCE. Oh, yes. Indeed he does. *(Oscar rises.)* You must hear this. Sit down. *(He does.)* For your own protection. He told me of that house on Little College Street. He said it was talked of among the actors. He told me of that man Taylor. Of men dressing as women. Of boys dressing as girls. He described the mock marriages between men. He described how trousers were cut to allow men to—fondle one another. He said you and Douglas frequented this place. He said, and this was his word, that you both hunted working-class men. I had this vision of a pack in a field. *(More slowly still.)* Funny thing. I never questioned why he should feel free to torment me with all this. He was like a messenger in the last act of an old play.

OSCAR. *(Utterly lost, an old joke dead.)* What is it I once said? A man cannot be too careful in the choice of his enemies. *(She is not amused.)* Sorry.

CONSTANCE. Instead, I asked, is it true, Mr Brookfield, that they have their own kinds of medical problems? I mean because of what they do to one another?

OSCAR. Exactly like women in other words.

CONSTANCE. He said, the delicate Mr Brookfield, that he did not defile his mind by thinking of such things. And no, it is not like women.

OSCAR. By God I shall kill him, Brookfield! *(Pause.)* Particularly since I can't sack him from my play.

CONSTANCE. I think he was quite shocked, actually, that I didn't disintegrate in tears at his feet. He is one of those men, our Mr Brookfield, who likes to cause women to suffer. So that he can then console them. I wept later, of course. Alone.

OSCAR. Brookfield. What did you do with him?

CONSTANCE. I ordered him out of the house.

OSCAR. I am grateful that you've told me this.

CONSTANCE. Then I pulled myself together. And I discovered something quite startling. I wasn't—surprised—that you were capable of—all this. No. It was as if it simply completed my knowledge of you. In a horrible kind of way, of course. You are in great danger. You know that?

OSCAR. Yes.

CONSTANCE. What will you do?

OSCAR. Don't divorce me, Constance.

CONSTANCE. I keep thinking. What is the connection? What is the connection between his foul behaviour and the beauty of what he writes? Can anyone ever answer that question?

OSCAR. We are all in the gutter but some of us are looking at the stars.

CONSTANCE. I think that's too easy. What I'm thinking of cannot be put in a single phrase.

OSCAR. *(Unable to conceal his irritation.)* Do you actually enjoy correcting me? I merely ask. You are the only person who does this, the only one!

CONSTANCE. Oh, don't be so touchy, Oscar, for heaven sakes. We know one another.

OSCAR. What an understatement. Energy. It is all a question of energy. There is energy in the muscle. There is energy in the loop of syntax. The one feeds the other.

CONSTANCE. Even when you are doing something gross?

OSCAR. There is no distinction, my dear, between what is gross and what is sublime in art.

CONSTANCE. *(Weeping.)* And what about love? Is love gross, too?

OSCAR. Ah, Constance, how I have made you suffer!

CONSTANCE. And after all your protestations you're back with Douglas again—

OSCAR. Yes—

CONSTANCE. He's a monster, you know. It's going to destroy you.

OSCAR. Yes, he is. And yes, it will. Don't divorce me, Constance, for God's sake, don't—

CONSTANCE. Give me one good reason why I shouldn't.

OSCAR. *(Very distressed.)* The children! The children! So that I may see them.

CONSTANCE. Divorce. No divorce. What does it matter?

OSCAR. It matters! Divorce would annihilate me! You're a long line to the shore when I'm far out at sea.

CONSTANCE. I've decided something about you. I said this to someone the other day. He's absolutely deficient, I said, in certain areas of feeling. And absurdly intense in others. A sort of imbalance which is extremely dangerous . . . If you have anything to do with him, that is.

OSCAR. Don't you see what these visits mean to me? The rest of my life is madness! Madness! *(Whisper.)* No divorce, then?

CONSTANCE. *(Pause.)* No divorce.

Music. Two of the attendants lead her off the circular space into darkness. Then, as he stands there, alone, he too is led off to the side. Constance sits to one side, 'reading' to the two 'children.' This shadowed image remains throughout the following speech, fading before it ends. A hanging cage is flown in. It hangs over what follows.

The mobile staircase is pushed onto the disk once more but now reversed, with the steps hidden from the audience. The back of the staircase resembles a simple dock. Puppets of judge, lawyers and gentlemen are brought forward, crowding around the dock, waving arms. The impression is of frenzy.

Wilde climbs the stairs onto the dock. He speaks off as if in memory.

OSCAR. And, you, Wilde, have had the audacity to prosecute a father for libel, knowing full well that he was merely protecting his son from your foul influence. That the father was a peer of the realm, Lord Queensberry, and his son, Lord Alfred Douglas, a member of the aristocracy, simply gives some indication of the range of your upstart insolence. You, Wilde, have been the corruptor of young men. That many of them were of the lower classes, grooms, newspaper boys, valets, and the like, gives some indication of your vulgarity. That you dressed some of these youths to resemble the sons of gentlemen, putting some public school colours in their hats, elevating them above their proper sphere, gives some indication of your contempt for the ordering of society. You, Wilde, have been a family man and the father of two children. You have violated your family and stained, beyond cleansing, the lives of your wife and children. You, Wilde, have failed in all things. You have failed in your action against the Marquis of Queensberry. You have failed in your subversion of society. You have failed as a husband. You have failed as a father. You now have six hours and fifty minutes before the departure of the boat train from Victoria. If you have not fled this kingdom by then you will be arrested, tried. And condemned.

The dock/staircase is trundled off into darkness with Wilde still on it to the distant, echoing sound of the courtroom response, cheers, jeers, hand clapping, various cries, insults.

Two elegant chairs are put in place on the white disk. Constance is led on, limping badly and supporting herself on a cane. She sits. Douglas, in outdoor clothes, is conducted on behind her. He stands. At first she doesn't look at him.

CONSTANCE. If what you tell me is true, then he is doomed.

DOUGLAS. But, surely, you knew all this already?

CONSTANCE. They told me that the painted women of the streets danced in triumph. After the trial. Outside the Old Bailey. Is that true? Would you believe it, I even asked: why? Silly me. Competition, I was told. There's great competition on the streets between the men and women streetwalkers. Where is he now?

DOUGLAS. The Cadogan Hotel. In Sloane Street.

CONSTANCE. So. Your father has triumphed. They always do, don't they, fathers? And they've given him the chance to run away, have they, the authorities?

DOUGLAS. Yes. He could follow all the other friends of ours into exile but he mustn't. That is why I came.

CONSTANCE. I see. And did he send you here?

DOUGLAS. Good Lord no!

CONSTANCE. How long has he got?

DOUGLAS. Three hours. He's wavering. I know it. He's wavering. There is a half-packed suitcase open on the bed. The room is like a

Jane Brennan in *The Secret Fall of Constance Wilde*.
Courtesy Amelia Stein.

railway station, comings and goings. Everyone screaming advice. Get
the boat train, Oscar! I fled. Couldn't stand it a moment longer. Said
I was going to Westminster to get help. To my cousin, George Wyn-
dham. But what I really wanted was to come here. To you. I knew that
you, of all people, would stand firm at this time.

CONSTANCE. I detest the sight of you.

DOUGLAS. I've changed, Constance.

CONSTANCE. Indeed? Why are you trying to stop him from leaving for France?

DOUGLAS. For his sake, of course!

CONSTANCE. Not to prolong that absurd farce with your father?

DOUGLAS. Everyone says that! Why will no one believe me? My father is a mad little man. He doesn't know it but he's only the mouthpiece, the pawn, of the larger enemy. There is only one person who can fight that larger enemy. Oscar.

CONSTANCE. Even if he is destroyed in the process?

DOUGLAS. Yes.

CONSTANCE. How very brave of you. There's no danger of *your* arrest, is there?

DOUGLAS. I am in terrible danger.

CONSTANCE. What's this greater enemy that you speak about?

DOUGLAS. It's a body of powerful interests in this country which hates love.

CONSTANCE. I see. And you know this larger enemy, do you, Lord Douglas?

DOUGLAS. I was born into it, Mrs Wilde.

CONSTANCE. Why did it all go so utterly wrong? Why? Oscar seemed so confident he would win.

DOUGLAS. Someone betrayed us.

CONSTANCE. What do you mean?

DOUGLAS. Well, when we first took the case there was no doubt that we would defeat my wretched father. Everyone said that he had libelled Oscar. We were so confident that we left at once for Monte Carlo. When we got back it was all horror. Someone had given the other side, well, information. All lies, of course. But *(shrugs)* it worked with that wretched jury.

CONSTANCE. *(Pause.)* Our Mr Brookfield.

DOUGLAS. Who did you say?

CONSTANCE. I happen to believe that information, you know. What does that make me, then? Another member of the jury?

DOUGLAS. What on earth do you know about it?

CONSTANCE. Oh, never mind. What is it that you want me to do for Oscar?

DOUGLAS. You are the only one he will listen to!

CONSTANCE. I don't trust you.

DOUGLAS. I can understand that. I know what I've been like. Oscar has made me see that. He has that gift of making people see themselves. Don't you think so? That is why they hate him. Most people can't bear to look at themselves.

CONSTANCE. Why! You're trying to make me share him with you!

DOUGLAS. But we do that already, don't we?

CONSTANCE. What can you know of me?

DOUGLAS. A lot, actually. I mean I think I know you terribly well. How? Well, he never stops talking about you, for one. Used to hate it, of course. Until I listened to what he was actually saying.

CONSTANCE. My life is private!

DOUGLAS. You misinterpret. Never, not once, has Oscar betrayed the privacies between you two. What he does talk about, endlessly I have to say, is your capacity to—accept.

CONSTANCE. Of course. Accept! In that way I may be abused, humiliated!

DOUGLAS. Oh, do let's stop talking about ourselves! This is infinitely bigger than any one person. How Oscar conducts himself now will determine the future of many, many people. Many of them frightened little people in lonely rooms. They will see him stand his ground. And his example will give them hope. Only Oscar is capable of that because of the immense hate that he has provoked.

CONSTANCE. You sound extraordinarily disinterested, Lord Douglas. Well, I'm not. I'm only interested now in the survival of my two boys. For that, I want him as far away as possible. At the very least, the south of France.

DOUGLAS. Constance, Constance! You don't know what you're condemning him to. I do. You don't know the deathly life of the invert in exile. I do. I know it so well. Imprisonment in a villa above Monte Carlo with the likes of Podge Somerset. The perpetual whine, the perpetual, futile plans to return home. Capri, Taormina, Tangiers. Splendid to visit, but what if there were nothing else? Ever? Oscar would go insane. Apart at all from the fact that he would see it as cowardice.

CONSTANCE. You'd prefer him to be a victim?

DOUGLAS. I'd prefer him to be Oscar.

CONSTANCE. Perhaps I have underestimated you.

DOUGLAS. I have never threatened you. Oscar says that, you know. He says, at some level she is never threatened.

CONSTANCE. No, not threatened. Hurt, yes.

DOUGLAS. Well, then. We can have an understanding, can we not?

CONSTANCE. I hate hypocrisy and all the dangerous, malevolent hypocrites sitting in high places. Tell him I said he should fight them! Fight them! Fight them to the bitter end.

DOUGLAS. *(Producing paper and pencil.)* Would you write a short letter to him?

CONSTANCE. A letter!

DOUGLAS. Yes, you know how Oscar adores letters. *(She takes the paper and pencil and writes.)* It would mean so much to him to read your actual words. There is only one thing he prefers to receiving letters. That is, tearing up the bad ones.

CONSTANCE. *(Handing him the note.)* You may read it if you wish.

DOUGLAS. I always read other people's letters. *(Reading.)* 'Dear Oscar, Fight them to the end. Constance.' I feel as if I'm carrying a last-minute reprieve to the gallows.

CONSTANCE. Well, then, you should hurry along, shouldn't you? *(He turns to go.)* I want him to read that before he leaves that room.

He looks at her as she steps off the circle. Then he steps off and they stand to one side in darkness, watching.

A loud sound of clappers as the attendants lead Oscar onto the centre of the circle. He is wearing a fur overcoat and top hat. His costume is such that it will come apart in pieces during what follows. As he speaks the attendants crouch at his feet, like dogs.

OSCAR. Certain melodramas rise to the Aristotelian, others descend to the depths of realism. Mine was somewhere in between. The policeman's knock on the door. The heavy hand on one's shoulder. *(Outburst.)* Where is Bosie? Why isn't he here? Room Number 53, the Cadogan Hotel. My rather vulgar Upper Room. From now on my fate would be determined by numbers. Why do all these people keep urging me to go abroad? It is deafening. I have just *been* abroad. One cannot keep going abroad. Unless one is a missionary. Or a commercial traveller. That sounded so much better the first time round. The boat train departed from Victoria at 5:45 P.M. The knock on the door came exactly at ten minutes past six. They wished me to cut and run, you see. Mr Wilde, I presume? Yes? I must ask you, sir, to accompany me to the police station. Decent opening lines, no? When the policeman finally confronts his quarry there is always this exchange between

equals. A sort of civility that can only be born out of a shared famil-
iarity with transgression. My coppers. Inspector Richards with his
warts, his doleful sergeant holding on to a scrap of paper for dear life.
Splendid fellows, those two! *(Anguish.)* Why isn't Bosie back? For
God's sake, go and find him, someone! I wrote to Constance. Told her
to protect the children. Lock the house. I told her that no one should
have access to my study but the servants. Perhaps I was thinking that
only servants should read what I had written from this day out?
(Great cry.) Bosie! He has abandoned me! He wasn't up to it when the
chips were down. Funk! Well, my dear, cheers! Why am I not running away? They do not understand, you see, that it was long past all
that. I was already condemned. I was already in that filthy cell, stink-
ing of diarrhoea and the smell of every inmate who had ever been
there down the endless years. The Community of Man, oh, yes, indeed. I was already staggering on the treadmill, I was already turning
the crank, my daily duty. When men set out to destroy their own
kind they give them tasks of exquisite uselessness. I already knew all
this before I put on my topcoat with my two coppers in tow. I knew
the future. I knew the past. I knew what it was to be among the olives
in that garden at eventide, the fake kiss, the hysterical disciples and
the violent sacrifice of the one for the many.

*The cage is lowered. A piercing cacophony of sound and discordant notes,
canned laughter and applause, night screams and cries of agony and, as a bass
tone, endless opening and banging shut of prison cell doors, feet shuffling along
stone corridors, indecipherable shouts of command.*

*The attendants have leaped upon Oscar, tearing at his clothes and hair. The
clothes come apart in strips, the hair comes off in tufts. He is dragged, half-
naked, half-mutilated, back to the cage which is now the only thing on stage
that is lit. He is pushed naked into the cage, and it swings aloft. In there, he
is hosed down by the attendants.*

*Constance and Douglas watch all this in silhouette, backs to audience. Lights
down on all but Constance. She turns to the audience walking well downstage.*

CONSTANCE. It was as if I married him a second time in that disgusting prison but this time not the bride in cowslip yellow crowned
with myrtle in St James's Church, oh no, this time naked in the bed of

filth. You see, I saw Papa, too, in that cage, degraded, loving, generous, reviled, monstrous Papa. I loved two criminals, you see. Papa-Oscar. Oscar-Papa. And he said to me, from that cage, nothing can be concealed here, Constance, poor, naked wretches, nothing to cover them, no words, no love.

People keep asking me questions: What will you do now, Constance? And what will you tell the children?

She stands there as the lights come down.

END OF PART ONE

PART TWO

Music: Organ, variations on the Missa in Commemoratione Omnium Fidelium Defunctorum. Rising and falling through the following: Constance is still standing where she was at the end of Part One, still facing the audience. The iron cage has been pushed forward, downstage. The white disk hangs above it, a large moon or gigantic wafer. There is a hidden ramp behind the cage, beneath the disk.

Oscar is in the cage, bedraggled prison uniform, a worn, beaten figure on his knees, praying, back to audience. One ear is bandaged with a filthy cloth.

CONSTANCE. The children! The children! he cried. The children! And I remembered how one day on the beach at Brighton I was alone on a deck chair, the children at my feet among the sandcastles. And suddenly this large figure appeared in the distance in inappropriate black, it being high summer, the hot sun, flapping like a monstrous bird. It was Oscar. He ran across the strand, waving his arms so that I thought something quite dreadful had happened. The children! he cried. The children! Tears streaming down his face. Are they all right? Yes, of course they're all right, I said. Oh, my God, he cried, collapsing on the sand beside me. I was asleep and dreamt that they had been swept out to sea!

Pause.

That, too, you see, is Oscar. The other question people keep asking me is: *(Voice.)* You saw him in prison, Constance, what was it really like? Was it really so very dreadful? *(Self again.)* They make it sound like a slightly disagreeable tea party. I cannot raise my left arm anymore. Did I really fly? Or was I cast down? *(Voice.)* What did he look like, Constance? Did he have to wear those awful duds, the ones with those funny arrows? *(Self again.)* Actually—I said to them in my best nonchalant, wife-of-a-celebrity voice—Christ came to him in his cell. That stopped them in their tracks, I can tell you. Always managed to have the best of company, our Oscar. Wherever he found himself. *(Shrill, deep distress.)* Dirt, they said, dirt—he is dirt, stained bed linen, well, then, stick him in the dirt, rub his face in it, diarrhoea and urine. Christ came in the dirt, obvious, isn't it? I followed him! Followed him down into the dirt. And loved him there in my bowels. Human, indeed!

She turns and watches what follows. The six attendants in black chasubles, white gloves, lead on Douglas in procession, along the ramp, beneath the white disk, above Oscar's head. Douglas is dressed in the full black, traditional vestments of the Mass of the Dead, chasuble, stole, cincture etc.

Two of the attendants carry tall, black-stemmed altar candlesticks with lit candles. A third carries a large display of lily of the valley and ciborium, a fourth, the large, traditional Mass missal. This is held open before Douglas, resting on the attendant's head so that Douglas, as priest, may read from it.

The total effect is of a fantastic dream or nightmare.

DOUGLAS. *(Intoning, hands outstretched.)* Requiem aeternam dona eis, Domine: et lux perpetua luceat eis. In memoria aeterna erit iustus, ab auditione mala non timebit. Absolve, Domine, animas omnium fidelium defunctorum ab omni vinculo delictorum. Et lucis aeternae beatitudine perfrui.

A massed male choir breaks out into the opening verses of the Dies Irae and it runs through the following: the attendants strip Douglas of the outer vestments so that he is now a Christlike figure in long white alb. One of them hands him the ciborium. They conduct him down into the cage where he gives Communion from the ciborium to a reverential Oscar. The attendants take the ciborium from Douglas. Oscar kisses Douglas on each of his proferred palms, prostrates himself and kisses his feet. Douglas raises Oscar and kisses him on the mouth. At this the attendants applaud noisily and sweep Douglas away, out, up and across the ramp into darkness while the choral singing is sharply cut off.

OSCAR. *(On his knees.)* Domine, non sum dignus! Domine, non sum dignus!

Sound: marching along prison corridors, steel doors swinging open, banged shut. A second cage is moved in beside the first. Constance is conducted into this. Puppet gaolers. The other attendants stand to either side, guards or macabre waiters. One of them takes a piece of paper from Constance and carries it to Oscar.

CONSTANCE. *(Cry.)* Why will you not let me touch him? *(Rising, holding the bars of her cage.)*

OSCAR. *(Reading, voice breaking.)* It says here that she simply turned her face to the wall and died. Just like that. Oh, my God, poor Mama! Is this my brother's handwriting?

CONSTANCE. Yes.

OSCAR. Still trying to write lurid journalism, that brother of mine. You know she came to me, Mother, as an apparition in the cell but she didn't speak.

CONSTANCE. I wanted to be the one to tell you, Oscar. About her death.

OSCAR. Thank you.

CONSTANCE. She was a deeply serious person, your mother. Underneath those outlandish clothes. *(Pause.)* Can you still not eat the food they give you?

OSCAR. I eat the soup. And a little bread.

CONSTANCE. How is your ear infection?

OSCAR. It has stopped draining. I think.

CONSTANCE. *(Cry: to attendants.)* Please! Let me touch him!

OSCAR. Don't, Constance. They punish each indiscretion. I would get solitary for three days. I cannot bear it anymore. Oh, Mama, Mama, what have I done to you!

CONSTANCE. You've suffered enough, Oscar.

OSCAR. I cannot suffer enough.

CONSTANCE. Why, that's simply not true.

OSCAR. *(Hard laugh.)* Constance still correcting me! Sorry. Didn't mean that. Joke.

CONSTANCE. I was simply thinking of the great courage you always have.

OSCAR. I had. Past tense. She never lost her dignity, you know. Mother. Even when she was down on her uppers. Not a brass farthing in the house. Alone in that darkened room waiting to die. Couldn't bear to let people see her poverty. She was always capable of the right gesture. Even with that monster, my father. Do you know, when he was dying she conducted one of his mistresses to the bedside and left them alone together? She belonged to a future. A future that may never materialize, alas.

CONSTANCE. There's another reason that I came.

OSCAR. *(New anxiety.)* Is it the boys? Has something happened to them? Are they safe?

CONSTANCE. Yes—yes—yes—they're perfectly fine.

OSCAR. *(Pause.)* Constance. *(Pause.)* What have you told them? About me?

CONSTANCE. I say that you are away on a long journey.

OSCAR. But there was something else, why you came.

CONSTANCE. *(Distress.)* I came to confess.

OSCAR. To what?

CONSTANCE. Confess! Confess! *(Very distressed.)* I kept saying to myself—throughout all the horrors—I kept saying, remember, remember, it's all human, Constance! Human! That way I could somehow accept it all. *(Bitter.)* Constance's great capacity to accept everything. Then one day, I don't know why, I don't even remember when—I saw this for what it was. Flattery. I was simply flattering myself with my own— *(Contempt.)* goodness.

OSCAR. Constance—

CONSTANCE. No, hear me out. Suddenly there was nothing between me and absolute horror, something monstrous within me, some squat creature. It was terrifying.

OSCAR. But why are you telling me all this now?

CONSTANCE. Because it has to do with you.

OSCAR. How with me?

CONSTANCE. Don't know, really. I mean I detest the life you've been living. I find it utterly disgusting. And yet I know that this facing myself or whatever it is, exposure, or something, has to do with

the way you've exposed yourself. Isn't that strange? I felt so utterly se-
cure when I first met you, all that brilliant camouflage, all that mask-
ing. And now that you're broken I am broken, too. Very odd, actually.

OSCAR. It takes great suffering to see that.

CONSTANCE. Oh, it's not a bit grandiose like that. It's infinitely
more mundane. Actually quite ugly, as a matter of fact. One day in
Genoa it was. The pain from my spine particularly severe. One
minute I was crouching there, unable to straighten up. But congrat-
ulating myself, of course! Bravo Constance! You can do it, there's a
good girl. Put up with anything. Yes, you can! Next moment I
straightened up in unimaginable pain, my mouth screaming out the
most frightful obscenities. At myself. At you. Gross words I didn't
know I possessed. Spewing out of me. Like a sewer. I believe I blas-
phemed. Yes! I certainly swore at God for this thing called existence.
I felt utterly degraded. The funny thing is I also felt somehow—ex-
hilarated. All at the same time.

OSCAR. It is Christ!

CONSTANCE. I beg your pardon!

OSCAR. We are born to live with contradiction. When Christ said:
Forgive thine enemy, it wasn't for the relief of the enemy, it was for
the healing of oneself. Oh, Constance, I've learned so much in here! I
used to hold contradiction in a single phrase. Now I am learning to
hold contradiction in my heart. Everything in this life threatens to
contradict something else.

CONSTANCE. As man and woman.

OSCAR. That too, that too.

CONSTANCE. I love you, Oscar, the way you once said you loved
me. Remember? That day in Dublin, in Merrion Square?

OSCAR. *(Eagerly.)* You mean we can be together again with the
two boys!

CONSTANCE. They miss you frightfully.

OSCAR. Please tell me more about the two of them, Constance.
What do they do each day?

CONSTANCE. Well, Cyril still wants to be a sailor. Royal Navy.
He's got lots of books about it. Practises his salute in front of the mirror. Terribly brave. Each day we must spin the globe and sail all
around the world. That makes me feel young again.

OSCAR. And Vyvie?

CONSTANCE. Oh, he's very imaginative, actually, makes things with bits of coloured paper. But he keeps asking: where are my tin soldiers, Mummy? Do you know all the children's toys fetched thirty shillings at the auction?

OSCAR. Thirty pieces of silver. Where have I heard that before! (*Pause.*) I did all that!

CONSTANCE. You are not responsible for the evil of other people, Oscar.

OSCAR. I gave them licence.

CONSTANCE. Our splendid civilization has given them licence, Oscar. (*Pause.*) When you waited in the hotel. Before your arrest. Did you receive a letter from me?

OSCAR. No. What was in it?

CONSTANCE. I told you not to run away.

OSCAR. Oh, if only I had received it—

CONSTANCE. I gave it to Douglas—

OSCAR. I see. (*Pause.*) I'm afraid he is particularly irresponsible in the matter of correspondence. Something to do with public schooling, I believe.

CONSTANCE. Oscar, have you finished with him?

OSCAR. I was mad, Constance. For four whole years, I was out of my mind. Didn't you see it? I see it now with the most awful clarity.

CONSTANCE. (*Whisper.*) What about Douglas?

OSCAR. He is trying to sell my letters, you know. Can you believe it! He is offering his story for money to newspapers! But no one wants anything to do with him.

CONSTANCE. (*Almost breaking.*) What about you and Douglas?

OSCAR. If he were here this instant I'd kill him. They talk about my crime. Ha! My only crime is that I made a god out of common clay. That is unforgivable.

CONSTANCE. (*Scream.*) Answer me!

Blare of music. Constance's cage is thrown open and she is led out. The cage is quickly taken off while Oscar, sunken, remains in his own cage. Douglas, in long travelling coat, white hat and cane appears upstage in a bright spot.

A frenzied movement: attendants with puppets of travellers, complete with suitcases, valises, portmanteaus. Rushing train sounds. Engine smoke. Douglas is swept up in this travel. Constance, in travelling coat and hat, with the two child puppets, travelling in a cutaway railway carriage that heaves and shudders to loud train noise and reeling, flashing light. Train comes to a halt. Attendants/porters conduct Constance and her luggage off the carriage. An hotel entrance. Hôtel de la Gare. Constance and the children are turned away from the hotel door by an attendant/hotel manager and attendant/doorman.

Back in the carriage once more. Repeat of the shuddering journey, train whistle. Again the journey comes to a halt. Silence. A dazed Constance is brought forward. The child puppets and her travelling coat and hat are removed. A white garden seat is placed for her but first she addresses the audience. Douglas finishes his travelling, coat and hat off.

CONSTANCE. Somewhere between Switzerland and the Italian plain I knew he would never answer me. I decided to change our name. Never again could we call ourselves Wilde. It was an ending but not *the* ending. You see I hadn't confessed all to him. I was unable to. And there could be no ending until I did so. Confess. Secret. To fall again. *(Pauses, glances off.)* Who is it? Who is that? *(She turns in shock. Douglas steps forward and they are lit in bright sunlight.)* How did you know where I was?

DOUGLAS. Why are we both living abroad? Hmm? Apart from the insufferably dull world of commerce, there are only two reasons why people travel. Culture and criminality. You and I are abroad for the same reason. His name is Oscar, the cultured criminal. Our circuits may be different, true. I may fancy Capri with odd diversions to Monte Carlo to play the tables at the casino. Or Sicily with odd diversions to Algiers for the Arabs. While you move from Germany to Switzerland to Monaco to Italy, hobnobbing, I believe, with the Ranee of Sarawak and Princess Alice of Monaco.

CONSTANCE. Why are you here?

DOUGLAS. *(Pauses.)* To settle our differences.

CONSTANCE. *(Impatience.)* We are utterly different.

DOUGLAS. My dear, in your desperate need to have everything black and white, you utterly miss the point.

CONSTANCE. Oh? Really? And what might that be, may I ask?

DOUGLAS. That there are no absolutes except in the desperate imaginations of men and women. No black. No white. No good. No evil. No male. No female. Everything runs together and runs in and out of everything else. But human beings cannot abide such glorious confusion. So, they invent what is called morality to keep everyone and everything in place. I am quoting, I believe, from the testament of the beloved apostle, St Oscar.

CONSTANCE. *(Cry.)* Oscar has changed. I know it. I've seen him in prison. What's more, he is contemptuous of you. *(Douglas laughs.)* Why do you laugh?

DOUGLAS. Why do I ever laugh? Oh, Oscar, Oscar!

CONSTANCE. You mock him!

DOUGLAS. *(Fiercely, complete change in tone.)* I *know* him! And he knows me. He has taught me everything I know. Everything! Like most aristocrats I was raised in boorishness. He taught me that anything unearned is not only without value, it is the source of corruption. He taught me that we must learn our true nature and be true to that or else we are damned. He taught me to live when I was merely breathing. He taught me to love. What every human creature may have. If she has the courage, that is.

CONSTANCE. I see. That is quite extraordinary. Somehow I always thought of you as superficial. I was wrong, obviously.

DOUGLAS. You see! We can be friends.

CONSTANCE. Don't talk nonsense, please! I shouldn't allow you near me, if I could help it. All you've done is convince me that whatever it is between you and Oscar, well, it's substantial, if nothing else. And, therefore, my relationship with him becomes that much less. That's all.

DOUGLAS. You talk like a clerk. Adding up. One column on one side, one on the other.

CONSTANCE. That's the only way you can understand it, isn't it? Do you realize, Lord Douglas, how essentially vulgar you are?

DOUGLAS. My! My! Vulgar now, are we?

CONSTANCE. Get out of my—home!

DOUGLAS. And tantrums, too! Heavens!

CONSTANCE. At once! Do you want me to call someone to eject you? Do you?

DOUGLAS. Just a moment. Before I leave. May I see the two boys?

CONSTANCE. *(A long, long pause while she studies him in growing fury.)* What did you say?

DOUGLAS. What? What?

CONSTANCE. Get out of here!

DOUGLAS. What is it now?

CONSTANCE. Out! Out!

DOUGLAS. You're—unwell!

CONSTANCE. *(Shrill.)* Why have you asked to see the two boys?

DOUGLAS. To say hello. Good-bye.

CONSTANCE. Why—why—why?

DOUGLAS. *(Almost speechless.)* Oscar's children—

CONSTANCE. *My* children!

DOUGLAS. That is incontestable. What is going on here?

CONSTANCE. *(Trying to calm herself.)* Why did you ask to see the children?

DOUGLAS. Why do *you* think I wish to see them, Constance? Yes. Why? Go on. Do tell me.

CONSTANCE. *(Sudden, total calm.)* They are safe.

DOUGLAS. Safe from what?

CONSTANCE. From all that—filth!

DOUGLAS. Filth is it? The only filth, madam, is what is presently in your own mind. How dare you make such insinuations. Typical, how typical of you women. Tight, tight!

CONSTANCE. *(Lost in her own thought.)* Protected—

DOUGLAS. But I'm not going to let this pass. No! You've made a dreadful insinuation against me. I would never harm a child. Never! What gives you the right? To imply such things?

CONSTANCE. If Oscar were here he would—

DOUGLAS. If Oscar were here he would be pleased that I admire the beauty of his sons. Very simple. Very pure.

CONSTANCE. He would physically eject you if he were here! He has turned his back on your kind.

DOUGLAS. Oscar is positively surrounded, my dear, with, as you put it, my kind. We call them the sorority of St Mary Magdalen. Robbie Ross, Reggie Turner, More Adey. The wonder is how they find room for all of them in that cell of his. What a crush!

CONSTANCE. Not true—not true—

DOUGLAS. He is incapable of wiping his nose without their advice. Why, they have even succeeded in turning him against me. The little—

CONSTANCE. *(Whisper.)* It's not true!

DOUGLAS. I'm afraid it is, my dear.

CONSTANCE. I know an Oscar that no one else can know!

DOUGLAS. Precisely. There are many Oscars. That is what makes him so seductive.

CONSTANCE. But I spoke to him in prison—

DOUGLAS. Prison is one thing, freedom is another. Besides, he is now about to reemerge, I believe, like that other beloved one, from the tomb.

CONSTANCE. He has lied to me again! Lied to me!

DOUGLAS. My dear, you mustn't distress yourself. You know it's not lying. It's just that Oscar has to reinvent everything as he goes along. One simply has to work around his creativity.

CONSTANCE. (*Utterly lost.*) We both said that it would be the same as before.

DOUGLAS. Nothing, my dear, nothing is ever the same as before. That is my lesson for the day. (*Whirling away.*)

CONSTANCE. (*Screaming after him.*) Why should I believe you, of all people?

She stands a moment and then walks off.

Music. A great peal, a hallelujah. The attendants use their clappers loudly. Two of them lead Oscar out of his cage, into the light.

Chairs on the white disk, Oscar is now seated on it and given a drink by the attendants. Douglas comes forward and is just about to step onto the disk when an attendant touches his arm and hands him a letter. He holds it up to the light, searching its contents. No good. Looks about and then delicately pries open the envelope and takes out the letter. Constance stands to one side in a fading light. She speaks, as Douglas reads silently, the light gradually going down on her as he takes over.

CONSTANCE. 'Dear Oscar, It is so difficult for me, but I am trying to understand, to forgive. That's what is important, isn't it? To forgive? The only hope for us is that we close the door on the past. Can you do that, Oscar? Can you?'

DOUGLAS. (*Reading.*) 'In particular, I must insist that you never see Lord Alfred Douglas again—Constance.' (*He carefully refolds the letter, puts it back in the envelope, reseals and hands it to the attendant.*) See that Mr Wilde gets that, would you? In about three weeks' time.

(Aside to audience.) The whole history of our dramatic literature is dependent upon the inadequacies of the postal service. *(Steps onto the disk: to Wilde)* I'm here!

OSCAR. Bosie! I've been thinking. But when you visited with her that time, what exactly did she say to you? About my seeing the boys again? What were her exact words?

DOUGLAS. Never! Never!

OSCAR. Never! Oh, what a word! My two boys! Never!

DOUGLAS. Do let's forget about her, darling. It's such a bore—

OSCAR. I simply cannot understand it. Her letters to me have been so—warm. And now, this silence.

DOUGLAS. But I'm here now, darling—

OSCAR. It was worse than prison, waiting for you here in Berneval. Oh dear boy, you've no idea what excruciating tortures they devise for one at the lesser French seaside resorts—table d'hôte with the English spinsters at six, dominoes and spittle with the village elders by the quayside—

DOUGLAS. But what about me!

OSCAR. *(Looks at him for a moment.)* Oh, dear sweet, beautiful boy! Hush! I'd be suicidal if you hadn't come, you know that.

DOUGLAS. But do I? You spend every waking hour talking about her.

OSCAR. You're being cruel again, Bosie—

DOUGLAS. It's a pain in the neck, that's what it is! It's like living in a ghastly domestic novel in three volumes.

Oscar laughs, a bit forced, and clicks his fingers at an attendant who promptly produces more drinks, the perfect waiter.

OSCAR. You adorable boy! My goodness, we are going to have such fun—I am so happy, Bosie—how I've missed your—sharpness, your—attack! Let's demolish everyone and everything!

DOUGLAS. Let's begin by forgetting this family of yours, shall we?

OSCAR. But you said yourself you'd love to have the boys come and visit—

DOUGLAS. *(Pause.)* Yes. *(Pause.)* No!

OSCAR. We could take them boating and swimming. Cyril is terrifically athletic, you know—

DOUGLAS. *(A savage turn: outburst.)* What utter nonsense!

OSCAR. May take time, of course. But I know Constance. She moves slowly and now that she is away from sniggering, malevolent England—

DOUGLAS. *(Fury.)* I'm not talking about her! I'm talking about us!

OSCAR. Why are you so angry?

DOUGLAS. Who do you think we are? Some kind of holy family? We are outside the law, my friend. We trawl the streets. We pick fruit where we can.

OSCAR. I hate this cynicism in you, Bosie! Hate it! It demeans you—I will not be brutalized! They tried that. Every conceivable disgusting way, they tried. And failed—

DOUGLAS. Allow me to make a list for you. Your marriage has ended. You are extremely lucky that your wife continues your allowance, paltry as it is, subject to good behaviour. You are an ex-con. You are extremely lucky that your lover finds you—irresistible. You are a permanent exile. You are extremely lucky that police procedures are as variable as the European climate. *(Clincher.)* And your boys are gone. Forever.

OSCAR. Why are you doing this to me, Bosie!

DOUGLAS. Truth.

OSCAR. I've spent a lifetime expressing the truth.

DOUGLAS. Indeed. But always in the most delightfully ambivalent fashion.

OSCAR. You abuse me!

DOUGLAS. Don't whinge, Oscar. I detest whingeing.

OSCAR. You're so cold, cold—

Oscar is still in the chair. Douglas goes behind him, taking him, fiercely, by the hair, pulling the head back, sharply, exposing the throat. Oscar is completely passive throughout all this, face up.

DOUGLAS. *(A full-tongued kiss.)* But you love my coldness, don't you, my love? You find it intensely—satisfying. You said so yourself. *(Each single word tasted.)* Marble. Muscle. *(Again, the tongued kiss.)* I love your mouth. Mouth. It is as if all the senses of your body were drawn into this single organ. What a mouth you have, Oscar! Have you ever thought? This is where your real genius resides. Mouth. This is where your soul is. Soul. Hole. Tongue. Lick. *(Another tongued kiss.)*

La vipere rouge. When your mouth opens, I would go in, in, in. Swallow. More than any other kiss, I love the kiss of betrayal.

Constance crosses the stage at the back, walking with difficulty, holding the child puppets, in sailor suits, by the hands. Suddenly the puppeteers whisk the puppets away in a wild, childish run and then they are gone.

CONSTANCE. *(Turns to audience.)* They keep running away from me and I cannot follow. They see it as a game. Mummy cannot run! Mummy cannot—. The other day I overheard them. Behind the orange tree. Whispering. About him. He might as well be dead, Cyril said. Vyvie wept. I couldn't move towards them. The pain in my back became so bad that I cried out. I heard this sort of braying come from my mouth. They came around the orange tree, two very dusty little boys. I said sometimes one's papa can be cruel. I don't care, Cyril said. Was your papa cruel, Mummy, Vyvie asked? I shook and shook as if I were perishing in that perfect sunshine. Standing there. We three in silence. *(Pause.)* He never answered my last letter. Weeks passed. Not a word from him. Then I realised that there was nothing left. Except my need to confess.

She walks back into darkness. She will now be dressed exactly as in the opening of the play, with a cane. Douglas breaks away from Oscar.

DOUGLAS. Do we have anymore cash?

OSCAR. You mean you've spent the rest of it? All of it? On what? Those little boy bitches down on the waterfront?

DOUGLAS. Now—now! Now—now!

OSCAR. You've spent our last bloody penny—

DOUGLAS. But where's all this other money you were promised?

OSCAR. Is that the only reason you have stayed with me? Money?

DOUGLAS. You said my darling mother was to give you two hundred quid—

OSCAR. Indeed. Provided I stay away from you.

DOUGLAS. Oh, Mother, Mother, you excel yourself. What about all those bucks you were to make from the land of Uncle Sam? Wasn't that well-known pornographer Smithers going to make your fortune for you? America awaits your great poem, Mr Wilde.

OSCAR. It hasn't—happened—

DOUGLAS. I see. Of course, if you'd played your cards right with that wife of yours—

OSCAR. Played my cards! Played my cards!

DOUGLAS. —she wouldn't have withdrawn that damned allowance, such as it was!

OSCAR. Played my cards! How vulgar!

DOUGLAS. You're such a snob, Oscar! It's laughable—enter the duchess! It doesn't wash, dearie, not with me, luv, it don't.

OSCAR. You're despicable.

DOUGLAS. Of course. How predictable! I'm despicable. Do you know, your snobbery has brought us to this?

OSCAR. What rubbish!

DOUGLAS. That actor. Brookfield. Remember? How he gathered the dirt on us, so to speak? And why? Because you humiliated him. I heard about it. One should not wear gloves during afternoon tea, Brookfield. That's what you said to him. In public! And in America, of all places! You committed the cardinal sin. You corrected an Englishman in a matter of etiquette. One never does that. Particularly if one is not English oneself. Particularly if he is an actor and trained to imitate his betters.

He clicks his fingers. The attendants come forward with a cape and hat. One of the attendants will also offer him a smart travelling bag.

OSCAR. Poor Brookfield! What are you doing?

DOUGLAS. Dressing.

OSCAR. But why?

DOUGLAS. One always dresses properly for the outdoors.

OSCAR. Why are you leaving?

DOUGLAS. There is nothing left here. Is there?

OSCAR. Oh, Bosie! Bosie!

DOUGLAS. Oh—Oscar—Oscar— (*He comes up beside Oscar. Oscar lifts a hand towards him but Douglas brushes it aside.*) The truth is, m'dear, you are only of interest when you are on a pedestal—

Douglas steps off the disk, leaving Oscar slumped behind him. He seems to be about to leave but then returns and addresses the audience directly. Constance steps out of the darkness.

DOUGLAS. You're wondering, aren't you? How it all ended? Not him. We all know what happened to him on the streets of Paris. No, not him, her! Well, she died. The pain became excruciating. She made the mistake of entering an Italian clinic and like many another who did so she never came out again. I liked her, really liked her. If only we had met at another time, another place. Pity. Because, you see, when it all ended I felt as if I had been released from a malevolent white circle. Free at last! And I outlived them both. By nearly half a century, as a matter of fact. Married, settled down. Dabbled in the horses, bit of shooting here and there. Perfectly normal human being once more. Not like that dreadful little shit I used to be. Absolutely not. No. Normal! Normal! Normal!

He walks back and off into the darkness. The attendants come and dress Oscar in hat and cloak and hand him a cane. Constance and Oscar are now in exactly the same scene as in the opening of the play but on the forestage, not the white disk. The attendants have rolled off the white disk, hanging it stage left. Beneath it they set up an outdoor Parisian café scene.

CONSTANCE. No! No! No!

OSCAR. I must see them, Constance, must, must. They're my children too.

CONSTANCE. This is no longer about the children.

OSCAR. Well? What is it about, then?

CONSTANCE. You know he said to me that you had the gift to make others see themselves.

OSCAR. Who said that?

CONSTANCE. Douglas.

OSCAR. Bosie! What a burden I placed upon him.

CONSTANCE. I didn't quite know what he meant. Then. I know now.

OSCAR. (Pause.) Your fall. Why you fell?

CONSTANCE. Yes.

OSCAR. But something else?

CONSTANCE. On the landing—

OSCAR. What did you see, Constance?

CONSTANCE. *(Low.)* Unspeakable—

OSCAR. I am here, Constance—

CONSTANCE. You are here, Oscar. Then I am not alone.

OSCAR. No. You are not alone. What was it, Constance?

CONSTANCE. Can't be told. Can only be—acted out. Little girl. On the stairs. Waiting for Papa to come home. Papa came home early. Always early. He gave me gifts. On the landing. *(Girlishly.)* What is it, Papa? Me, please! Me, please! Ribbons. Paper, gorgeous paper show—love—touch—secret—secret—fall—

She drops to her knees. A great, thumping beat of sound. We watch as Oscar watches and the attendants bring on a gigantic puppet: Victorian gentleman, red cheeks, black moustache, bowler hat, umbrella, frock coat. Bright paper package dangling from one puppet arm.

The procession reaches Constance and the puppet is made to squat or kneel before her, it and the attendants blocking her from view. The whole group heaves and humps several times and Oscar turns away in distress. Then the attendants, very quickly, carry off the puppet, a lifeless thing, and we see Constance, retching, on her knees. Oscar tries to reach out to her but she gestures him away.

CONSTANCE. I have loved evil! I have loved evil!

OSCAR. No, Constance! No!

CONSTANCE. You said to me, you're different, Constance. Remember? You're uncontaminated by life, Constance. That's what you said. What utter rot! How more contaminated could I be?

OSCAR. *(Cry of pain.)* You were but a child! An innocent child!

CONSTANCE. Child—children! You—I. Connected. Everything connected.

OSCAR. It's finished, over. He's dead, finally dead. Let me help you, Constance.

CONSTANCE. No Oscar. No. it's all so different now. I used to think: nothing can touch me, married to this brilliant, outrageous man. I am safe beneath this glittering surface! Whereas the truth was you were drawing me into horror, step by step, like a dangerous guide. The horror of myself. You have made me brave Oscar. And now that it is all out, our marriage has finally and utterly ended. All that remains now are the children.

OSCAR. I must see them before I die! Why are they hidden from me? Why?

CONSTANCE. Because I will not have them exposed.

OSCAR. Exposed to what, may I ask?

CONSTANCE. No black. No white. No right, no wrong! No male, no female! That's what you believe, isn't it? You and Douglas? Everything in confusion! How wrong you are!

OSCAR. I am finished with Douglas. Finished. You're simply disturbed, Constance, confused. That horrible man—your father!

CONSTANCE. Confused? Confused? I am absolutely and totally clear. I'm clear enough to draw a line and say that's it. Are you? Can you draw a line even if it cuts you in two? Can you? Do you know what it costs me? To deny my children their own father? Do you? It's like bleeding inside.

OSCAR. You've even changed their name!? Not Wilde anymore.

CONSTANCE. They and I have to live in the real world.

OSCAR. What is the real world?

CONSTANCE. Oh my God, you have learned nothing! Nothing!

OSCAR. I've learned what it is that separates us. *(Pause.)* Constance, I am still their father.

CONSTANCE. And what does that mean?

OSCAR. *(More uncertainly.)* Duty—

CONSTANCE. The only duty of a parent is to make childhood possible. For as long as possible. But you haven't an inkling of what that means.

OSCAR. No? Perhaps not. Perhaps you are right. Perhaps you are wrong. Perhaps. But you will never tolerate the world of perhaps, will you, Constance? *(Pause.)* There is one final thing I must ask of you.

CONSTANCE. What is it?

OSCAR. I want you to think of me as— *(Pause.)* Will you be my sister now, Constance? *(She nods her head dumbly, beyond words.)* I will go back to the streets of Paris, then. I'm like a monument now, you know. I sit, daily, on the pavement outside the Café de Flore. They allow me to sit there, you see, with saucer and empty cup. A monument. What am I waiting for? A few francs? The end of the century? The fall of night? Do you know, I dread the thought of living beyond the century? The very thought of putting nineteen hundred and something atop one's notepaper gives one the willies! And yet! There are times when I see the mist of the future lift. I see them there, in rows, standing. And, you know something? They are applauding me—

He turns and leaves her and disappears from view. She still stands there, her eyes still closed. As she speaks, two attendants, figures of death, gather close about her, one pushing a surgical trolley, another carrying a white sheet.

At the same time, lights up on the Paris street scene: the figure of Oscar, long cloak, long hair, wide black hat, seated at the outdoor café table, back to audience.

CONSTANCE. 'Dearest Cyril, Dearest Vyvyan, my two darling boys, I am writing this letter because tomorrow I must go into the clinic at Genoa. Please don't be frightened. I am— *(Pause, going on with difficulty.)* They are going to—it's just a matter, really, of taking away Mummy's pain. That's good, isn't it? I wanted to write about your father. All his troubles arose from his own father, from the way his father crushed something within the soul of his own son. But your father is a great man. He had this terrible, strange vision. He sacrificed everything to reach out to that vision—that was very brave, wasn't it? You see what he did was to try to release the soul from his body, even when his body was still alive—'

She turns and the two attendants lay her out upon the trolley and cover her with the sheet. Music. The Parisian outdoor café scene fully lit. Four attendants bring on puppets of gentlemen who pass by Oscar at his café table. Oscar stretches out his hand to beg. Various reactions from gentlemen puppets as they sweep by. Some give him money, others sweep by contemptuously. Then silence.

The figure of Oscar rises to full height, back to audience, and throws both hands in the air. A piercing sound and light change, high, white spot. At once all the costume, together with the hat and wig, fall off to reveal the naked Androgyne who now poses before the white disk, a flare of white light, then black out and the play ends.

END OF PLAY

Alex Johnston.
Courtesy Amelia Stein.

Melonfarmer

ALEX JOHNSTON

1997

Original Cast

Charlie Bonner	Niall Shanahan
Gertrude Montgomery	Patrick Leech
Elizabeth Kuti	Tony Flynn
Pauline Hutton	Amelia Crowley

Characters

SEAN

BRIAN (doubles UNDER THE BED)

SIOBHAN

STEPHEN

RAY

KIRSTEN

KATHY (doubles WOMAN'S VOICE: LOW)

MARTINA (doubles WOMAN'S VOICE: HIGH)

RADIO DJ (voice only—also doubles TV PRODUCER's voice)

This script represents the play as originally performed in the 1997 Peacock Theatre production. The script was revised in 2000 for a production by the Theatre Royal Plymouth, and the author regards this later version as definitive. Copies of the revised version are available from the author's agent.

Everything has to be changed.

—Joseph Beuys

For A. K.

Scene 1

Darkness. A cheery radio DJ speaks cheerily.

DJ. Ahh . . . what a great song that was, Men Without Hats there with 'Safety Dance,' one of my favourite singles of the eighties. And if you've just tuned in a very good morning to you from myself and Gerry. And this flashing light tells me it's time for our £10,000 cash call!

114

TAPED VOICES. Cash call! Ooh! Aah! etc.

DJ. This is your chance to win ten thousand pounds so remember to say, 'I listen to FM 93, the station of the nation,' and ten thousand pounds can be yours: Okay I'm dialing now, hmm, a Dublin number. There we have it. And now let's see.

TAPED VOICES. Cash call! Ooh! Aah!

A phone rings. Lights up on Sean's flat. It rings and rings.

DJ. Hmm. Is there anyone there? Is there anyone there? Doesn't look like there's anyone there. I'm giving it five more rings or we go to someone else.

Sean comes in in a dressing gown. He has just been woken up.

Oooo! So near and yet so far—

Sean picks up the phone.

SEAN. Hello?
DJ. Hello to you! Is this Sean Spence?
SEAN. Yeah.
DJ. Sean it's Chris Guiney here from FM 93, this is the FM 93 cash call.
SEAN. Yeah.
DJ. Have you anything to say to me? . . . Are you there Sean?
SEAN. Yeah.
DJ. Ah Sean! Gimme a hand here!
SEAN. Yeah.
DJ. Nnngghh Sean. I'm very sorry.

Taped sound: Bwaa bwaa bwaa bwaa.

SEAN. Yeah.
DJ. You just lost ten thousand pounds Sean.
SEAN. *(Beat.)* Yeah.
DJ. You were meant to say 'I listen to FM 93, the station of the nation.'
SEAN. Yeah.

DJ. Sorry Sean.

SEAN. Yeah.

DJ. Ten grand up the chimney. How do you feel about that Sean?
. . . Well thanks anyway for being such a good sport.

SEAN. Yeah.

DJ. Ha ha ha, great. Thanks again Sean.

SEAN. Yeah.

DJ hangs up. Silence. Sean goes back to bed.

Scene 2

Stephen alone.

STEPHEN. When I was about thirteen I used to stay sometimes with this cousin of mine who had an air rifle. It was a pretty good one, BSA .22. Anyway they live in Wicklow and the whole property was totally beautiful, you know this house and a big hill behind, which they'd climb. One summer I remember especially they had this big tree at the back of the house and it got a wasps' nest. Every so often the place would just fill up with wasps. They had apple trees and by the middle of August the wasps were just destroying the whole crop of apples. So my cousin used to do this thing. He'd put an apple on the patio and sprinkle it with sugar, and he'd get the air rifle and lie on the grass. After a while, a wasp would come and settle on the apple and start to eat. Then my cousin would take the empty air rifle, cock it and very slowly take the muzzle up until it was just right over the wasp. Then he'd pull the trigger and the blast of air would stun the wasp, like *(Does stunned look.)*. Then he'd open up the rifle, take a pair of tweezers, pick up the wasp and load it into the rifle. Then he'd shoot it against the wall. He wrote his name on the wall, in wasps. Admittedly his name was Ken. If his name was Bartholomew he probly woulda run out of wasps.

Scene 3

The flat of Brian and Siobhan, Sean's neighbours. Late evening, Brian and Siobhan are reading magazines. Sean is fixing a small piece of electrical equipment. The TV is on.

Silence.

Siobhan puts down her magazine and speaks.

SIOBHAN. Brian. Will you make the tea please?

BRIAN. In a minute.

SIOBHAN. D'you want tea Sean?

SEAN. I'm cool thanks.

BRIAN. *(To Sean.)* Oh did you hear about Patrick?

SEAN. Patrick on the Net?

BRIAN. Yeah, he had this supposed girlfriend called Joni who everybody thinks is really him posting from a different address? And meanwhile he was into this woman in Chicago called Cheng?

SEAN. I vaguely . . .

BRIAN. Well he flew to Chicago, porked Cheng and apparently then told her that Joni doesn't exist because Cheng then went and cross-posted every group Patrick has ever been on saying, Patrick told me Joni doesn't exist. And now Patrick's frantically mailing everyone going, the vicious bitch betrayed me, she deserves to be buggered with a pointed stick, and anyway, it's, uh, not true at all.

The door buzzer rings briefly. Brian goes to answer it.

SEAN. That's fucked.

SIOBHAN. I know, isn't it great?

BRIAN. *(To intercom.)* Hello? *(Beat.)* Piss off.

SEAN. Oh well, I never liked him.

Brian returns to his seat.

SIOBHAN. Yeah. He is one of the almightiest spas ever to walk the surface of the planet. And yet Jordan's always saying she wants to shag him.

SEAN. Does Jordan know he looks like a frog in a wig?

SIOBHAN. Good question. *(Of the door.)* Who was it?

BRIAN. Oh. Fucking scangers.

SEAN. Anyway when Jordan really fancies someone she never says she wants to shag him. That's why she never said she wanted to shag me.

SIOBHAN. You reckon?

SEAN. Fuckin' A.

SIOBHAN. Actually she did say she wanted to shag you.

SEAN. *(Interested.)* Really?

SIOBHAN. I got mail from her and she said, tell Sean he's a babe.

SEAN. Oh well.

BRIAN. *(Reading aloud.)* 'Alive: Based on the true story of a plane crash in the Andes. Faced with starvation and cold, the survivors are confronted with a terrible decision.' Breast or a leg?

SIOBHAN. Make the tea.

BRIAN. I made it last time.

SIOBHAN. No you didn't.

BRIAN. Yes I did.

SIOBHAN. No you didn't.

BRIAN. Yes I did.

SIOBHAN. No you *didn't.*

SEAN. Very good. Work *through* the conflict, not against it.

SIOBHAN. I made tea this morning. Remember?

BRIAN. *(She did.)* Are you sure?

SIOBHAN. Yes.

BRIAN. Well I don't want any.

SIOBHAN. *(Getting up.)* Shithead.

BRIAN. Yes dear.

Siobhan goes into the kitchen. Sean finishes.

SEAN. That's me.

BRIAN. Okay.

SEAN. See you.

Sean goes.

BRIAN. *(To Siobhan.)* Put another bag in.

He reads and grins.

Scene 4

The pub. Terrible music. Sean is drinking with Ray. Ray is better dressed.

RAY. Mmmmmm.

SEAN. What?

RAY. Eleven o'clock. Short blonde hair. Dark vest. Uh . . . sort of legging things.

SEAN. *(Looks.)* Wow.

RAY. That's obscene.

SEAN. I'd have her children, I'd have the operation.

RAY. Oooooooo.

SEAN. Don't think about it.

RAY. I . . . can't . . . help . . . it.

SEAN. *She's* nice.

RAY. Who?

SEAN. At the bar. Red hair. Check shirt.

RAY. *(Looks.)* Mmnnh. D'like red hair.

SEAN. Good on her though. I like the little black necklace.

RAY. Wait.

SEAN. What?

RAY. Fu-cking hell.

Sean starts to look.

Don't look! She's facing this way.

SEAN. Fuck off, if I can't look, why bother.

RAY. *Down* boy.

SEAN. All right. Let me know when she's not looking over here.

RAY. Okay. Very carefully. Look at the clock. Right, under that. Long hair. Star on the T-shirt.

Sean looks.

SEAN. *(Unimpressed.)* Yeahhhhhh . . . yeah, she's alright.

RAY. Alright?

SEAN. Yeah. She's, I dunno, great . . . build.

RAY. *She* is *beautiful.*

SEAN. No. She's good-*looking.*

RAY. Here we go.

SEAN. Well, beautiful is somebody I'd definitely be *attracted* to, you know, good-looking is just, what, decorative spunkbucket. Good-looking is cheap. Beautiful is meaningful.

RAY. What the fuck are you like?

SEAN. Well, beautiful, I think I have some connection with, let's say, whereas good-looking is . . . sort of plasticky. They look like they're on TV or something; that's not beauty.

RAY. It's a good thing she can't hear you saying, I think you're really beautiful but not in a good-looking way.

SEAN. I never said that—

RAY. You know what that's like? Someone saying to you 'I love your face, it's so *open.*'

SEAN. I never said she didn't look good, I'm saying I use 'beautiful' in a particular way.

RAY. I really don't think she'd thank you for saying this to her.

SEAN. Nah, well, I'm not going to.

RAY. Why not?

SEAN. I don't know her.

RAY. Fuck *that* shite. You don't *need* to know her.

SEAN. So how do you talk to her?

RAY. Very simply, go up to her, with a mate if you need one, *(Acting it out.)* 'Excuse me, dja have a light?' And either it's— *(Stares hard into Sean's eye with a long cool smile.)* 'Sure,' *(Produces lighter from cleavage and lights it up.)* or, it's *(Curtly.)* 'Yep.' *(Mimes flicking on lighter. Gives Sean the cold shoulder.)* See? If it's the second, depending how you pissed you are, you might go ahead anyway.

SEAN. Oh.

RAY. Don't tell me you never tried this when you were in school.

SEAN. I wanted to be a comedian didn't I? I just used to stand in the corner and collect material.

Enter Kirsten.

KIRSTEN. *(To Ray.)* Hi!

RAY. Jesus. Hi. What are you doing here?

KIRSTEN. *(Very fast.)* I'm back down, I found a new place in, whatsit, Terenure. Terenure? Yes! Terenure! It's a new building, it's all very, wooo! New. I don't *know* myself. A bathtub. A washer-dryer. I'm clean! It's brilliant. I'll cook you dinner!

RAY. Hey—

KIRSTEN. So what are you up to, are you working?

RAY. Yeah. I'm currently appearing in the Savoy One having ice cream licked off my chest.

KIRSTEN. Well that's work isn't it?

RAY. Dirty job but yadda yadda yadda. You wanna drink?

KIRSTEN. Eee—aaa, I'll come back. I'm with some friends, where did they— *(Looks.)*

RAY. Whatever. You up to anything?

KIRSTEN. *(With renewed enthusiasm.)* Oh I've got this, it's very, have you heard of Angel? I'm doing a devised thing, it's almost, uh, more of a dance thing? cause I didn't want to do anything too . . . *(Taps head.)* this. Not after *The Wild Duck,* God what was I thinking when I took that? But I just needed—

RAY. I know.

SEAN. You did *The Wild Duck?*

KIRSTEN. Yeah.

SEAN. Which. What, uh, part, were you?

KIRSTEN. Hedwig.

SEAN. Ah.

Pause.

KIRSTEN. But the main thing is, the *Angel* thing is directed by Richard Beckett.

RAY. *Oh.* Well pardon me if I touch the hem of your garment.

KIRSTEN. Oh stop. Sure you get to have ice cream licked off you.

RAY. Yeah, ah, unfortunately that actress is not normally interested in licking ice cream off *men.*

KIRSTEN. Oh. Still. How are YOU?

RAY. In that respect? Mmnnh.

RAY. What about you?

KIRSTEN. Ohh God, don't start. I'm not really, I've *no* time, me and men, we never quite, I'm a disaster area reely. I'm just gathering my energies. I'm actually trying to get stuff together for this show, so if ya hear any good stories will you let me know?

RAY. Course.
KIRSTEN. Look I better get back to them. Bye-bye.
RAY. Okay. Look *(Kisses her.)* give me a call, alright?
KIRSTEN. I will of course. Take care. *(To Sean.)* Bye.

Kirsten exits.

RAY. Lovely girl.
SEAN. Yes.
RAY. Cousin.
SEAN. Oh.
RAY. Mind you. Mad as a *fucking doorknob.*
SEAN. Maybe. I kinda like that though.
RAY. Hey. Go for it.

Silence. They drink.

Scene 5

A bus stop. Kathy is the only person waiting. It's cold.

Sean arrives.

They stand. Sean stands on tiptoe to look over her head, and glances at her face on the way down.

Kathy takes out a cigarette. She can't get her lighter to work. Sean takes out his Zippo and is just about to offer it when she asks him.

KATHY. Sorry, do you've a, thanks. *(Smiles.)*

Sean smiles. He holds it to her cigarette. It doesn't work. She cups her hands around it and it still doesn't work.

SEAN. I paid fourteen quid for it and it's guaranteed not to work in all weathers.
KATHY. That's always the way.

It still doesn't work.

Let me.

She looks at it.

Could be the flint's run down. Or else it's empty.
    SEAN. Possible.

She flicks it. It lights.

    KATHY. There we go.
    SEAN. Well done.

Kathy lights her cigarette. She gives him back the lighter. Pause.

I have this theory about why they issue these to the U.S. military. It's that they'll get so pissed off trying to get 'em to light that they'll kill anything that moves.
    KATHY. Makes sense. *(Beat.)* Sorry—

She offers him a cigarette. He takes one.

    SEAN. Thanks.

He lights it. Pause.

I didn't know you could get these here.
    KATHY. Oh yeah. *(Beat.)* Used to be only France. They're every-where now.
    SEAN. Oh.

Pause.

Were you . . . in . . . France?
    KATHY. Yeah.
    SEAN. Where?
    KATHY. Paris.
    SEAN. Ah.

Pause.

I like Paris. *(Beat.)* Em, how'd you find it?

Beat.

> KATHY. It's good.
> SEAN. Mm.

Beat.

> KATHY. French men are fucking horrible bastards, mind you.
> SEAN. Really?
> KATHY. Oh yeah.
> SEAN. What's wrong with them?
> KATHY. Well, friend of mine was coming home from work one evening and a guy behind her wanked off over her shopping bag.
> SEAN. Fuck that's disgusting.
> KATHY. I know. At least Irishmen usually keep it in their socks.
> SEAN. Although I've seen some bizarre shit, I was in the pub last night and I went to the toilet and I'd swear that somebody jacked off into the urinal. These little threads of white stuff in the . . . thing, swimming around.

Pause.

> KATHY. Really.
> SEAN. Sorry.
> KATHY. Mm.
> SEAN. My name's Sean by the way.
> KATHY. Oh. Kathy.

Pause.

Are you a student?

> SEAN. Nah. I'm sort of a musician?
> KATHY. Only sort of one?
> SEAN. Well, I try out all this stuff but it always ends up as this kind of genre-confounding burble.
> KATHY. *What* confounding?

Gertrude Montgomery and Niall Shanahan in *Melonfarmer.*
Courtesy Amelia Stein.

SEAN. Genre. I mean, shite, really. Thinking of moving to something a bit more in my line.

KATHY. What, are you in a band?

SEAN. No, I, uh, work with this community group.

KATHY. Great.

SEAN. Not really, it's a FAS scheme.

KATHY. Oh. Is that so unbearable?

SEAN. No, it's a good crowd, like, but the endless everyday hassle of having to deal with—

KATHY. Oh shit, there's a 47. I'd better run, sorry. It was nice talking to you.

She moves away.

SEAN. Bye. "I like Paris." Jesus.

A party. Loud music. Sean drinks beer with a thousand-yard stare. Kathy comes up to him.

KATHY. *(Calm.)* Hello.
SEAN. *(Beaming.)* Hello.
KATHY. *(Trying to remember his name.)* . . . Sean?
SEAN. *(Also trying to remember his name.)* Sean Spence. Kathy.
KATHY. Yeah. Are you a friend of Michael's?
SEAN. Yeah, are . . .
KATHY. I'm the new flatmate. God this city's a bit too small isn't it?
SEAN. That's fucking eerie.
KATHY. Very.
SEAN. How do you know Michael?
KATHY. I used to go out with his sister.

Pause.

SEAN. Right. So . . . eh . . . how . . . was she?
KATHY. *(Didn't hear.)* Sorry?
SEAN. *(Gabbling.)* How'd you, what did you, did you, doesn't matter. Beer?
KATHY. Absolutely.

Sean gives her a beer. She drinks.

SEAN. So.

Pause.

KATHY. Do you know many people here?

SEAN. Not really, I sorta know Michael.

KATHY. How?

SEAN. Long story, not very interesting.

KATHY. Oh. Oh well.

SEAN. Whenever I go to parties, I always imagine that I'm gonna act off with someone, and I never have.

KATHY. You've never got off with anyone?

SEAN. Never at a party.—No. Once at UCG in 1990.

KATHY. Oh yeah?

SEAN. It was no fun though.

KATHY. Well you're just sitting here. You're not exactly going out of your way.

SEAN. *(Uncomfortable.)* Yeah . . . isn't this music fuckin' manky?

KATHY. I mean look around. Loads of babes ripe for the picking.

SEAN. She's cute. *(Points.)*

KATHY. *(Looks.)* Yeah. She's queer though.

SEAN. Oh. Well there you go, I fancy someone, wrong shaggin' gender. Story of my life.

KATHY. You too, huh?

SEAN. You get that too.

KATHY. I do, funnily enough.

SEAN. Pisser isn't it?

KATHY. Yeah.

SEAN. Cheers.

KATHY. Cheers.

They clink cans.

Wanna come out to the garden?

SEAN. No, I think I'm fine—

KATHY. There's food.

SEAN. I'm kinda nice and warm and—

KATHY. *(Grabbing his wrist.)* Oh don't be such a veg. You have to see the garden.

SEAN. I don't really—

KATHY. The garden is fucking brilliant.

She drags him away.

Scene 6

Brian and Siobhan are tripping for the first time in their lives. Brian is sitting. Siobhan is sitting on the floor between his legs, staring at the cover of a book.

SIOBHAN. Wow.

Pause.

BRIAN. What?

Pause.

SIOBHAN. This. Fucking stunning.

Pause.

BRIAN. You know . . .

Pause.

SIOBHAN. What?

Pause.

BRIAN. I'm getting a bit bored of this now.

Pause.

SIOBHAN. Why?

Pause.

BRIAN. Well there are bats in here. And I know there aren't. So I kind of wish they'd go away. Well either it's the drugs or it's just us, but look up there.

Siobhan looks at where he is staring.

SIOBHAN. What the fuck is that?
BRIAN. I don't know but I don't think it's very happy.
SIOBHAN. Oh Jesus.
BRIAN. Be cool.
SIOBHAN. Oh Jesus.

He holds her.

BRIAN. Okay. Be cool.
SIOBHAN. Oh my God.
BRIAN. Calm down. Close your eyes.

She closes her eyes. Pause.

SIOBHAN. Nah, it's still there.
BRIAN. Well then it must be me.

He holds her hands.

There. You're okay.

She pulls her hands away.

SIOBHAN. I am never doing this again.
BRIAN. What time is it?

Siobhan looks at her watch. She keeps looking at it. Pause.

SIOBHAN. Fuuuuuck.
BRIAN. What's happening?
SIOBHAN. My watch. It's gone mental.

He looks.

BRIAN. Wow.
SIOBHAN. I think . . . didn't I read . . . Vitamin C shortens the effect?
BRIAN. Yeah.
SIOBHAN. I think there's Vitamin C in the bedroom.

BRIAN. I'm not going in there. There's a fucking man-eating tiger on the bed.

SIOBHAN. It's Claudia's copy of *Calvin and Hobbes*. Shit. I don't even know what it's doing in there. Alright, I'll get the Vitamin C.

BRIAN. Cool.

SIOBHAN. I'll go. If I'm not back before the summer you can tell my parents.

Siobhan rises to her feet. Pause.

BRIAN. Well?

SIOBHAN. Yeah?

BRIAN. I thought you were going to get Vitamin C?

Pause.

SIOBHAN. That was ages ago.

BRIAN. Was it?

SIOBHAN. Wasn't it?

BRIAN. I can't remember.

SIOBHAN. I'll give it another go.

She goes out. Pause.

BRIAN. Siobhan?

Silence.

She's gone. She left me. She's gone back to Claudia. She's fucking got back together with Claudia. The bitch. SIOBHAN!

Pause. Siobhan enters.

SIOBHAN. What?

BRIAN. Oh thank Christ. I thought you'd left me.

SIOBHAN. Didn't I?

She sits down next to him.

I can't find it.

    BRIAN. The Vitamin C?

    SIOBHAN. Yeah.

    BRIAN. Bollocks. We'll have to sit it out.

She shifts in her seat. Pulls out the bottle of Vitamin C.

    SIOBHAN. Oh here it is.

    BRIAN. Good. Give us some.

She gives him a capsule and takes one.

    BRIAN. Wow.

Scene 7

Sean in bed reading. Box of tissues next to the bed. He puts the book down and lies back. Hand under sheet. Movement.

Stops.

    WOMAN'S VOICE — LOW. Hello Sean.

    SEAN. Hello.

    LOW. Why have you summoned me?

    SEAN. Us.

    WOMAN'S VOICES — LOW and HIGH. Why have you summoned us?

    SEAN. I'm bored.

    LOW and HIGH. Let us see what we can do. Be our master Sean. We want to take you higher.

    SEAN. Yes.

    LOW. Do you like what we have done to make you comfortable?

    SEAN. It's okay.

    HIGH. Feel the soft furnishings. They are made from the fur of an African deer which is in a constant state of arousal.

Sean feels the sheets.

LOW. Sean. Did you know that there are cases reported of male dolphins attempting to copulate with human females? Imagine that.

SEAN. Must be quite painful.

LOW. Oh no no no. Far *from* it. Imagine that. Being in the water.

HIGH. The heat.

LOW. The water.

HIGH. The feel.

LOW. Imagine *that.*

SEAN. Yeah.

HIGH. Put your hands on us.

Sean puts his hand under the sheet. Movement.

Oh yes.

LOW. *Oh* yes.

HIGH. Oh *yes.*

SEAN. Talk to me.

LOW. You have beautiful eyes.

HIGH. Strong shoulders.

LOW. A broad chest.

HIGH. Powerful legs.

LOW. And yet sensitive.

HIGH. You respond to us.

LOW. As we respond to you.

Sean's hand moves faster.

You know our secrets.

HIGH. Our rituals.

LOW. We can hide nothing from you.

HIGH. Come to us.

LOW. Come to us.

HIGH. Yes.

LOW. Yes.

HIGH. Higher.

LOW. Higher.

HIGH. Take us higher.

LOW. Higher!

HIGH. Higher!

LOW. Yes!
HIGH. Higher!
LOW. Yes!
HIGH. Higher!
LOW. *(Peaking.)* Yes.

Sean comes. Fireworks, space travel, industrial light and magic. The women's voices die away as he relaxes.

Pause. He leans over, pulls out a tissue and cleans himself. He rolls over and goes to sleep.

LOW. So good.

Scene 8

Siobhan and Kathy in a club. They have been dancing. Loud music.

KATHY. Oh God.
SIOBHAN. Phew.
KATHY. It's too hot out there.
SIOBHAN. Yeah.

Kathy looks around.

KATHY. I have to say, you're a fucking great dancer.
SIOBHAN. Sorry?
KATHY. You're a great dancer.
SIOBHAN. Thanks. So are you.
KATHY. Thank you.
SIOBHAN. Do you know what time it is?
KATHY. Beg pardon?
SIOBHAN. Do you know what time it is?
KATHY. . . . Quarter to one.

Pause.

SIOBHAN. Fancy a game of table football?
KATHY. Of what?

SIOBHAN. Table football. Wanna game?

KATHY. Oh Jesus no thanks. Do they have one here?

SIOBHAN. Yeah, it's inside.

KATHY. God. I haven't been here in yonks. Everything's changed.

SIOBHAN. Neither have I. Well not to one of these nights anyway, for ages.

KATHY. I've met so many old mates it's unreal.

SIOBHAN. Isn't it great? Why haven't you been in?

KATHY. I was studying in Maynooth. Teacher training.

SIOBHAN. Oh great.

KATHY. I'm Kathy.

SIOBHAN. I'm Siobhan.

KATHY. How you doin, Siobhan?

SIOBHAN. Not too bad.

KATHY. Why haven't *you* been in?

SIOBHAN. I wanted to get my boyfriend to come but he wouldn't.

KATHY. I see.

SIOBHAN. I call him a boyfriend. I suppose he is a sorta one.

KATHY. Well I don't blame him. If I were a bloke I wouldn't want to see my girlfriend bopping with half the lesbians in Dublin.

SIOBHAN. Oh no he'd be into that. He just can't be arsed to go out much anymore.

KATHY. Not even to check up on his girlfriend?

SIOBHAN. Long story. I think he assumes I'm not gonna get into trouble.

KATHY. And have you?

SIOBHAN. I don't know.

KATHY. What I mean is, are you wanting to get into trouble?

SIOBHAN. I'm just here to have fun.

KATHY. I'll drink to that.

They drink.

SIOBHAN. I'm thinking of getting a tattoo on the palm of my hand with A.S.F.H.A. Whenever I might start enjoying myself I can look at it and go, Ah Sure Fuck Him Anyway.

KATHY. Did you used to come here a lot?

SIOBHAN. A good bit. Before I went out with Brian.

KATHY. How did you get together with him?

SIOBHAN. Well we were friends before, and then one night, sorta, happened, and one thing I will grant him, he has a gorgeous penis, so that clinched it, for the first few months anyway. Now it's all gone a bit pear-shaped. (*Laughs.*) Sorry, was that a really weird thing to say?

KATHY. Naah no.

Pause.

Ya know Siobhan, you're extremely beautiful.

SIOBHAN. (*Grinning.*) Fuck off.

KATHY. Had to be said. You are.

SIOBHAN. So are you.

KATHY. On a good night I am, yeah. Do you train a lot or something?

SIOBHAN. (*Worried.*) Why, are my thighs really enormous?

KATHY. No, I just—

SIOBHAN. Yeah, em, I'm a Tae Kwon Do instructor.

KATHY. Shit. So you could, like, break people's legs?

SIOBHAN. In theory yeah. I mean I never actually have.

KATHY. So if, say, you were to walk home with me, we'd be perfectly safe?

SIOBHAN. (*Considers.*) Totally safe.

KATHY. Brilliant.

Pause. They snog.

SIOBHAN. Want another drink?

KATHY. Yeah.

SIOBHAN. I'll get them.

KATHY. I'll go in with you. I'm getting chilly.

SIOBHAN. Isn't it freezing? I shoulda worn more.

KATHY. I love that top.

SIOBHAN. It's more for the summer but it's the only clean thing I had.

They go.

Scene 9

Stephen in pub, drinking. Sean enters.

SEAN. Hi.
STEPHEN. Hi.
SEAN. Sorry I'm late. My excuse is I'm an arsehole. Pint.

Sean goes to the bar.

STEPHEN. He's a lot different. He's got really arty. 'Oh I'm so unself-conscious.' I probly knew he'd get like this, it's depressing. So many people I went to school with, fucking insufferable by now. He's gonna tell me about his 'work.' He's gonna pretend to be interested when I tell him about Canada. I wonder has he a girlfriend? Some wispy arty type with a floral skirt and Docs. Or maybe he's got in touch with his sexuality and he'll try and hit on me. He better not.

Sean returns with a pint. Stephen sits facing downstage. Sean sits turned to him.

SEAN. There.
STEPHEN. So.
SEAN. So. How the hell are you?
STEPHEN. Ah. Grand. Keeping myself busy.
SEAN. What's this engineering you were saying?
STEPHEN. I've been doing this civil engineering project in Alberta, basically a question of building a canal from one lake to another. They called me in to help with the mapping of this, the company I was with contracted me out and I helped them work it out, on the system they had, which was pretty antiquated actually. It probly sounds a lot more fun than it was, basically extremely boring, except for lots of money.
SEAN. Right.
STEPHEN. And hordes of Canadian totty. That was the other good thing about it.
SEAN. No no no no no, it, it, it, it sounds interesting. And what, this was a couple of months or—

STEPHEN. Eighteen months, in fact, it took.
SEAN. Wow.

Pause.

STEPHEN. So what have you been doing?
SEAN. Just tryna do music, not much else. I've been working with this music collective a friend of mine's in, mostly doing administration but also music for parades and stuff. Which I don't set much store by. But it's a way of getting known, you know? Get your name up there, see your stuff being done. See what's wrong with it, and then you can use that to build on.
STEPHEN. Right.

Pause.

SEAN. So um—
STEPHEN. This thing, the thing in Canada it was run by this amazing guy from Edmonton. He looked like a roadie for Lynyrd Skynyrd, big fucker, hair down to here—Harley Davidson belt buckle but in *fact* a genius in his field. Which was mainly producing this kind of 3-D topography on the basis of photographs and measurements. And nothing he didn't know about computers. Like you'd be working away and all of a sudden, as occasionally happened, the system would crash and you'd go Ross! and he'd come in eating a chili dog or something, 'Has it gone down again, man? Shit' and he'd sit down, tweak tweak and I dunno what but forty-five seconds later it's up and running again. Great guy, used to take us out for beers every Friday night. Tell you the most incredible fuckin' stories. He was on the Net, he'd finish work at like eleven and be on the Net till five in the morning.
SEAN. Oh yeah, a couple of friends of mine are on the Net.
STEPHEN. Yeah?

Pause.

SEAN. So.

Pause.

STEPHEN. When did you have your ear pierced?

SEAN. Oh. Last year. Time had come. But one day about a month after it was done, I came into a room and there was this curtain hanging in front of the door and somehow, it got caught in the threads and was ripped out and flew across the room.

STEPHEN. Really.

SEAN. Not for the fainthearted.

STEPHEN. Tell me about it. *(Stands.)* Slash. *(Goes.)*

Pause. Sean glances at his watch.

Scene 10

Ray and Martina in Ray's flat. They have had dinner.

RAY. You know what's the worst? Films dubbed for bad language.

MARTINA. Yeah.

RAY. I did this play once and it had this brilliant speech which was, like, *as if* dubbed for bad language. Like I had to team all the lip movements and whatnot. I never quite got it right but it was great.

MARTINA. Do you still know it?

RAY. I might do.

MARTINA. Do it.

RAY. Now?

MARTINA. Yeah.

RAY. Okay.

He stands up.

Em. I'm like a policeman who's been told not to carry out this investigation. And I have this big, like, standup speech in the squad room to my lieutenant. *(Readies himself.)* 'I've been a cop for thirty *fudgin* years. What kind of *fudgin* moron do you think I am? Do you think I'm gonna stand here and suck your *corn* for you? I don't come in here so you can *flick* me in the ear and *hiss* in my mouth. I'm gonna go about this the only way it can be done, and that's my way. And no *corn*sucking *face*wipe is gonna tell me what that is, so *flip* you, *melon-farmer!*'

Pause. Martina drinks wine.

Very funny.

    MARTINA. I'll take your word for it.

    RAY. It was good *then*.

    MARTINA. I only know one thing, like a speech or a song or. 'Western Wind.'

    RAY. What's that?

    MARTINA. It's a folk song.

    RAY. Go on.

Martina closes her eyes and sings softly and beautifully.

    MARTINA.
Western wind, when will thou blow
the small rain down can rain,
Christ that my love were in my arms
And I in my bed
Again.

Pause. Ray moves in a little.

    RAY. That was beautiful.

Martina opens her eyes. Beat.

    MARTINA. I'd fuckin' love to have sex with you now.

Ray is a bit startled. Pause.

    RAY. Okay.

Scene 11

Café. Brian and Siobhan are drinking coffee.

    SIOBHAN. That was brilliant.

Brian is sceptical.

I suppose when Death came down at the end with the scythe it was a bit *Seventh Seal.*

Brian stirs his coffee.

I take it then you didn't like it.

Brian didn't like it.

What about the bit when she holds up the supermarket, and they all pull out guns?

BRIAN. Saw that a mile off.

SIOBHAN. You did in your hole.

BRIAN. It was shite.

SIOBHAN. It was good!

BRIAN. Okay, for a start it was completely in the style of David Lynch. Meets *Thelma and Louise.* Secondly. I don't like films where ordinary speech patterns are willfully abandoned. Thirdly there was a lesbian sex scene which happened in total darkness so you couldn't even see anything. Fourthly it was all over the place.

SIOBHAN. It was bloody funny.

BRIAN. Yeah, you may have noticed me rolling off my chair and beating the ground with my fists in convulsions of hilarity.

SIOBHAN. You only didn't like it cause it was such a women's film.

BRIAN. It was written by a man.

SIOBHAN. It was directed by a woman.

BRIAN. Women's film, that's bollocks. There's no such thing as a women's film.

SIOBHAN. What!?

BRIAN. By its very nature it's the most collaborative art form.

SIOBHAN. It doesn't have to be completely made by women.

BRIAN. So what makes it a women's film? That all the men in it are total fuckwits? Or it doesn't have any recognisable plot or believable characters or motivation?

SIOBHAN. It did!

BRIAN. No it didn't.

SIOBHAN. It did but you didn't see it.

BRIAN. I *believe* we saw the same film?

SIOBHAN. We saw the same film but the way we made sense of it, each of us, is not, it didn't, neither of us brings the same kind of, of, of way of seeing it, to it, and so, the preconceptions we have of what makes a good film—are not always the same.

BRIAN. The preconception I have of what makes a good film is that it shouldn't be a loada wank.

SIOBHAN. You see, that's it, you thought it was a loada wank. I thought it was extremely carefully structured.

BRIAN. An extremely carefully structured loada wank.

SIOBHAN. You didn't like anything in it at all?

BRIAN. She was a babe. The main one. But no, the whole thing was a mess. She was a whinge.

SIOBHAN. I think maybe you would have to be a woman to make much sense of it.

BRIAN. Now that is true bollocks. What you're saying is, a women's film is a women's film if I, as a man, think it's crap.

SIOBHAN. All I can say is, to me it made a lot of sense and was a great film.

BRIAN. Well your sense of a great film must be up your hole.

Pause.

It's not as if I don't like any films made by women.

SIOBHAN. Name one.

BRIAN. *(After some thought.)* Blue Steel. Point Break. Tank Girl. The Loveless. Go Fish. Fast Times at Ridgemont High. Near Dark. The Decline of Western Civilisation. The Politicians.

SIOBHAN. Right, in the first place, I remember you telling me you thought *Go Fish* was a load of crap. In the second place—

BRIAN. It may have been crap but it was full of hot girl-girl action.

SIOBHAN. In the second place, *The Politicians* wasn't made by a woman.

BRIAN. Yes it was.

SIOBHAN. No it wasn't. Rainer Stewart. He's a man.

BRIAN. Well.

SIOBHAN. And in the third place, two of those films are by the same director.

BRIAN. Who is a woman. Kathryn Bigelow. And it was four of them.

SIOBHAN. *Yes,* but—

BRIAN. Ah! I rest my case.

SIOBHAN. But she's not—

BRIAN. I suppose you're gonna say she's not a real woman. Her name's actually Kevin Bigelow.

Kathy enters and registers Siobhan.

SIOBHAN. No, but as a woman director, in terms of the argument I'm making, she's problematic.

BRIAN. Because *she* makes *good* films.

SIOBHAN. Now this is the kind of shit I'm talking about!

Kathy comes over.

KATHY. Hello.

SIOBHAN. Oh. God you gave me a fright.

KATHY. Oops. Sorry.

SIOBHAN. Hi—ah don't worry. Em, Kathy, this is Brian.

KATHY. *(Oh fuck!)* Oh hi!

BRIAN. *(Friendly.)* Hi.

SIOBHAN. Kathy's a friend of Sean's.

BRIAN. *(Rising to his feet.)* Like a coffee?

KATHY. Uh, I can't really, em, stay, I'm just literally streaking through the place. Well not literally, ha. I've just got to—

BRIAN. I'm just going up, take a seat. *(To Siobhan.)* Want another?

SIOBHAN. Nnnno thanks. Gotta get to the gym.

BRIAN. Sure?

SIOBHAN. Yeah, I mean no. Thanks.

BRIAN. Biscuit? Juice? Anyone?

SIOBHAN. No thank you.

BRIAN. Oh well. Know when I'm not wanted.

Brian goes up to get another. Kathy sits down.

KATHY. Oh shit.

SIOBHAN. Ah well.

KATHY. Is this bad timing?

SIOBHAN. No.

KATHY. Yeah?

SIOBHAN. Yeah.

KATHY. Good. Em . . . fuck. I've got to go to a fucking computer thing. How are you?

SIOBHAN. I'm okay. We went to the pictures.

KATHY. What'd you see?

SIOBHAN. *Corona.* In the IFC.

KATHY. Oh. I don't know it.

SIOBHAN. I think you'd've liked it.

KATHY. Listen, em, what I wanted to say was, I had a great time in the place there the other night. And I'd like to do it again if you're on for it.

Siobhan is silent.

And that was pretty much it so I'd better head. *(Gathers her things.)* You can give me a call during the week if you want—

SIOBHAN. No, I, eh, I am on for it. Definitely.

Pause.

KATHY. Oh noo. The pregnant silence.

SIOBHAN. And . . . can I talk to you about it again?

KATHY. Of course you can.

SIOBHAN. I'll call you then.

KATHY. Do. *(Smiles.)* I've got to go. Talk to you soon.

SIOBHAN. Bye.

Kathy goes. Brian returns with a fresh cup.

BRIAN. *(Sitting down.)* I wonder what *Strange Days* is like. I heard it's not that good.

SIOBHAN. We have to talk.

BRIAN. Yeah?

SIOBHAN. Seriously.

BRIAN. Okay.

SIOBHAN. You know it's getting on for nearly a year now we've been seeing each other.

BRIAN Yyyeahhh . . .

SIOBHAN. Just wondering how you feel about it.

BRIAN I take it you wouldn't be asking me if you didn't have a problem.

SIOBHAN. Well exactly.

BRIAN. What's the problem?

SIOBHAN. I don't really feel I can do this anymore.

Pause.

BRIAN. I see. What exactly?

SIOBHAN. The you and me thing. I em, I don't . . . fancy you. As such. Anymore.

BRIAN. Ah.

SIOBHAN. I'm really sorry, there isn't any other way of putting it.

BRIAN. Right. What, you don't enjoy the, uh, the . . . sex?

SIOBHAN. Em no . . . not the sex . . . I just don't . . . really . . . like you. No, fuck, not 'like,' I . . . don't . . .

BRIAN. You don't get on with me?

SIOBHAN. No, well, we've had a lotta rows lately but that's not it. It's just. I can't help thinking there should be *more*.

BRIAN More . . .

SIOBHAN. To what we do. To what happens between us. Than what we have.

BRIAN. You wish we did more together?

SIOBHAN. No, aagh, it's not that. Em, what's the best way of putting it. I don't love you. Does that sound. . . ?

BRIAN. Well, *love* . . . it's hardly . . .

SIOBHAN. I don't want to go to bed with you anymore.

BRIAN. Yeah . . .

SIOBHAN. I don't find you attractive.

BRIAN. No?

SIOBHAN. God this sounds so crap—I don't want to see you anymore.

Silence.

BRIAN. Right.

SIOBHAN. And my feeling is that we should stop seeing each other. I'm sorry.

BRIAN. No, no, I see. I see. *(Pause.)* So, what are we going to do about it?

SIOBHAN. Well like I say. I think we should stop seeing each other.

BRIAN. Yeah I know, but how are we gonna 'work through that'?

SIOBHAN. I just said. I think we should stop seeing each other.

BRIAN. Yes I understand Siobhan, but what I'm *asking* is, what are we going to do about your feeling that we should stop seeing each other?

SIOBHAN. Jesus you're not listening. I'm—

BRIAN. I am listening, and what I'm trying to establish is how we can find a way—

SIOBHAN. *No. Brian.* Fuck that shit. *I'm not going* to see you anymore. I'm going home tonight and I'm *not* going to come back tomorrow. Do you *understand?*

Pause.

BRIAN. May I ask a question?

SIOBHAN. Of course you can. What?

BRIAN. Why?

Pause.

SIOBHAN. I don't know. You . . . I don't know.

BRIAN. I what?

SIOBHAN. I don't know. That's it.

She stands.

BRIAN. You seeing somebody else?

Pause.

I thought so.

SIOBHAN. But that's nothing to do with it, it's—

BRIAN. A man or a woman?
SIOBHAN. Oh for fuck's sake.
BRIAN. I hope you're both very happy.
SIOBHAN. Good-bye.
BRIAN. Yeah.
SIOBHAN. Say good-bye.

Brian reads. Siobhan leaves. Brian stops reading.

Scene 12

Sean in bed, reading. Puts down book. Lies back. Hand under sheet. Movement. Kirsten is there, wrapped in a sheet. She's a fantasy.

SEAN. Oh. What are . . .
KIRSTEN. What?
SEAN. I'm just surprised.
KIRSTEN. Why? You thought I was cute.

Pause.

SEAN. Are you gonna do anything, or are you just gonna stand there and look at me?
KIRSTEN. Well it's your wank fantasy. That's up to you, isn't it? Come on, shirt off.

Sean removes his T-shirt. Hand under sheet. Movement. Kirsten gets onto the bed.

Okay, what am I wearing?
SEAN. What you were when I met you.

Kirsten drops the sheet. She's wearing almost the same clothes as she was in the bar, earlier, but the details are all blurred. She lies on the bed facing him.

KIRSTEN. Good. What's the situation?
SEAN. We're in here, no, we met for a meal earlier.

KIRSTEN. Right, so we're—not pissed but—happy. And now we're in here. Murmur murmur . . .

SEAN Yeah . . .

KIRSTEN. Who kisses who first?

SEAN. You kiss me.

KIRSTEN. Oo, I am masterful aren't I? How are we doing? Are you a bit tense? You seem to be holding back.

SEAN. It's okay, uh, I don't want the bed to creak. People next door.

KIRSTEN. Forget them. Concentrate. We're on the bed, mmm. Who's getting undressed first?

SEAN. You undress me.

Kirsten lies on top of Sean and covers them both up to the shoulders with the sheet. She undresses Sean.

KIRSTEN. Thaat's it.

SEAN. Em, can you get where I can see you, just . . .

KIRSTEN. Now now. Didn't I say imagine? Now where were we?

SEAN. I'm taking your clothes off.

KIRSTEN. *Yees.* Any details you want to linger over?

Sean's hand under the sheet moves faster.

SEAN. Yeah . . . slight problem with the bra strap . . .

KIRSTEN. About which I giggle in a low husky voice.

SEAN. Nah, that's . . .

KIRSTEN. You're right. Cliché. Okay, hang on.

She disappears under the sheet. Reappears.

Jesus, there's some serious elbow action going on down here, does that not hurt your willy?

SEAN. No no no, I need, it's only to get me started—

She disappears under the sheet and undresses. Reappears.

KIRSTEN. Now we're right. (*Shifts about.*) Ahh. You animal.

Sean is getting there. He starts to move his hips. She moves with him.

Yes, very good, right up into the spine, up through the legs, the pelvis, the back, the ribs, throat, mouth, lips, the taste of the mouth, together, the hips, arms, fingers, arse, the cunt and wait and up in the hips and wait and hold and wait and . . . that's weird, I think I can hear the dryer going downstairs.

    SEAN. Fuck!!!

    KIRSTEN. No! Yes! Come on! Supreme effort! Yes! Yes! Up and yes and up and yes and—

Sean comes. It's nothing special.

Yes! And relax it back, yes, and breathe, yes.

Sean lies back. Pause.

Do I get to come too?

    SEAN. Yeah. Several times.

    KIRSTEN. Good.

Sean leans over, gets a tissue and wipes himself.

You're probly going to sleep now?

    SEAN. Well . . .

    KIRSTEN. Okay.

She wraps herself in her sheet and gets off the bed. Sean puts his T-shirt and shorts on, puts out the light and turns on his side.

Well that was deadly. Night Sean.

She picks up her clothes and leaves.

Pause. A voice comes from under Sean's bed.

    UNDER THE BED. Sean.

Pause.

Sean.

Pause.

SEAN. Often when you lie in bed and you close your eyes, you can hear your name in your head. Like I usually hear it in my mother's voice.

UNDER THE BED. Sean?

Pause.

SEAN. What?

UNDER THE BED. It's really filthy down here.

SEAN. I'll hoover at the weekend.

UNDER THE BED. It'll get dirty again Sean.

SEAN. Don't call me by my name.

UNDER THE BED. What if you bring someone back and she looks under here? It's disgusting.

A hand comes from under the bed and throws out a crumpled tissue.

Filthy.

SEAN. Shut the fuck up.

UNDER THE BED. I'm only telling you. Look at this.

Under the Bed starts throwing out great masses of crumpled tissues, plastic bags, bits of paper.

SEAN. Put that back. I'm not getting up.

UNDER THE BED. *(Whiny.)* I can't sleep. I'm bored.

SEAN. So am I. Now shut up.

Pause.

UNDER THE BED. Remember when you were a kid and you'd have friends to sleep over, telling stories until late into the . . .

SEAN. Will you go to sleep! Fuck's sake. I'm not gonna start reminiscing.

UNDER THE BED. Sean. Sean.

Sean puts on the light and reads.

When was the last time there was a woman in here? I can remember. Eleven months ago. She was lovely as well. But you can't sleep when there's somebody else in the bed, can you?

SEAN. It's not a bed made for two people.

UNDER THE BED. Even so. You were really hot and you woke up and you saw her face. All shiny. The sweaty hairs on her upper lip.

Pause.

You had a moment there, didn't you? You said to yourself, my God, look at her. She looks ropey as fuck.

Pause.

That was the last time you slept with anyone, wasn't it?

SEAN. Your point being?

UNDER THE BED. Sean Sean Sean.

SEAN. *(Levelly.)* I said don't call me by my fucking name.

Pause.

UNDER THE BED. *(Ruminatively.)* Those who knew Spence at this period of his life often commented at the air of fatalism that hung around him. Even at twenty-five he seemed like a man for whom happiness was at best a theoretical concept, something like UFOs, a phenomenon he'd heard of but couldn't seriously bring himself to believe in.

SEAN. *(Irritably.)* Fuck off.

UNDER THE BED. His music of the period, with its obsessive recourse to the tonic, is marked by an almost total lack of harmonic movement.

Sean gets out of bed, cleans up the mess and gets back into bed while Under the Bed talks.

This dronelike insistence on the tonic is perhaps a reflection of Spence's essentially melancholy personality, although it does lend an ultimately fucking boring quality to his work of this period. It was as if his most personal music was also his most completely tedium-inducing. Small wonder then that Spence was so unhappy during this period, as it was the time of his life when he was forced to confront the fact that he was fundamentally second-rate, a hopeless loser, a crap musician and altogether a minor player in the story of his own life.

SEAN. *(Angry.)* FUCK OFF!

Pause.

UNDER THE BED. So anyway Sean. Tell us again how you broke up with her.

Pause.

Lovely girl she was.

Pause.

Sean?

Pause.

Sean?

Sean lies in bed, staring out. There is no way he's getting to sleep.

Scene 13

Stephen's car. Night. Stephen and Kirsten are in the front, Martina in the back.

MARTINA. Jesus I'm slaughtered.
STEPHEN. Belt.
KIRSTEN. Sorry?
STEPHEN. Your belt's not done.
KIRSTEN. Oh sorry. *(She fixes it.)*
MARTINA. Okay. Now first we have to go to . . . em . . . oh fuck where do I live? Kirsten where do I live? Phibsborough.

STEPHEN. Phibsborough.

Stephen puts the car in gear. Throughout, he pays careful attention to his driving.

MARTINA. Fuck this is great. A lift home. Must be me fuckin' birthday.

STEPHEN. You wouldn't want to be out in a night like this.

MARTINA. What's that?

STEPHEN. I said you wouldn't want to be out on a night like this, it's vicious.

MARTINA. Well you're a gentleman, whatever your name is.

STEPHEN. Stephen.

MARTINA. Hello Stephen, I'm Martina.

Martina rummages in her bag.

Jesus that was useless. If I hear fuckin' 'This Is Cult Fiction' one more time, I'm gonna . . . I dunno what I'm gonna do. Where the fuck's my purse? *Bollocks.* Kirsten I think I left my purse in the fuckin' . . .

KIRSTEN. Seriously?

MARTINA. Seriously, the fuckin' . . . *Bollocks.* I've left the fuckin' thing.

KIRSTEN. Is there stuff in it?

MARTINA. My smokes are in it's the most important thing. Ah *fuck.* Stephen ya wouldn't have a cigarette wouldja?

STEPHEN. Yep.

He hands her the packet.

MARTINA. You're a star.

He hands her a lighter. She lights up.

Mmmm. Here.

STEPHEN. Keep them.

MARTINA. Seriously? Okay, your fuckin' loss. Isn't he a nice man Kirsten? Fuck's sake. What a shit night. All they had was that fuckin' blue label vodka I *hate*. Oh well, drank it anyway. *(To Kirsten.)* Did you know who half of them were?

KIRSTEN. Which ones?

Stephen brakes for the lights.

MARTINA. All the studenty ones in the living room.

KIRSTEN. I think, friends of Louise.

MARTINA. Jesus. What a pack a spas. They all fuckin' talked to *each other* the whole time. There was one I thought was quite good-lookin' and I got talkin' to him and then I ran out of drink and I started to see he was about twelve years old. Are they all students?

STEPHEN. *(To himself.)* Come on.

KIRSTEN. Yeah.

MARTINA. Jeezus. *Fuckin'* students. *(To Stephen.)* You aren't a student are ya?

STEPHEN. Nooo no.

He drives.

MARTINA. Thank fuck. What's your name again?

STEPHEN. Stephen.

MARTINA. Hello Stephen. I'm Martina. What are you if you aren't a student? I'd say yous were in computers.

STEPHEN. I am indeed.

MARTINA. I knew it. What are you in computers?

STEPHEN. I'm a software designer.

MARTINA. That's astonishin'. *(It's not.)* I'm a drunk bitch in case ya hadn't noticed.

STEPHEN. Each to his own. *(To Kirsten.)* What do you do?

KIRSTEN. Oh nothing much.

MARTINA. She's an actress. Stephen Kirsten Kirsten Stephen. She's a fuckin' brilliant actress too, I've seen her. And I'm not a real theatrey person, but I always go and see what she's doin'. She's fuckin' amazin'.

STEPHEN. Have you been in anything—

KIRSTEN. Not really, just here and there.

STEPHEN. Are you working at the moment?

KIRSTEN. Just a fringe thing, it's not big or anything.

STEPHEN. Oh I think, uh, fringe theatre, it's not to be sniffed at. Isn't there a lot of that happening more recently?

KIRSTEN. Yeah.

STEPHEN. I don't get to see much . . . but . . . *(Turning the car.)* I think it's good to have it there. Shows there's a bit of life in the country still.

MARTINA. Well *she* is fuckin' amazin'.

Silence. Stephen drives. Martina lies on the backseat.

STEPHEN. If you want some music go ahead.

Silence.

MARTINA. Put it on so.

KIRSTEN. Sorry, I didn't know you wanted any.

Kirsten turns on the radio music. Martina sings along with it.

STEPHEN. *(To Kirsten.)* How do you know Hanna?

KIRSTEN. We're just friends from around the place. We were both waitresses at one time.

STEPHEN. Ah, Hanna's okay. I'm just making contacts again. I'm back from Canada three months ago. Looking up a lot of people again.

KIRSTEN. Oh.

STEPHEN. I was there a year and a half. Fucking beautiful country. British Columbia. Do you know it?

KIRSTEN. No.

STEPHEN. Great place. Spent a couple of months in Seattle, for the music, you know? But it's not that interesting anymore, very full of itself. Bit like Dublin come to think of it. And I always kept an eye on what was goin' on at home. I reckoned if the country got its shit together enough I'd come back. And what did it in the end was the divorce referendum, the Yes vote. I thought, the place has finally copped onto itself.

Pause.

What did you think of that?

KIRSTEN. What—the divorce?

STEPHEN. Yeah.

KIRSTEN. I thought we should have it.

STEPHEN. Yeah. You know, *(Gestures.)* staring us in the face. A dose of reality for a change. But the state of some of the people who were against it. *(Laughs.)* Did you see the one on the news, 'You're all a bunch of wife-swapping sodomites!' *Fuck.*

KIRSTEN. *(Smiles.)* Yeah.

Stephen is looking to see where he is.

STEPHEN. Round 'em all up and stick 'em in a fuckin' oven some-where . . . I think we're here, isn't this Phibsborough? *(To Martina.)* Hello?

MARTINA. Oh are we here? Okay, listen, thanks a million Simon.

STEPHEN. Stephen.

MARTINA. Stephen. Whatever, *(To Kirsten.)* I'll give you a call to-morrow or the next day, okay? God. I'm fuckin' ill now. See ya.

Martina goes. Stephen pulls away and drives.

STEPHEN. *(Grinning.)* She's great.

KIRSTEN. *(Apologising.)* She's just very drunk.

STEPHEN. But she's a laugh though . . . right? Where to?

KIRSTEN. Em, Terenure.

STEPHEN. Terenure. Terenure. Terenure.

KIRSTEN. It's a bit out of the way, you can just drop me off—

STEPHEN. Not at all. I know Terenure. So what's the name of this thing you're working on?

KIRSTEN. It's kind of a long title, *The Downward Motion of the Evening Land.*

STEPHEN. Of the?

KIRSTEN. *The Evening Land.*

STEPHEN Right. And what, it's a play or—

KIRSTEN. Well yeah, it's devised, it's not really written as such. We're working it out at the moment.

STEPHEN. *Right.* So have you done any of the, like, famous plays? The great classical—

KIRSTEN. I was in *The Wild Duck,* by Ibsen.

STEPHEN. Oh. I don't know it.

KIRSTEN. Oh. Well that's the only really classical stuff I've done. I was in *King Lear* but that was in drama school.

STEPHEN. Oh right. I think I did that in my Leaving. Who were you in it?

KIRSTEN. Cordelia.

Pause.

King Lear's daughter.

STEPHEN. *(Smiles.)* I know, yeah. It's just there's a car coming up—

KIRSTEN. Sorry.

STEPHEN. Cordelia—that must be a bit of a shit role? I mean she gets hung in the end doesn't she?

KIRSTEN. Well it's a great play. It's true she's a bit of a victim, but I liked doing the play, it was a good thing to be doing, you know.

STEPHEN. Mmmm.

DJ. Mmmm, 'Judy in Disguise' there by John Fred and the Playboys, and that's from the motion picture soundtrack of *Drugstore Cowboy,* great movie, starring Matt Dillon and Kelly Lynch and directed by Gus Van Sant, wasn't it Gerry? Gerry says yes. Kelly Lynch, I wonder where she is now, there's a question, of course it goes without saying, folks, don't mess around with drugs, uh, they're a menace, and I've lost a lot of good friends to them, so if you're thinking of getting involved with them, don't, cause believe me, it's a mug's game. The time is a quarter past three on a Sunday morning and the temperature is eight degrees over the bay area with widespread rain. Here's Aerosmith with 'Sweet Emotion.'

STEPHEN. I *hate* that.

KIRSTEN. What?

STEPHEN. Calling Dublin 'the bay area.'

He turns off the radio.

So where are we going exactly?

KIRSTEN. Mayfield Road, it's just off—

STEPHEN. Oh I know it, yeah.

Pause.

KIRSTEN. The quickest way is probably straight down Harold's Cross Road.
STEPHEN. Yeah.

Silence.

KIRSTEN. Em . . .

Silence.

I think . . . the turning was back there.
STEPHEN. I don't think . . .
KIRSTEN. I don't think you can get there from here.
STEPHEN. You can . . . you go up Kimmage Road.
KIRSTEN. Just bear left here.
STEPHEN. Nah this is quicker.
KIRSTEN. No it's back and turn.
STEPHEN. No this is definitely quicker. I grew up round here, I know what it's like.

Silence.

KIRSTEN. Now go left here.
STEPHEN. No it's a one-way.
KIRSTEN. No it's not.
STEPHEN. We'll just see.
KIRSTEN. Okay thanks you can stop here.
STEPHEN. *(Smiling.)* No really.
KIRSTEN. It's fine I can walk.
STEPHEN. What's wrong?
KIRSTEN. It's okay really I can walk from here. Just stop the car. Please. I'm not upset, just, you can let me out here, I'm fine. I'm not—I just wanna walk from here.
STEPHEN. *(Overlapping Kirsten.)* Look it's just a quicker way. We'll

get there. What are you getting so upset about? But you're miles away. Just calm down. I just want to show you—

He takes her arm.

KIRSTEN. *(Snatching it away.)* STOP THE FUCKING CAR! RIGHT NOW!
STEPHEN. What the *fuck* is the matter with you?

Kirsten is unfastening her seat belt. She takes her bag and opens the car door. Starts to get out.

(Braking.) Jesus Christ! *(He tries to stop her.)*

She falls out of the car and rolls. She gets up and runs away. The car has stopped. He watches her go in the rearview mirror. Lights a cigarette. Drives away. Fade-out.

Spotlight on Kirsten. She gasps for breath, takes an inhaler from her bag and uses it. Puts her hands over her face to calm herself. Breathes.

INTERVAL

Scene 14

Stephen's flat. He opens the door to Sean.

STEPHEN. Excuse the unsightly filth and squalor. Wanna cup of tea?

Sean sits. Stephen makes tea.

So you're still playing the old geetar?
SEAN. Trying to. I tried a bit of busking but I never got the hang of it. And myself and the other guy could never agree about songs. He was always saying you've gotta do the classics, man, the classics, Dylan and the Beatles, that stuff really gets the cash in and I wanted

to do like John Cale and Elvis Costello but he didn't know any of their stuff, plus I fuckin' hate Bob Dylan. The Speedy Gonzales of popular music.

STEPHEN. The what?

SEAN. You know Speedy Gonzales. *(Nasal.)* 'Arrriba arrriba! The answer my frriend is blowin' in de wind!'

STEPHEN. Oh. Wasn't he the one based on that sitcom?

SEAN. *Bilko*? Nah that was *Boss Cat.*

STEPHEN. *(Doesn't remember.)* Yeah?

SEAN. You know! *Boss Cat*! It was actually called *Top Cat* but they had to retitle it for the UK because there was a kind of pet food called Top Cat. Unfortunately in the programme itself he's still called Top Cat cause they couldn't go through it having all the characters call him something else. So thousands of British and Irish kids grew up with the trauma of having like Boss Cat at the beginning of the programme and calling him Top Cat all the way through.

STEPHEN. I see.

He gives Sean tea.

SEAN. You see many films?

STEPHEN. Nah not really. I'm not that interested. I tend to watch the same ones over and over.

SEAN. Which ones?

STEPHEN. I like . . . eh . . . nothing much. Nothing in particular like. I like stuff with . . . there's not a lot of stuff around these days with a lot of bite to it. It's all got very fuckin' tame. You know?

SEAN. You think? I'd've said if anything it's got *more* violent, you know we take less seriously than in the seventies. Like a film like *La Haine,* for example, which is about—

STEPHEN. It's not violence as such. It's more to do with the attitude behind it.

SEAN. What like—

STEPHEN. *(Not an outburst.)* There's just such bullshit out there. People are so full of shit.

Beat.

SEAN. About what?

STEPHEN. Hold on a sec, I wanna show you something.

Stephen leaves and returns with a shoe box. He takes out some paper. Underneath is something wrapped in cloth. He unwraps a large handgun and hands it to Sean by the barrel. Sean holds it. Pause.

SEAN. *Fuck* me.
STEPHEN. Nice, isn't it?
SEAN. I wouldn't say nice exactly.
STEPHEN. You know what to do when somebody gives you a gun?

Sean checks the cylinder. It's empty.

SEAN. Fuck.
STEPHEN. Give it a go.
SEAN. Can I?
STEPHEN. Go ahead.

Sean pulls the trigger a few times.

SEAN. Where did you get it?
STEPHEN. I found it.
SEAN. You found it.
STEPHEN. I found it. Nah I did actually. I was hiking in Wicklow. Found it in a forest. Along with these.

He unwraps a box of rounds in a polythene bag. Sean puts the gun down.

SEAN. Fucking *hell.*
STEPHEN. Some scanger musta dropped them. Probly if I'd looked I'd've found more. Maybe an arms stash nearby. You know the General used to hide a lot of his guns in the Dublin mountains. But I didn't wanna look, I thought, tempting fate. Cut my losses and take 'em.
SEAN. Why?
STEPHEN. Come on. Too good to leave lying around. I mean I'm not gonna go round with it tucked in my belt. Thought I might take it somewhere, use it all up and chuck it away. That'd be the safest. Loads of places to go to, miles from anywhere. No one's gonna hear and if they did they'd probly think it was fireworks.

Stephen picks up the gun, points it at the audience and pulls the trigger a few times.

You wanna come?

SEAN. And like—

STEPHEN. Yeah. I don't wanna do it by myself, it'd be boring. Blow some shit out of stuff.

SEAN. I dunno.

STEPHEN. Go on. You know you want to.

SEAN. I dunno I *do* want to. You guarantee this place is safe, no one's gonna find it? I mean *you* found it.

STEPHEN. Ah think about it, you hear somebody firing a gun, you're really gonna go and look who's doing it? The fucking 'Ra in training most likely. It'll be fun.

SEAN. It'll be fuckin' freezing.

STEPHEN. So we'll wear woolly jumpers.

SEAN. I can't believe you're serious. It's such a guy thing.

STEPHEN. Get to fuck, a guy thing. You're a guy aren't you? Look, if it gets weird you'll be able to write a fuckin' song about it. Every guy should be irresponsible with a gun once in his life. Every woman come to that.

SEAN. I'm not gonna play Russian roulette.

STEPHEN. Oh. Well we'll go anyway—seriously.

SEAN. Why me?

STEPHEN. Cause you're the only person I'd trust. Come on, that is a BFG.

SEAN. It is a big fucking gun. When are you thinking of?

STEPHEN. What about Saturday week?

SEAN. I really should work.

Stephen looks at Sean. Sean looks at the gun.

Scene 15

Martina's flat. Ray and Martina are having sex. She is on top. He comes. They relax.

RAY. You never come.

MARTINA. No. *(Laughs.)*

RAY. I wish I could make you.

MARTINA. I dunno. You're not bad.

RAY. Still. I don't want . . .

MARTINA. What?

RAY. In a way I'd rather you came and not me. Sometimes.

MARTINA. I'm not bothered. One day I'll just get fed up and find a fella who can, that's all.

RAY. *(Grabbing her.)* Oh yeah? Not before I learn how to do it.

Martina laughs and breaks free.

Is there anything you'd like me to do? How about a visit from Mister Tongue?

MARTINA. No thanks. No. I dunno. I'm never relaxed enough. It's weird.

RAY. What about anybody else? Could they do it?

MARTINA. There was one.

RAY. What did he do?

Martina smiles.

What?

MARTINA. Didn't work out. Doesn't matter. I can do it meself whenever. I don't need to with you.

RAY. But you'd like to?

MARTINA. *(Considers.)* Yeah.

RAY. So. What?

MARTINA. There is one thing always gets me goin'.

RAY. Yeah?

Martina whispers in his ear. He laughs.

(Like a cat.) Rrrrrr.

MARTINA. Every time.

RAY. Sorry?

MARTINA. Think I'm jokin'?

RAY. Well . . . you are.

Martina smiles at him. He stops smiling.

I mean, you are? Seriously?

She laughs. He laughs.

Ya bitch.

    MARTINA. What? What's funny?

He stops laughing.

    RAY. Wait. You're *not* joking?
    MARTINA. Of course I'm not joking.
    RAY. You'd like to do that?
    MARTINA. Yeah.
    RAY. With me?
    MARTINA. Yeah.
    RAY. I see.

Beat.

    MARTINA. So?
    RAY. Yeah?
    MARTINA. Dja want to?
    RAY. Of course I don't want to.
    MARTINA. Why not?
    RAY. I'm not into it.
    MARTINA. What's wrong with it?
    RAY. It's fuckin' dangerous.
    MARTINA. No it's not. You've just to be careful.
    RAY. It's not just dangerous, it's insane.
    MARTINA. What's insane about it?
    RAY. It's . . . the whole thing. Just thinking about it. Eeuuh.
    MARTINA. It's not insane. It's about trust.
    RAY. There's trust and there's playing with your fucking life.
    MARTINA. It's really not that dangerous.
    RAY. Forget about it. It's not gonna happen. *(Pause.)* God.
    MARTINA. Look, we don't have to do it, but if you want me to come that's the way to go about it.
    RAY. Well in that case I'm never gonna make you come cause I am *not* up for that. *(Beat.)* I can't stay here. Jesus.

Ray gets up and gets dressed.

MARTINA. C'mon. You don't have to go, I don't need it that much. I'm just tellin' you.

RAY. Look . . . I don't know what the fuck is going on, but if this is gonna . . . this is getting just a lit-tle bit weird, and I think I have to go now.

MARTINA. *(Pause.)* Are you gonna call me tomorrow?

RAY. Maybe. *(To himself.)* Jesus.

MARTINA. Fuck off then.

RAY. *Okay.* I'll call you tomorrow.

MARTINA. FUCK OFF!

Ray leaves.

Scene 16

Sean and Kathy in a café.

SEAN. So how are you?

KATHY. Wrecked. This kid brought an air pistol into class today and shot another kid with it.

SEAN. Fuck.

KATHY. Not badly but. He's a little prick, I hate him anyway so it was great to be able to drag him off and bang him up.

SEAN. I remember in school we had a student teacher and somebody threw a burning paper aeroplane at her.

KATHY. You little animals. Mind you others get it worse than me cause at least they fancy me. Well some of them.

SEAN. The boys or the girls?

KATHY. Don't be cheeky.

SEAN. Have you come out? To the teachers, like?

KATHY. Fuck no. You can lose your job for that. PTA would go through the roof. It's shit but— *(Beat.)* How are you?

SEAN. Oh, I'm . . . uh . . . I'm, I'm . . . I, I've lately . . .

KATHY. It's just a conventional question, you don't *have* to tell me exactly how you are.

SEAN. No I, uh . . . I've started to, uh . . . well you know that bit in *Taxi Driver* when Robert De Niro says to Peter Boyle, I'm startin' to get some weird ideas in my head? I'm like that.

KATHY. Weird ideas like . . .

SEAN. Ah that's a bit melodramatic. Em. I dunno. I dunno. I'm just—

KATHY. You're not thinking of shaving your head and assassinating someone?

SEAN. Oh no no no no no no. Just a sort of—like I'm missing a sense, or something like hearing or whatever.

KATHY. Oh?

SEAN. Dja know what I mean?

KATHY. Not really.

SEAN. Ya know like . . . just like . . . nothing that happens to me, *happens* to me. Kinda thing. Fuck, sorry, I dunno what I'm talking about.

KATHY. Is it just like you're depressed?

SEAN. I dunno. Maybe.

KATHY. Everyone gets depressed, Sean.

SEAN. I know. I know.

KATHY. I mean. That doesn't help, but we all have it.

SEAN. I know.

KATHY. So just—

SEAN. I know.

KATHY. I mean if you want to [talk.]—

SEAN. Nah. Nah.

KATHY. You sure?

SEAN. Yeah.

KATHY. Positive?

SEAN. I'm fine. I'm fine.

KATHY. Okay.

Pause. Kathy stretches.

Ahhh. Isn't it fuckin' bizarre though?

SEAN. What?

KATHY. Stuff. Oh guess what I'm doing tomorrow.

SEAN. Can't guess.

KATHY. Cooking dinner for your sexy neighbour.

SEAN. Who's that?
KATHY. Siobhan.
SEAN. Oh right.
KATHY. Be a little bit happy for me.
SEAN. *(Not smiling.)* Think you'll get to fuck her?

Pause.

KATHY. Are you pissed off with something?
SEAN. No.
KATHY. Cause don't take it out on me, Sean, it's not fair.
SEAN. Sorry.
KATHY. I'm gonna get some more milk. When I come back I want you to be in a good mood.
SEAN. Yes miss.

She leaves. Sean picks up the cup and spoon in front of him. In a little tiny voice he plays with them.

'Hello Mr. Cup.' 'Hello Mrs. Spoon.' 'How are you today?' 'I'm all depressed. My life is completely without meaning.' 'Oh dear, we can't have that. Let me help you.'

He puts the spoon in the cup and pretends to stir.

'Oh that's better. Oh uh uh.' 'Oh yes! Oh yes! Harder! Harder!' 'Beat me! Beat me!'

He taps the spoon on the rim of the cup.

'Yes! Yes! Aaaa!'

Kathy comes back with two cups.

KATHY. What are you doing?
SEAN. Getting some distance on my angst. Good isn't it? 'Uh! Uh! Uh!'
KATHY. You're a sad man.

She sits down and squeezes his hand.

Your hands are freezing.

Scene 17

Kathy and Siobhan are drinking wine. They've just eaten.

> SIOBHAN. That was delicious.
> KATHY. Thanks.

Pause. They drink.

Well.

> SIOBHAN. Do anything interesting today?
> KATHY. I went to see *Corona,* actually. That one that you—? It was great.
> SIOBHAN. Wasn't it?
> KATHY. Oh *that* was a slightly freaky afternoon.
> SIOBHAN. *(Agreeing.)* Oh no. *(Beat.)* So do you—
> KATHY. In fact I had to run out of the cinema cause I'd forgotten to get the fish and it was nearly seven. So I missed the last ten minutes.
> SIOBHAN. Oh no! Well the end is a bit shite so you didn't actually—
> KATHY. But *she* was brilliant.
> SIOBHAN. The main one?
> KATHY. Yeah.
> SIOBHAN. Yeah.

Pause. They drink.

Em . . .

Kathy lights a cigarette and offers one to Siobhan. She takes one.

Ya know, that time, in the club, when we met, and I went off, to get fags, wasn't it, and we had that stupid thing about, who's gonna get them, but I remember, just for a moment, that I knew, I think, we were both thinking the same thing, and since then, I've actually been coming back, to the whole thing of, where we are, and what are we doing, and I don't totally know but, if I'm not mistaken, there is definitely—isn't there?—something going on, or potentially going on, and God I mean, you have no idea like, how much I would *love* to just, but, I have to say, even though I, you, whatever, and besides anything else I just like your company, that at the moment *(she drinks)* I'm just coming out of a very long-term thing, and I think what I need really, is time to get myself together, and I can't be so sure, that I should start getting involved, so soon after, which is mad I know, and I wish I were more myself, the way that I could—

KATHY. No no no no, um, I think, I'm glad you said it cause I have to say, I think, yes, I do, also, I feel like you *would,* just the perfect, *ridiculous* like, I mean it's *fucked,* but I think also you're right, and for myself, I haven't been, you know, *with* anyone, in such a long time, and what with the work, and other kinds of shit, I feel like, I really, for a start I'd just get so tired *(joke)*, and if only to try to sort it all out, I really don't want to see myself with anyone, at the moment, and I'll kick myself tomorrow, but . . .

SIOBHAN. *(Nodding.)* No.

Pause. They drink.

And then again . . .
    KATHY. *(Beat.)* Yeah?
    SIOBHAN Nah, it's . . .

They drink.

Well eh . . . I think I'd better head.
    KATHY. You sure?
    SIOBHAN. I've got work tomorrow morning.
    KATHY. Okay. You're very welcome to crash here.
    SIOBHAN. Mmmmm, nah, I think it'd be better if . . .
    KATHY. Sure—okay.
    SIOBHAN. Well I'll see you again. We'll go for coffee.
    KATHY. Yeah.
    SIOBHAN. Thanks for dinner. It was lovely.

KATHY. No problem. You do one for me, maybe.
SIOBHAN. Sure—where did I put my jacket?
KATHY. It's in the bedroom. Hang on.

Kathy goes off. Siobhan waits. Kathy comes back with the jacket.

SIOBHAN. Thanks. (*She puts it on.*)
KATHY. Well, okay, take it easy.
SIOBHAN. Yeah. Can I've a hug?
KATHY. Yeah.

They hug. They disengage.

SIOBHAN. Can I give you a kiss?
KATHY . . . Yeah.

They kiss. It turns into a snog. It pauses. Kathy breaks away slightly.

SIOBHAN. What's wrong?
KATHY. Em. I think we should fuck now before I explode.
SIOBHAN. Finally. Jesus.

They start to undress each other.

Scene 18

Derelict building. Storm lamp on ground. Ghetto blaster plays tapes. Sean and Stephen sit. They have a bottle of whiskey, mostly full. They eat crisps and drink from mugs. Sports bags in which they brought all this stuff. They smoke.

STEPHEN. See you think too much. Women don't like guys who know exactly what's going on.

Sean drinks and refills his mug.

I tell ya. Women aren't stupid. The contract, between a man and a woman, it's gotta be almost unconscious. If the woman likes the look of you but what she gets off you is, I know this is bullshit and you know this is bullshit, let's just play along until we can be honest with each other, which let's face it doesn't happen very often, I mean how often do you meet like the perfect woman it's a fuckin', it's a *creation*, up here, *(Taps head.)* anyway, what was I saying?

SEAN. The contract.

STEPHEN. Yeah. It's like . . . a woman doesn't like to think that you're sort of laughing at the little ritual of getting to know each other and sharing secrets because say you only really want to get into her *pants,* that's like assuming you've got a God-given right to fuck her. No no. They can smell you being superior. This is why women fall for dumb fucks, cause every time those guys talk to a woman they're so fucking ignorant it's like it's the first time, and one thing women love, is seein' guys making arseholes of themselves. That fumbling thing. They love that.

Sean drinks.

SEAN. So how do *you* talk to women?

STEPHEN. Plunge in there. Take the reins. Always works. They respect that. I don't sit back *worrying* about how should I, ohh oh, 'changed roles,' or that the whole thing is a joke.

SEAN. I think nowadays it's a bit more—

STEPHEN. No. No. Fuck nowadays. *Fuck* nowadays. Cause what I'm saying is, *deep down,* the outside stuff changes, the *clothes,* but deep down what's going on is always the same.

Sean changes the tape.

But *you,* I dunno. You're much too hung up on this fuckin' sex thing. A good cigarette is nearly as good as a good shite, which is a lot better than a bad fuck.

SEAN. You reckon?

STEPHEN. Defnitly. The thing I love about cigarettes is when you take a good blast *(does so)* the tingling in the face around the mouth. Cigarettes. Fucking extraordinary. Every time you take one, a little death to let you know you're alive. *(Takes a drag.)* Why do you think antismoking ads're so stupid? 'Smoking kills.' Of course it kills, that's why we *do* it. Obsessed with health and safety. That's why we've had so many wars this century, cause we're so up our arses about health the whole time, we're not being relaxed about hey, I'll have a cigarette, I'll do myself a bit of harm rather than do some other fucker a lot of harm. Don't you think?

SEAN. Get the gun out, go on.

STEPHEN. All right, all right. I'm getting the gun out. The gun is being got out now.

Stephen gets the gun out and loads it.

I love this. The ultimate tool. A time-honoured device for blowing shit out of stuff. Okay. It's my gun so I'm having first go.

Stephen stands. He points the gun upstage.

As the owner of this gun I have a right . . . I'm gonna aim for that bit of wall over there.

SEAN. Pretend it's a bunch of, em . . .

STEPHEN. No no, I'm pretending it's all the wankers who've annoyed me the last week. Eat lead death motherfuckers!

Stephen fires the gun twice. Sean is slightly stunned by the noise.

There. I think that said something.

He gives the gun to Sean.

You try.

SEAN. Em . . .

STEPHEN. I think we've got a new therapeutic tool here. Gun therapy. Fire something and feel better.

SEAN. Wait. I know— *(He suddenly fires.)*

STEPHEN. The fuckin' ricochet! Ya see it?

Sean gives the gun to Stephen.

What's wrong?

SEAN. Not sold on it. Kind of expected more of a—

STEPHEN. Of a what? Look at this.

He holds the muzzle to the ground and fires.

Class. I'm gonna see if there's any bottles. Don't drink everything.
Fact, I'll take this.

He takes an unopened bottle from the bag, puts the gun down and exits.

Sean drinks. He picks up the gun. Tries out various moves. Tries to do a hand-stand. Can't. Drinks. Lies on the floor.

Fade.

As before. Loud music. Sean dances his arse off.

Fade.

As before. Silence. Sean lies on the floor.

> SEAN. On my birthday a few years ago I was in Galway.
> Great time. Sessions, singing, playing guitars, not usually
> things I really enjoy but I fuckin' had a great—
> really enjoyed myself.
> The next day myself and the girl whose house I was in and a cou-
> ple of friends
> went for a walk
> clear our heads.
> The beaches in Galway
> big storm beaches
> these massive boulders all the way up
> get blown in off the sea
> Anyway
> big wind comin' off the sea
> we all split up
> everybody by themselves just walkin'
> lookin' out the ocean
> sitting on these massive boulders
> I was on my own
> climbed up this huge boulder and just sat and looked out to sea
> thought about my life and the way

it was going
an' what I wanted to do with it
an' I mean this beach
an' the sea going out thousands of miles
you look out
all the bullshit falls away
an' you have to look at
the truth.
So I sat
an' I let everything fall away
an' I relaxed
cleared myself completely
an' you know what came to me?
Absolutely fuck all.

Sean raises the gun, takes aim and shoots himself in the foot. Blackout.

Scene 19

As before. Sean is lying on the ground in extreme pain. Blood leaks from his foot across the ground. Stephen enters. His bottle is half empty.

STEPHEN. Not a fuckin' bottle in the place. Fuckin' factory. Oh. What happened? Look at you. You hit your foot?

He leans over Sean's foot. Sticks a finger in the hole and wiggles it.

Widgy widgy. (*Chuckles.*) Y'see this what happens when you don't check's loaded? You're a fuckin' idiot Sean. Said this all along. We're gonna lose the gun now, cops're gonna know.

Stephen suddenly realises the significance of this. He shouts.

You fuckin' dipshit! You fuckin' ignorant fuckin' dipshit! What the fuck. (*He kicks Sean's injured foot.*) What you do that for? Gonna lose my *gun* now. Which I *found.* I leave you two minutes and some fucked up shit you're into, a thing like that. I *knew* I couldn't trust you with that. I fuckin' knew you'd pull somethin like this. You *cunt.* You fucking ignorant cunt.

Stephen puts his foot on Sean's injured foot and leans on it.

There you go. Tortured artist. Iznat good? What's your opinion bout violence in films now motherfucker? What about a bullet in your fuckin' face pal? Sort out your head once and for all?

Stephen drinks.

Don't worry. I'm not gonna. You'd only write a fuckin' song about it. Write about this, fucker.

Stephen leans on Sean's foot. He overbalances and staggers. Sean is making noise.

Whoa. I better stop fore you get bruises. I can't be arsed explaining. Shut up. Ring the ambulance in a minute. I gotta sit, I'm fuckin' locked.

Stephen sits down.

Jesus. Been a long day. For me. Tired.

He drinks.

I'm going back.

He looks around.

What a shithole.

He lies back. Falls asleep.

Scene 20

Ray and Kirsten are at breakfast.

KIRSTEN. You want tea?

Ray does not answer.

You're very quiet this morning.

RAY. Yeah, well maybe I don't feel like talkin'.

KIRSTEN. You felt like talkin' last night. You said a lot of things.

She goes behind him and starts to massage his shoulders. He shrugs her off.

RAY. Yeah well.

KIRSTEN. Somebody got out of bed the wrong side. And you didn't answer my question. You want tea?

RAY. *(Irritably.)* What? *(He runs a hand through his hair.)* Sorry doll. Got a lot on me mind.

KIRSTEN. And no time for me it seems.

RAY. Ah what is this? Me me me! Djever think of what I feel!

KIRSTEN. Well how can I have any idea if you won't tell me?

RAY. Yeah well if you'd shut up for a minute I might be able to get a word in!

KIRSTEN. So what's stopping you? *(Suspicious.)* Has this got anything to do with that phone call you had this morning?

RAY. Yeah well maybe it has and maybe it hasn't.

KIRSTEN. What's that supposed to mean?

RAY. Whatever you want it to mean.

KIRSTEN. You'd better start making some sense.

RAY. I got a phone call, right? From the hospital. One of me best friends might be dying. *That's* what's 'got into me.' So if I can have a bit of peace for a while I'm going to see him. Happy now?

KIRSTEN. I—I'm sorry.

Ray heads for the door.

RAY. Yeah well. Don't ask for what you want, because you might just get it.

He goes out. Kirsten looks troubled.

TV PRODUCER. *(Voiceover, megaphone.)* Cut! Thanks Ray, good stuff. Okay Conor? Bring it in for a tight CU on the coffeepot and we'll move on to the hospital scene quickly please, thank you.

Ray comes back in. He and Kirsten sit to the side.

KIRSTEN. This is kind of crap.

RAY. It's fuckin' arse. We could've improvised better than that, and I'm shite at improvising. (*Sotto voce.*) And I wouldn't mind only the cunt does everything the same way. Two-shot, head shot, reaction shot, two-shot, head shot, reaction shot. Does he know you can like *move* the camera?

KIRSTEN. Don't worry about it. Better things will come.

RAY. Second spear-carrier at The Gate? Spare me.

Pause.

KIRSTEN. It's weird about Sean. And everything.

RAY. I know, woof. Art imitates life, or rather wank imitates life.

KIRSTEN. How is he?

RAY. Oh. Okay, apparently. Extremely lucky. He'll lose the toe.

KIRSTEN. Oh Jesus!

RAY. It's not all that bad. You don't really need ten toes for walking, 'cept in flip-flops. And he's not really the flip-flop type.

KIRSTEN. God, that's horrible. Has he told anybody what happened?

RAY. Nah. When I talked to him he was on a lot of painkillers and wasn't really gonna say. Maybe he'll tell his family, or the cops . . . but I dunno. Nobody seems to be pressing charges. I think just they were fucking around and it went off, probly.

KIRSTEN. I must go and see him. Is he having visitors?

RAY. He doesn't want any till he's off the drugs. Slows him down.

KIRSTEN. Oh.

RAY. What about you?

KIRSTEN. Oh. I forgot to say, I'm moving. I didn't wanna stay, never liked that flat much. And I got a card asking to see my TV licence, so I thought, time to go.

RAY. Cunts.

KIRSTEN. So I found this really nice place and did out an ad to share cause nobody I knew was also looking, and a couple of people answered but one was really nice.

RAY. Who?

KIRSTEN. The flatmate? She's a waitress, she's lovely. And she does a lot of stuff like decorating I'm crap at? So it's cool. We're having a flatwarming so you'll see it then.

RAY. Excellent.

KIRSTEN. Bring Martina.

RAY. Oh no. I think not.

KIRSTEN. Oh. Didn't happen?

RAY. Happened up to a point. Then I think the chemistry was a *bit* wrong. No. History.

KIRSTEN. Oh. Well come and chat up all the waitresses then.

RAY. Sorted.

KIRSTEN. *(Beat.)* Poor Sean.

Ray agrees. Pause.

RAY. Sean bocht. Like something in the Irish reader.

KIRSTEN. Ray!

RAY. Bhris Sean an gcos leis an gunna.

KIRSTEN. Cos isn't foot, it's leg.

RAY. Oh yeah. What's foot?

KIRSTEN. Em . . . hand is lámh, and arm is mean or bean or something?

RAY. Foota. No. Shit. It's on the tip of my tongue as well. Ah God! Are you sure it's not the same word? Cos is foot as well?

KIRSTEN. I don't think so?

RAY. Okay. Lá amháin, bhí an ghrian ag taitneamh agus níl aon scamaill sa spéir. Chaith Sean an gunna. Ó, arsa sé, tá brón orm. Ní lig aon cailín sa leaba liom. Tá orm mé féin a gcaitheamh leis an gunna seo. Ach ní raibh Sean maith leis an gunna.

KIRSTEN. Sean wasn't happy with the gun?

RAY. No, he wasn't a good shot.

KIRSTEN. Is dóchas nach raibh sé aon fear gunna.

RAY. Mm, shadow of a fear gunna. Okay. Agus chuaigh an . . . an liathroidín isteach sa chois féin. Ochon! arsa sé!!

KIRSTEN. Ach, tiocfaidh an . . . inneall . . . dochtuir . . . agus chuaigh Sean go dtí an ospidéal. Cad amadán atá orm! a deir sé. And he lived happily ever after.

They fall about.

RAY. It'd make a good film. Madra na reiseirbheoir.

KIRSTEN. *(Thoughtfully.)* Yeah. It's mad.

Scene 21

Sean in hospital. Siobhan and Kathy round the bed.

KATHY. Okay, I didn't say this, but his wife is supposed to have come into his office one day and found him shagging some guy on the desk, and she was so amazed that she threw up all over the floor.

SIOBHAN. Jesus.

KATHY. This is what I heard. And when I see him now on TV I can't look at him without thinking of him on the desk between some guy's legs, and their trousers round their ankles, pumping away . . . (*Does their expression.*)

Brian enters.

BRIAN. (*To Sean.*) Hi.

SEAN. Hi.

Brian nods to Siobhan and glances at Kathy, who acknowledges him. Siobhan doesn't.

BRIAN. Gotcha this.

He gives Sean a CD in a plastic bag.

SEAN. Jesus, that's very nice. Thanks a million. The Goldberg Variations. Glenn Gould. Deadly.

BRIAN. I remembered you talkin' about him.

SEAN. Cool, I don't actually have a CD player but when I do—

BRIAN. Oh shit. I'll exchange it for cassette.

SEAN. No it's great. I'll find a way. (*Puts it aside.*) Well.

Silence.

BRIAN. How's the foot?

SEAN. Fine. Throbs kind of, when I wake up in the morning.

BRIAN. (*Sympathetically.*) No toe.

SEAN. No, well, I'll learn to live without it.

Silence.

SEAN. *(To Brian.)* So how are you?

BRIAN. Fine.

SEAN. Good.

Silence.

Ray and Kirsten enter. Ray has a parcel.

RAY. Hey hey. Look at you.

SEAN. Howieya.

Ray gives Sean the parcel. Sean unwraps it.

RAY. From all the kids at work.

SEAN. Ah God.

It's a cafetiere.

Ah that's lovely. Cheers.

RAY. It was a bit last-minute.

SEAN. You know Brian, Siobhan, Kathy don't you?

RAY. *(To Kathy.)* I know you. *(Kisses her, sits.)* So what's happening?

SIOBHAN. Well a while back there we were just swapping libels about famous public figures.

BRIAN. Of course you know the one about Jodie Foster? Not the famous Jodie Foster, this is a totally different one, worked in a café in Arklow?

RAY. No.

BRIAN. Well this other Jodie Foster, not the actress, went to Yale.

RAY. Oh. Same as the famous one.

BRIAN. Yeah, oddly enough. And while she was in Yale, every woman she slept with she used to give a Yale sweatshirt to. So now there are all these women with ten-year-old Yale sweatshirts all over America.

SEAN. *(Beat.)* That it?

BRIAN. Sounds to me like a good deal. Shag Jodie Foster, get a free sweatshirt. I wonder if you snogged her did she give you a baseball cap?

KATHY. Maybe if you gave her head you got a pair of shorts.

SIOBHAN. Giving someone head is worth more than that.

KATHY. What would you think?

SIOBHAN. Depends if it was good or bad head. For good head, shorts and a halter top.

BRIAN. What's a halter top?

KATHY. It's a sorta sleeveless top with a collar up to here *(Touches her neck.)*.

BRIAN. A vest, in other words.

SIOBHAN. It's not a vest.

BRIAN. Sounds like a vest.

SIOBHAN. You know *nothing.*

KATHY. *(To Sean.)* What do you think? Shorts and a halter?

SEAN. Dunno. I've never had good head.

KATHY. But the head you've had, what would you have given the person?

SEAN. *(Reflects.)* An Elastoplast.

RAY. Jodie Foster's never a lesbian!

Pause. They all look at him.

BRIAN. Well I can't speak for the famous Jodie Foster.

KATHY. Did you not hear? That's been going round for years.

RAY. Bollocks. That's so annoying. Not for her, I'm happy for her, it's just . . . Mr. Willy had been looking forward to meeting her. You'll be telling me next that k.d. lang is a lesbian.

SIOBHAN. Or Keanu Reeves.

BRIAN. Keanu Reeves is never a lesbian.

SIOBHAN. No, but you know what I, fuck off.

KATHY. Personally I'd go for that one in that film we saw *(to Sean)* who did I like in that? The one where the guy kills himself by wrapping dynamite round his head?

SEAN. *Anna Karina.*

KATHY. That's the one. I knew it couldn't be *Anna Karenina.*

Pause.

RAY. So.

Brian gets up.

BRIAN. Better go.

SEAN. Okay. Thanks for comin'.

BRIAN. When are you coming out?

SEAN. A week and a bit.

BRIAN. Okay. I'll give you a call. Come round for dinner. *(Beat. To Siobhan.)* Coffee?

SIOBHAN. No.

BRIAN. Okay.

Pause. Brian waves.

Have fun. See you.

He goes.

SIOBHAN. *(Sighs. To Sean.)* Sorry.

SEAN. *(Dismissing it.)* Ah.

KATHY. Go and have a coffee.

SIOBHAN. In my arse.

KATHY. Siobhan?

Pause.

SIOBHAN. I'm going out for a fag. If he's there, I'll talk to him, if he's not he can shag off.

Siobhan hugs Sean.

Look after yourself. Give us a ring when you're . . .

SEAN. Yeah.

KATHY. I'll be out in a bit.

She goes.

RAY. That's me too.

He and Kirsten stand.

SEAN. Awright. Thanks for the pot. *(To Kirsten.)* Bye-bye.

KIRSTEN. Yeah. Ah, *(Gestures.)* hospitals, eeuhh, wooo.

SEAN. I know.

She hugs Sean.

RAY. I'll be back in a coupla days. Take it easy wee man.
SEAN. Cheers.

Ray kisses Sean and Kathy. He and Kirsten leave.

KATHY. *(Deep breath.)* That was really trippy.
SEAN. Yeah.
KATHY. Sorry about all the domestic bullshit.
SEAN. Ah no. Nothing takes your mind off your troubles like constant agonising pain.
KATHY. Stop.
SEAN. Is there friction?
KATHY. She's only talked to him twice in the last four weeks.
SEAN. How's it goin' otherwise?
KATHY. It's okay. Look, I'm not bothered about me. It's you.
SEAN. Ah. What's to say.
KATHY. How Are You seems like a fairly cogent question.

Sean shrugs.

Sean.

SEAN. I never know how to answer that question.
KATHY. Well, *(Gestures at his foot.)* what's the fuckin' story here then?
SEAN. Seemed like a good idea at the time.
KATHY. Shut up.
SEAN. What can I say? I was drunk, I'd a gun in my hand and, and I didn't mind not ever being a tap dancer. It's—
KATHY. Okay, don't talk to me, you gobshite.

Pause. Sean picks up a book.

SEAN. I've been reading this, it's great. This is the guy who said, life is to be lived forward but understood backward. But in fact, I found the bit and what he also said is, I know I said life is to be lived forward and understood backwards, but the trouble is, I can't find the place where you stop, turn around and do the understanding.

KATHY. Tell me something. Do you think it does any good for people to talk to each other? I mean do you think, in general, what are the chances of communication between people, as opposed to nothing anyone says or doesn't say making a blind bit of difference, let's say in terms of *telling* people stuff in the hope that they may be able to *help* instead of bottling it all up and exploding? What are your thoughts on that particular subject?

SEAN. I dunno. Just cause I shot myself, doesn't make me a fuckin' oracle.

KATHY. Will you shut the fuck up with the jokes for five seconds? I'm trying to talk about this! I mean I am not in the best of moods at the moment, with a friend of mine going off and shooting himself, that says to me there is something seriously fucking wrong and I would quite like to get to the bottom of it, even if nobody else does, and you are not being any help. *Christ.* I can't believe that after all this drama you put everybody through you still have the nerve to sit there and make clever remarks like you don't even take your own *life* seriously.

SEAN. I don't.

KATHY. Don't talk shit! That is total shit. Of course you do, if you don't you would've killed yourself, so would you mind telling me what the *fuck* is the matter?

Pause.

Just don't go and do something like this and pretend that nobody gives a shit about it, 'cause they do. If something happens to you it matters. D'you not see that? I mean, fuck's sake, I knew you weren't happy, but I didn't know you were gonna pull something like this, and I mean I couldn't've known, but just tell me if there was something I could've done.

Pause. Sean stares at her.

Right.

Pause.

SEAN. I don't know.

Kathy takes out her cigarettes and lights one.

KATHY. Of course I can't smoke in here can I.
SEAN. No.

Kathy stubs it out and throws it away. She is on the verge of tears. Pause. She leans over and puts her arms round him. They embrace.

Scene 22

Martina's flat. Stephen is in bed with someone we can't see. He stares at the ceiling.

STEPHEN. I had this friend in school who was a total Unionist cunt. One summer he was in Dublin. This is when they still had traffic in Grafton Street. He was walking round town and it was a really hot summer so he was wearing this Union Jack T-shirt, eating a big fuckoff roll and drinking a pint of milk. So he's strolling down the middle of Grafton Street and this bus comes down the street and it gets level with him, and the driver looks out the window at him, and goes hah, bleedin Brit. And your man just goes *(mimes taking a big bite of roll)* and takes a big swig of milk and *(mimes chewing)* turns it into mush and then he just leans up and goes 'Bleeahhh!' *all over* the driver. *(Laughs.)* Driver's there for five minutes wiping the shit off. Friend of mine just walks off down the street.

The other person laughs indistinctly.

I swear. You can't make that shit up. Told me himself.

Pause.

I better wash.

He sits up and turns. There's a five-pointed star recently carved into his stomach. His torso is smeared with blood. He winces.

Ow. Ah, can't be arsed.

He lies down again. The other person gets up on one elbow and smiles down at him. It's Martina. Her face and T-shirt are smeared with blood.

MARTINA. You are so thick.
STEPHEN. Why?
MARTINA. He told you that and you believed him.
STEPHEN. So?
MARTINA. How old were you when he told you? Ten?
STEPHEN. Around ten.
MARTINA. Never thought he mighta been bullshittin'?

Stephen is silent. Martina licks her fingers and wipes her face. She takes from beside the bed an X-Acto knife in a foil wrapper. Stephen watches her. She unwraps it, heats it in a cigarette lighter and waves it to cool it down. She settles and puts the blade on his rib cage.

(Amused.) Dick.

She cuts him. He tenses and relaxes. She kisses the wound.

Scene 23

Kirsten alone.

KIRSTEN. I remember the first time I saw a naked man on TV.
I remember those headset yokes with little hearts on springs.
I remember pronouncing 'I remember' as 'I member.'
I remember the Cadbury's Icebreaker.
I remember the first time Christmas was no fun.
I remember when the Americans bombed Tripoli.
I remember wondering which if any of my schoolteachers were sleeping with each other.
I remember when suburban trains had hard red plastic seats like school furniture.
I remember when I was a kid, cleaning my teeth and getting all toothpaste froth in my mouth, pretending I had rabies.
I remember when the Challenger space shuttle exploded. And
I remember years later, hearing a rumour that they'd been alive in

the control cabin all the way down to the ocean and that NASA had tapes of what went on.

I remember a TV programme called *Vision On* and being puzzled by how slow and boring it was cause I didn't know it was meant for deaf people.

I remember feeling like I was part of a modern democracy because they were starting to have condom machines in pub toilets.

I remember little black flags hanging from lampposts when Bobby Sands died.

Some of them were there for years.

I remember when muesli seemed like it was new and fun.

I remember going to the theatre aged about five and not giving a shit about the play cause all I wanted to do was go backstage and see what they all got up to when they went off.

Scene 24

Sean's flat. The phone rings.

Sean enters in a dressing gown, on crutches, cast on his foot. Woken up far too early. He picks up the phone.

SEAN. I listen to FM 93, the station of the nation. Kathy! Sorry. Reflex action. Howieya.

It's okay, hurts when I wake up. But the pus doesn't seep through onto the sheet anymore.

It's a *joke.* God. So what's happening?

It's fuckin' nine forty-five.

No? Haven't seen her.

Ah don't do this to me. Tell me now.

Fuck! That's great news.

Fair play. Tell her I said well done.

So what, she can, like, break people's legs?

Hey, I'm there. Absolutely.

Listen, I'm gonna have breakfast.

Okay babe. You don't mind me calling you babe do you?

Okay. Bye-bye. Thanks for calling. See you later.

He hangs up. He looks out, expressionless. Beat. He heads for the kitchen.

Blackout.

END OF PLAY

Translation of Irish dialogue on page 177. NOTE: This dialogue is written in intentionally bad Irish.

RAY. Like something in the Irish reader. *(Poor Sean.)*

KIRSTEN. Ray!

RAY. *(Sean broke the foot with the gun.)*

RAY. Okay. *(One day, the sun was shining and there was not a cloud in the sky. Sean took the gun. Oh, he said, sadness is on me. No girl lies in my bed. It is on me to hit myself with this gun. But Sean was not good with the gun.)*

KIRSTEN. Sean wasn't happy with the gun?

RAY. No, he wasn't a good shot.

KIRSTEN. *(Not . . . it is supposed that he was no gunman.)*

RAY. Mm, shadow of a *(gunman.)*. Okay. *(And went the . . . the small ball (i.e., bullet) into his foot. Alas! he said!!)*

KIRSTEN. *(But, came the doctor engine (i.e., ambulance, from 'inneall dóiteáin,' fire engine) and Sean went to the hospital. What an idiot I am! he said.)* And they lived happily ever after.

RAY. It'd make a good film. *(Reservoir Dogs—'reiseirbheoir' is written as if in Irish orthography.)*

Marina Carr.
Courtesy Amelia Stein.

By the Bog of Cats

MARINA CARR

1998

Olwen Fouéré   Siobhan Cullen/Kerry O'Sullivan
Conor MacDermottroe   Pat Leavy
Pauline Flanagan   Tom Hickey
Fionnuala Murphy   Joan O'Hara
Pat Kinevane   Ronan Leahy
Conan Sweeny   Eamon Kelly
Gavin Cleland   Kieran Grimes

Director: Patrick Mason

Characters

HESTER SWANE, forty
CARTHAGE KILBRIDE, thirty
JOSIE KILBRIDE, seven, Hester and Carthage's daughter
MRS. KILBRIDE, sixties, Carthage's mother
MONICA MURRAY, sixties, a neighbour
CATWOMAN, fifties, lives on the bog
XAVIER CASSIDY, sixties, a big farmer
CAROLINE CASSIDY, twenty, his daughter
THE GHOST FANCIER, a handsome creature in a dress suit
THE GHOST OF JOSEPH SWANE, eighteen
YOUNG DUNNE, a waiter
FATHER WILLOW, eighty
TWO OTHER WAITERS
VOICE OF JOSIE SWANE

Time and Place

The present.

ACT I *takes place in the yard of Hester Swane's house and by the caravan on the Bog of Cats.*

ACT II *takes place in Xavier Cassidy's house.*

ACT III *opens in Hester's yard and then reverts to the caravan on the Bog of Cats.*

190

Accent

Midland. I've given a slight flavour in the text, but the real Midland accent is a lot flatter and rougher and more guttural than the written word allows.

Songs of Josie Swane

To be recorded and used during the play.

By the Bog of Cats
By the Bog of Cats I finally learned false from true,
Learned too late that it was you and only you
Left me sore, a heart brimful of rue
By the Bog of Cats in the darkling dew.

By the Bog of Cats I dreamed a dream of wooing.
I heard your clear voice to me-a-calling
That I must go though it be my undoing.
By the Bog of Cats I'll stay no more a-rueing.

To the Bog of Cats I one day will return,
In mortal form or in ghostly form,
And I will find you there and there with you sojourn,
Forever by the Bog of Cats, my darling one.
The Black Swan
I know where a black swan sleeps
On the bank of grey water,
Hidden in a nest of leaves
So none can disturb her.

I have lain outside her lair,
My hand upon her wing,
And I have whispered to her
And of my sorrows sung.

I wish I was a black swan
And could fly away from here,

But I am Josie Swane,
Without wings, without care.

ACT I

Scene 1

*Dawn. On the Bog of Cats. A bleak white landscape of ice and snow. Music,
a lone violin. Hester Swane trails the corpse of a black swan after her, leaving
a trail of blood in the snow. The Ghost Fancier stands there watching her.*

HESTER. Who are you? Haven't seen you around here before.

GHOST FANCIER. I'm a ghost fancier.

HESTER. A ghost fancier. Never heard tell of the like.

GHOST FANCIER. You never seen ghosts?

HESTER. Not exactly, felt what I thought were things from some
other world betimes, but nothin' I could grab onto and say, 'That is a
ghost.'

GHOST FANCIER. Well, where there's ghosts there's ghost
fanciers.

HESTER. That so? So what do you do, Mr. Ghost Fancier? Eye up
ghosts? Have love affairs with them?

GHOST FANCIER. Dependin' on the ghost. I've trailed you a while.
What're you doin' draggin' the corpse of a swan behind ya like it was
your shadow?

HESTER. This is auld Black Wing. I've known her the longest
time. We used play together when I was a young wan. Wance I had to
lave the Bog of Cats and when I returned years later this swan here
came swoopin' over the bog to welcome me home, came right up to
me and kissed me hand. Found her frozen in a bog hole last night, had
to rip her from the ice, left half her underbelly.

GHOST FANCIER. No one ever tell ya it's dangerous to interfere
with swans, especially black wans?

HESTER. Only an auld superstition to keep people afraid, I only
want to bury her. I can't be struck down for that, can I?

GHOST FANCIER. You live in that caravan over there?

HESTER. Used to; live up the lane now. In a house, though I've never felt at home in it. But you, Mr. Ghost Fancier, what ghost are you ghoulin' for around here?

GHOST FANCIER. I'm ghoulin' for a woman be the name of Hester Swane.

HESTER. I'm Hester Swane.

GHOST FANCIER. You couldn't be, you're alive.

HESTER. I certainly am and aim to stay that way.

GHOST FANCIER. *(Looks around, confused.)* Is it sunrise or sunset?

HESTER. Why do ya want to know?

GHOST FANCIER. Just tell me.

HESTER. It's that hour when it could be aither dawn or dusk, the light bein' so similar. But it's dawn, see there's the sun coming' up.

GHOST FANCIER. Then I'm too previous. I mistook this hour for dusk. A thousand apologies.

Goes to exit. Hester stops him.

HESTER. What do ya mean you're too previous? Who are ya? Really?

GHOST FANCIER. I'm sorry for intrudin' upon you like this. It's not usually my style. *(Lifts his hat, walks off.)*

HESTER. *(Shouts after him.)* Come back! I can't die—I have a daughter.

Monica enters.

MONICA. What's wrong of ya, Hester? What are ya shoutin' at?

HESTER. Don't ya see him?

MONICA. Who?

HESTER. Him!

MONICA. I don't see anywan.

HESTER. Over there. *(Points.)*

MONICA. There's no wan, but ya know this auld bog, always shiftin' and changin' and coddin' the eye. What's that you've there? Oh, Black Wing, what happened to her?

HESTER. Auld age, I'll wager, found her frozed last night.

MONICA. *(Touches the swan's wing.)* Well, she'd good innin's, way past the life span of swans. Ya look half frozed yourself, walkin' all night again, were ya? Ya'll cetch your death in this weather. Five below the forecast said and worser promised.

HESTER. Swear the age of ice have returned. Wouldn't ya almost wish if it had, do away with us all like the dinosaurs?

MONICA. I would not indeed—are you lavin' or what, Hester?

HESTER. Don't keep axin' me that.

MONICA. Ya know you're welcome in my little shack.

HESTER. I'm goin' nowhere. This here is my house and my garden and my stretch of the bog and no wan's runnin' me out of here.

MONICA. I came up to see if ya wanted me to take Josie down for her breakfast.

HESTER. She's still asleep.

MONICA. The child, Hester, ya have to pull yourself together for her, you're goin' to have to stop this broodin', put your life back together again.

HESTER. Wasn't me as pulled it asunder.

MONICA. And you're goin' to have to lave this house, isn't yours anymore. Down in Daly's doin' me shoppin' and Caroline Cassidy there talkin' about how she was goin' to mow this place to the ground and build a new house from scratch.

HESTER. Caroline Cassidy. I'll sourt her out. It's not her is the problem anyway, she's just wan of the smaller details.

MONICA. Well, you've left it late for dealin' with her for she has her heart set on everythin' that's yours.

HESTER. If he thinks he can go on treatin' me the way he's been treatin' me, he's another thing comin'. I'm not to be flung aside at his biddin'. He'd be nothin' today if it wasn't for me.

MONICA. Sure the whole parish knows that.

HESTER. Well, if they do, why're yees all just standin' back and gawkin'? Thinks yees all Hester Swane with her tinker blood is gettin' no more than she deserves. Thinks yees all she's too many notions, built her life up from a caravan on the side of the bog. Thinks yees all she's taken a step above herself in gettin' Carthage Kilbride into her bed. Thinks yees all yees knew it'd never last. Well, yees are thinkin' wrong. Carthage Kilbride is mine for always or until I say he is no longer mine. I'm the one who chooses and discards, not him, and certainly not any of yees. And I'm not runnin' with me tail between me legs just because certain people wants me out of their way.

MONICA. You're angry now and not thinkin' straight.

HESTER. If he'd only come back, we'd be alright. If I could just have him for a few days on me own with no wan stickin' their nose in.

MONICA. Hester, he's gone from ya and he's not comin' back.

HESTER. Ah you think ya know everythin' about me and Carthage. Well, ya don't. There's things about me and Carthage no wan knows except the two of us. And I'm not talkin' about love. Love is for fools and children. Our bond is harder, like two rocks we are, grindin' off of wan another and maybe all the closer for that.

MONICA. That's all in your own head, the man cares nothin' for ya, else why would he go on the way he does?

HESTER. My life doesn't hang together without him.

MONICA. You're talkin' riddles now.

HESTER. Carthage knows what I'm talkin' about—I suppose I may bury auld Black Wing before Josie wakes and sees her. *(Begins walking off.)*

MONICA. I'll come up to see ya in a while, bring yees up some lunch, help ya pack.

HESTER. There'll be no packin' done around here.

And exit both in opposite directions.

Scene 2

The sound of a child's voice comes from the house. She enters after a while, Josie Kilbride, seven, barefoot, pyjamas, kicking the snow, singing.

JOSIE.
By the Bog of Cats I dreamed a dream of wooing.
I heard your clear voice to me a-calling
That I must go though it be my undoing.
By the Bog of Cats I'll stay no more a-rueing—
  Mam—Mam— *(Continues playing in the snow, singing.)*
To the Bog of Cats I one day will return,
In mortal form or in ghostly form,
And I will find you there and there with you sojourn,
Forever by the Bog of Cats, my darling one.

Mrs. Kilbride has entered, togged up against the biting cold, a shawl over her face.

MRS. KILBRIDE. Well, good mornin', ya little wagon of a girl child.

JOSIE. Mornin' yourself, y'auld wagon of a granny witch.

MRS. KILBRIDE. I tould ya not to call me Granny.

JOSIE. Grandmother—did ya see me Mam, did ya?

MRS. KILBRIDE. Aye, seen her whooshin' by on her broom half an hour back.

JOSIE. Did yees crash?

MRS. KILBRIDE. Get in, ya pup, and put on some clothes before Jack Frost ates your toes for breakfast. Get in till I dress ya.

JOSIE. I know how to dress meself.

MRS. KILBRIDE. Then dress yourself and stop braggin' about it. Get in. Get in.

And exit the pair to the house.

Scene 3

Enter Hester by the caravan. She digs a grave for the swan. Enter the Cat-woman, a woman in her late fifties, stained a streaky brown from the bog, a coat of cat fur that reaches to the ground, studded with cats' eyes and cats' paws. She is blind and carries a stick.

CATWOMAN. What're ya doin' there?

HESTER. None of your business now, Catwoman.

CATWOMAN. You're buryin' auld Black Wing, aren't ya?

HESTER. How d'ya know?

CATWOMAN. I know everythin' that happens on this bog. I'm the Keeper of the Bog of Cats in case ya forgotten. I own this bog.

HESTER. Ya own nothin', Catwoman, except your little house of turf and your hundred-odd mousetraps and anythin' ya can rob and I'm missin' a garden chair so ya better bring it back.

CATWOMAN. I only took it because ya won't be needin' it any-more.

HESTER. Won't I? If ya don't bring it back I'll have to go down meself and maybe knock your little turf house down.

CATWOMAN. You just dare.

HESTER. I'll bring down diesel, burn ya out.

CATWOMAN. Alright! Alright! I'll bring back your garden chair, fierce uncomfortable anyway, not wan of the cats'd sleep on it. Here, give her to me a minute, auld Black Wing.

Hester does.

She came to my door last night and tapped on it as she often did, only last night she wouldn't come in. I bent down and she puts her wing on me cheek and I knew this was farewell. Then I heard her tired auld wingbeat, shaky and off-kilter and then the thud of her fallin' out of the sky onto the ice. She must've died on the wing or soon after. *(Kisses the black swan.)* Good-bye, auld thing, and safe journey. Here, put her in the ground.

Hester does and begins shovelling in clay. Catwoman stands there leaning on her stick, produces a mouse from her pocket.

A saucer of milk there, Hester Swane.

HESTER. I've no milk here today. You may go up to the house for your saucer of milk and, I told ya, I don't want ya pawin' mice around me, dirty auld yokes, full of diseases.

CATWOMAN. And you aren't, you clean as the snow, Hester Swane?

HESTER. Did I say I was?

CATWOMAN. I knew your mother, I helped her bring ya into the world, knew ya when ya were chained like a rabied pup to this auld caravan, so don't you look down on me for handlin' a mouse or two.

HESTER. If ya could just see yourself and the mouse fur growin' out of your teeth. Disgustin'.

CATWOMAN. I need mice the way you need whiskey.

HESTER. Ah, go on and lave me alone, Catwoman, I'm in no mood for ya today.

CATWOMAN. Bet ya aren't. I had a dream about ya last night.

HESTER. Spare me your visions and dreams, enough of me own to deal with.

CATWOMAN. Dreamt ya were a black train motorin' through the Bog of Cats and, oh, the scorch off of this train and it blastin' by and all the bog was dark in your wake, and I had to run from the burn. Hester Swane, you'll bring this place down by evenin'.

HESTER. I know.

CATWOMAN. Do ya now? Then why don't ya lave? If ya lave this place you'll be alright. That's what I came by to tell ya.

HESTER. Ah, how can I lave the Bog of Cats, everythin' I'm connected to is here. I'd rather die.

CATWOMAN. Then die ya will.

HESTER. There's sympathy for ya! That's just what I need to hear.

CATWOMAN. Ya want sugarplum platitudes, go talk to Monica Murray or anyone else around here. You're my match in witchery, Hester, same as your mother was, it may even be ya surpass us both and the way ya go on as if God only gave ya a little frog of a brain instead of the gift of seein' things as they are, not as they should be, but exactly as they are. Ya know what I think?

HESTER. What?

CATWOMAN. I been thinkin' a while now that there's some fierce wrong ya done that's caught up with ya.

HESTER. What fierce wrong?

CATWOMAN. Don't you by-talk me, I'm the Catwoman. I know things. Now I can't say I know the exact wrong ya done but I'd put a bet on it's somethin' serious judgin' by the way ya go on.

HESTER. And what way do I go on?

CATWOMAN. What was it ya done, Hester?

HESTER. I done nothin'—or if I did I never meant to.

CATWOMAN. There's a fine answer.

HESTER. Everywan has done wrong at wan time or another.

CATWOMAN. Aye, but not everywan knows the price of wrong. You do and it's the best thing about ya and there's not much in ya I'd praise. No, most manage to stay a step or two ahead of the pigsty truth of themselves; not you though.

HESTER. Ah, would ya give over. Ya lap up people's fears, you've too much time on your own, concoctin' stories about others. Go 'way and kill a few mice for your dinner, only lave me alone—or tell me about me mother, for what I remember doesn't add up.

CATWOMAN. What ya want to know about big Josie Swane?

HESTER. Everythin'.

CATWOMAN. Well, what ya remember?

HESTER. Only small things—like her pausin'.

CATWOMAN. She was a great wan for the pausin'.

HESTER. 'G'wan to bed, you,' she'd say. 'I'll just be here pausin'.' And I'd watch her from the window. (*Indicates window of caravan.*)

Times she'd smoke a cigar which she had her own particular way of doin'. She'd hould it stretched away from her and, instead of takin' the cigar to her mouth, she'd bring her mouth to the cigar. And her all the time pausin'. What was she waitin' for, Catwoman?

CATWOMAN. Ya'd often hear her voice comin' over the bog at night. She was the greatest song stitcher ever to have passed through this place and we've had plenty pass through but none like Josie Swane. But somewhere along the way she lost the weave of the song and in so doin' became small and bitter and mean. By the time she ran off and left ya I couldn't abide her.

HESTER. There's a longin' in me for her that won't quell the whole time.

CATWOMAN. I wouldn't long for Josie Swane if I was you. Sure the night ya were born she took ya over to the black swan's lair, auld Black Wing ya've just buried there, and laid ya in the nest alongside her. And when I axed her why she'd do a thing like that with snow and ice everywhere, ya know what she says, 'Swane means swan.' 'That may be so,' says I, 'but the child'll die of pneumonia.' 'That child,' says Josie Swane, 'will live as long as this black swan, not a day more, not a day less.' And each night for three nights she left ya in the black swan's lair and each night I snuck ya out of the lair and took ya home with me and brung ya back to the lair before she'd come lookin' for ya in the mornin'. That's when I started to turn again' her.

HESTER. You're makin' it up to get rid of me like everywan else round here. Xavier Cassidy put ya up to this.

CATWOMAN. Xavier Cassidy put me up to nothin'. I'm only tellin' ya so ya know what sourt of a woman your mother was. Ya were lucky she left ya. Just forget about her and lave this place now or ya never will.

HESTER. Doesn't seem to make much difference whether I stay or lave with a curse like that on me head.

CATWOMAN. There's ways round curses. Curses only have the power ya allow them. I'm tellin' ya, Hester, ya have to go. When have I ever been proved wrong? Tould ya ya'd have just the wan daughter, tould ya the day and hour she'd be born, didn't I now?

HESTER. Ya did alright.

CATWOMAN. Tould ya Carthage Kilbride was no good for ya, never grew his backbone, would ya listen? Tould Monica Murray to stop her only son drivin' to the city that night. Would she listen?

Where's her son? In his grave, that's where he is. Begged her till she ran me off with a kittle of bilin' water. Mayhap she wanted him dead. I'll say nothin'. Gave auld Xavier Cassidy herbs to cure his wife. What did he do? Pegged them down the tilet and took Olive Cassidy to see some swanky medicine man in a private hospital. They cured her alright, cured her so well she came back cured as a side of ham in an oak coffin with golden handles. Maybe he wanted her dead too. There's many gets into brown studies over buryin' their loved wans. That a fact, Hester Swane. I'll be off now and don't say the Catwoman never tould ya. Lave this place now or ya never will.

HESTER. I'm stoppin' here.

CATWOMAN. Sure I know that too. Seen it writ in a bog hole.

HESTER. Is there anythin' them blind eyes doesn't see writ in a bog hole?

CATWOMAN. Sneer away. Ya know what the Catwoman says is true, but sneer away and we'll see will that sneer be on your puss at dusk. Remember the Catwoman then for I don't think I'll have the stomach for this place tonight.

And exit the Catwoman and exit Hester.

Scene 4

Josie and Mrs. Kilbride enter and sit at the garden table as the Catwoman and Hester exit. Josie is dressed: Wellingtons, trousers, jumper on inside out. They're playing snap. Mrs. Kilbride plays ruthlessly, loves to win. Josie looks on in dismay.

MRS. KILBRIDE. Snap—snap! Snap! *(Stacking the cards.)* How many games is that I'm after winnin' ya?

JOSIE. Five.

MRS. KILBRIDE. And how many did you win?

JOSIE. Ya know right well I won ne'er a game.

MRS. KILBRIDE. And do ya know why ya won ne'er a game, Josie? Because you're thick, that's the why.

JOSIE. I always win when I play me mam.

MRS. KILBRIDE. That's only because your mam is thicker than you. Thick and stubborn and dangerous wrongheaded and backwards to top it all. Are you goin' to start cryin' now, ya little pussy babby, don't you dare cry, ya need to toughen up, child, what age are ya now?—I says what age are ya?

JOSIE. Seven.

MRS. KILBRIDE. Seven auld years. When I was seven I was cookin' dinners for a houseful of men, I was thinnin' turnips twelve hour a day, I was birthin' calves, sowin' corn, stookin' hay, ladin' a bull be his nose, and you can't even win a game of snap. Sit up straight or ya'll grow up a hunchback. Would ya like that, would ya, to grow up a hunchback? Ya'd be like an auld camel and everyone'd say, as ya loped by, 'There goes Josie Kilbride the hunchback,' would ya like that, would ya? Answer me.

JOSIE. Ya know right well I wouldn't, Granny.

MRS. KILBRIDE. What did I tell ya about callin' me Grand-mother?

JOSIE. *(Defiantly.)* Granny.

MRS. KILBRIDE. *(Leans over the table viciously.)* Grandmother! Say it!

JOSIE. *(Giving in.)* Grandmother.

MRS. KILBRIDE. And you're lucky I even let ya call me that. Ya want another game?

JOSIE. Only if ya don't cheat.

MRS. KILBRIDE. When did I cheat?

JOSIE. I seen ya, loads of times.

MRS. KILBRIDE. A bad loser's all you are, Josie, and there's nothin' meaner than a bad loser. I never cheat. Never. D'ya hear me, do ya? Look me in the eye when I'm talkin' to ya, ya little bastard. D'ya want another game?

JOSIE. No thanks, Grandmother.

MRS. KILBRIDE. And why don't ya? Because ya know I'll win, isn't that it? Ya little coward ya, I'll break your spirit yet and then glue ya back the way I want ya. I bet ya can't even spell your name.

JOSIE. And I bet ya I can.

MRS. KILBRIDE. G'wan then, spell it.

JOSIE. *(Spells.)* J-o-s-i-e K-i-l-b-r-i-d-e.

MRS. KILBRIDE. Wrong! Wrong! Wrong!

JOSIE. Well, that's the way Teacher taught me.

MRS. KILBRIDE. Are you back-answerin' me?

JOSIE. No, Grandmother.

MRS. KILBRIDE. Ya got some of it right. Ya got the 'Josie' part right, but ya got the 'Kilbride' part wrong, because you're not a Kilbride. You're a Swane. Can ya spell Swane? Of course ya can't. You're Hester Swane's little bastard. You're not a Kilbride and never will be.

JOSIE. I'm tellin' Daddy what ya said.

MRS. KILBRIDE. Tell him! Ya won't be tellin' him anythin' I haven't tould him meself. He's an eegit, your daddy. I warned him about that wan, Hester Swane, that she'd get her claws in, and she did, the tinker. That's what yees are, tinkers. And your poor daddy, all he's had to put up with. Well, at least that's all changin' now. Why don't yees head off in that auld caravan, back to wherever yees came from, and give your poor daddy back to me where he rightfully belongs? And you've your jumper on backwards.

JOSIE. It's not backwards, it's inside out.

MRS. KILBRIDE. Don't you cheek me—and tell me this, Josie Swane, how much has your mam in the bank?

JOSIE. I don't know.

MRS. KILBRIDE. I'll tell ya how much, a great big goose egg. Useless, that's what she is, livin' off of handouts from my son that she flitters away on whiskey and cigars, the Jezebel witch. (*Smugly.*) Guess how much I've saved, Josie, g'wan, guess, guess.

JOSIE. I wish if me mam'd came soon.

MRS. KILBRIDE. Ah g'wan, child, guess.

JOSIE. Ten pound.

MRS. KILBRIDE. (*Hysterical.*) Ten pound! A' ya mad, child? A' ya mad! Ten pound! (*Whispers avariciously.*) Three thousand pound. All mine. I saved it. I didn't frig it away on crame buns and blouses. No. I saved it. A thousand for me funeral, a thousand for the Little Sisters of the Poor and a thousand for your daddy. I'm lavin' you nothin' because your mother would get hould of it. And d'ya think would I get any thanks for savin' all that money? Oh no, none, none in the world. Would it ever occur to anywan to say, 'Well done, Mrs. Kilbride, well done, Elsie,' not wance did your daddy ever say, 'Well done, Mother,' no, too busy fornicatin' with Hester Swane, too busy bringin' little bastards like yourself into the world.

JOSIE. Can I go and play now?

MRS. KILBRIDE. Here, I brung ya sweets, g'wan ate them, ate them all, there's a great child, ya need some sugar, some sweetie pie sweetness in your life. C'mere and give your auld grandmother a kiss.

Josie does.

Sure it's not your fault ya were born a little girl bastard. D'ya want another game of snap? I'll let ya win.

JOSIE. No.

MRS. KILBRIDE. Don't you worry, child, we'll get ya off of her yet. Me and your daddy has plans. We'll batter ya into the semblance of legitimacy yet, soon as we get ya off—

Enter Carthage.

CARTHAGE. I don't know how many times I tould ya to lave the child alone. You've her poisoned with your bile and rage.

MRS. KILBRIDE. I'm sayin' nothin' that isn't true. Can't I play a game of snap with me own granddaughter?

CARTHAGE. Ya know I don't want ya around here at the minute. G'wan home, Mother. G'wan!

MRS. KILBRIDE. And do what? Talk to the range? Growl at God?

CARTHAGE. Do whatever ya like, only lave Josie alone, pick on somewan your own size. (*He turns Josie's jumper the right way around.*) You'll have to learn to dress yourself.

MRS. KILBRIDE. Ah now, Carthage, don't be annoyed with me. I only came up to say good-bye to her, found her in her pyjamas out here playin' in the snow. Why isn't her mother mindin' her?

CARTHAGE. Don't start in on that again.

MRS. KILBRIDE. I never left you on your own.

CARTHAGE. Ya should have.

MRS. KILBRIDE. And ya never called in to see the new dress I got for today and ya promised ya would.

Carthage glares at her.

Alright, I'm goin', I'm goin'. Just don't think now ya've got Caroline Cassidy ya can do away with me, the same as you're doin' away with Hester Swane. I'm your mother and I won't be goin' away. Ever. (*Exits.*)

CARTHAGE. Where's your mam?

JOSIE. Isn't she always on the bog? Can I go to your weddin'?

CARTHAGE. What does your mother say?

JOSIE. She says there'll be no weddin' and to stop annoyin' her.

CARTHAGE. Does she now?

JOSIE. Will you ax her for me?

CARTHAGE. We'll see, Josie, we'll see.

JOSIE. I'll wear me Communion dress. Remember me Communion, Daddy?

CARTHAGE. I do.

JOSIE. Wasn't it just a brilliant day?

CARTHAGE. It was, sweetheart, it was. Come on, we go check the calves.

And exit the pair.

Scene 5

Enter Caroline Cassidy in her wedding dress and veil. Twenty, fragile-looking and nervous. She goes to the window of Hester's house and knocks.

CAROLINE. Hester—are ya there?

Hester comes up behind her.

HESTER. Haven't you the gall comin' here, Caroline Cassidy.

CAROLINE. (*Jumps with fright.*) Oh! (*Recovers.*) Can come here whenever I want, this is my house now, sure ya signed it over and all.

HESTER. Bits of paper, writin', means nothin', can as aisy be unsigned.

CAROLINE. You're meant to be gone this weeks, it's just not fair.

HESTER. Lots of things isn't fair, daddy's little ice-pop.

CAROLINE. We're goin' ahead with the weddin', me and Carthage, ya think ya'll disrupt everythin', Hester Swane. I'm not afraid of ya.

HESTER. Ya should be. I'm afraid of meself—what is it ya want from me, Caroline? What have I ever done on you that ya feel the need to take everythin' from me?

CAROLINE. I'm takin' nothin' ya haven't lost already and lost this long while gone.

HESTER. You're takin' me husband, you're takin' me house, ya even want me daughter. Over my dead body.

CAROLINE. He was never your husband, he only took pity on ya, took ya out of that auld caravan on the bog, gave ya a home, built ya up from the ground.

HESTER. Them the sweet nothin's he's been tellin' ya? Let's get wan thing straight, it was me built Carthage Kilbride up from nothin', him a labourer's son you wouldn't give the time of day to and you trottin' by in your first bra, on your half-bred mare, your nose nudgin' the sun. It was me who tould him he could do better. It was my money that bought his first fine acres. It was in my bed he slowly turned from a slavish pup to a man and no frigid little daddy's girl is goin' to take him from me. Now get off of my property before I cut that dress to ribbons.

CAROLINE. I'll have to get Daddy. He'll run ya off with a shotgun if he has to.

HESTER. Not everyone is as afraid of your daddy as you are, Caroline.

CAROLINE. Look, I'll give ya more money if ya'll only go. Here's me bankbook, there's nearly nineteen thousand pounds in it, me inheritance from me mother. Daddy gave it to me this mornin'. Ya can have it, only please go. It's me weddin' day. It's meant to be happy. It's meant to be the best day of me life.

She stands there, close to tears. Hester goes over to her, touches her veil.

HESTER. What ya want me to do, Caroline? Admire your dress? Wish ya well? Hah? I used to baby-sit you. Remember that?

CAROLINE. That was a long time ago.

HESTER. Not that long at all. After your mother died, several nights ya came down and slept with me. Ya were glad of the auld caravan then, when your daddy'd be off at the races or the mart or the pub, remember that, do ya? A pasty little thing, and I'd be awake half the night listenin' to your girly gibberish and grievances. Listen to me now, Caroline, there's two Hester Swanes, one that is decent and very fond of ya despite your callow treatment of me. And the other Hester, well, she could slide a knife down your face, carve ya up and not bat an eyelid. (*Grabs her hair suddenly and viciously.*)

CAROLINE. Ow! Lave go!

HESTER. Listen to me now, Caroline. Carthage Kilbride is mine and only mine. He's been mine since he was sixteen. You think you can take him from me? Wrong. All wrong. *(Lets go of her.)* Now get out of me sight.

    CAROLINE. Ya'll be sorry for this, Hester Swane.

    HESTER. We all will.

And exit Caroline, running.

Scene 6

Hester lights a cigar, sits at her garden table. Enter Josie with an old shawl around her head and a pair of high heels. She is pretending to be her granny.

    JOSIE. Well good mornin', Tinker Swane.

    HESTER. *(Mock surprise.)* Oh, good mornin', Mrs. Kilbride, what a lovely surprise, and how are ya today?

    JOSIE. I've been savin' all night.

    HESTER. Have ya now, Mrs. Kilbride.

    JOSIE. Tell me, ya Jezebel witch, how much have ya in the bank today?

    HESTER. Oh, I've three great big goose eggs, Mrs. Kilbride. How much have ya in the bank yourself?

    JOSIE. Seventeen million pound. Seventeen million pound. I saved it. I didn't frig it away on love stories and silk stockin's. I cut back on sugar and I cut back on flour. I drank biled socks instead of tay and in wan night I saved seventeen million pound.

    HESTER. Ya drank biled socks, Mrs. Kilbride?

    JOSIE. I did and I had turf stew for me dinner and for dessert I had snail tart and a big mug of wee-wee.

    HESTER. Sounds delicious, Mrs. Kilbride.

    JOSIE. Ya wouldn't get better in Buckin'am Palace.

    HESTER. Josie, don't ever say any of that in front of your granny, sure ya won't?

    JOSIE. I'm not a total eegit, Mam.

    HESTER. Did ya have your breakfast?

    JOSIE. I had a sugar sammige.

    HESTER. Ya better not have.

    JOSIE. Granny made me disgustin' porridge.

    HESTER. Did she? Did ya wash your teeth?

JOSIE. Why do I always have to wash me teeth? Every day. It's so borin'. What do I need teeth for anyway?

HESTER. Ya need them for snarlin' at people when smilin' doesn't work anymore. G'wan in and wash them now.

Enter Carthage in his wedding suit. Hester looks at him, looks away.

JOSIE. Did ya count the cattle, Daddy?

CARTHAGE. I did.

JOSIE. Were they all there?

CARTHAGE. They were, Josie.

JOSIE. Daddy says I can go to his weddin'.

CARTHAGE. I said maybe, Josie.

HESTER. G'wan round the back and play, Josie.

JOSIE. Can I go, Mam, can I? Say yeah, g'wan, say yeah.

HESTER. We'll see, g'wan, Josie, g'wan, good girl.

And exit Josie. They both watch her. Silence.

CARTHAGE. I'd like to know what ya think you're playin' at.

HESTER. Take a better man than you to cancel me out, Carthage Kilbride.

CARTHAGE. Ya haven't even started packin'.

HESTER. Them your weddin' clothes?

CARTHAGE. They're not me farm clothes, are they?

HESTER. Ya've a cheek comin' here in them.

CARTHAGE. Well, you, missus, are meant to be gone.

HESTER. And ya've a nerve tellin' Josie she can go to your weddin'.

CARTHAGE. She's mine as well as yours.

HESTER. Have ya slept with her yet?

CARTHAGE. That's none of your business.

HESTER. Every bit of me business. Ya think ya can wipe out fourteen years just like that? Well she's welcome to ya and any satisfaction she can squeeze out of ya.

CARTHAGE. Never heard ya complainin' when I was in your bed.

HESTER. Ya done the job, I suppose, in a kindergarten sourt of way.

CARTHAGE. Kindergarten, that what ya call it?

HESTER. You were nothin' before I put me stamp on ya and ya'll be nothin' again I'm finished with ya.

CARTHAGE. Are you threatenin' me, Hetty? Because, if ya are, ya better know who you're dealin' with, not the sixteen-year-auld fool snaggin' hares along the Bog of Cats who fell into your clutches.

HESTER. It was you wooed me, Carthage Kilbride, not the other way round as ya'd like everywan to think. In the beginnin' I wanted nothin' to do with ya, should've trusted me first instinct, but ya kept comin' back. You cut your teeth on me, Carthage Kilbride, gnawed and sucked till all that's left is an auld bone ya think to fling on the dunghill, now you've no more use for me. If you think I'm goin' to let you walk over me like that, ya don't know me at all.

CARTHAGE. That at least is true. I've watched ya now for the best part of fourteen years and I can't say for sure I know the first thing about ya. Who are ya and what sourt of stuff are ya made of?

HESTER. The same as you and I can't abide to lose ya. Don't lave me. Don't—is it I've gotten old and you just hittin' thirty?

CARTHAGE. Ya know right well it isn't that.

HESTER. And I haven't had a drink since the night ya left.

CARTHAGE. I know.

HESTER. I only ever drank anyway to forget about—

CARTHAGE. I don't want to talk about that. Lave it.

HESTER. And still ya took the money and bought the land, the Kilbrides who never owned anythin' till I came along, tinker and all. Tell me what to do, Carthage, and I'll do it, anythin' for you to come back.

CARTHAGE. Just stop, will ya—

HESTER. Anythin', Carthage, anythin', and I'll do it if it's in me power.

CARTHAGE. It's not in your power—look, I'm up to me neck in another life that can't include ya anymore.

HESTER. You're sellin' me and Josie down the river for a few lumpy auld acres and notions of respectability and I never thought ya would. You're better than all of them. Why must ya always look for the good opinion from them that'll never give it? Ya'll only ever be Xavier Cassidy's workhorse. He won't treat ya right. He wouldn't know how.

CARTHAGE. He's treatin' me fine, signin' his farm over to me this evenin'.

HESTER. Ya know what they're sayin' about ya? That you're a jumped-up land-hungry mongrel but that Xavier Cassidy is greedier and craftier and he'll spancel ya back to the scrubber ya are.

CARTHAGE. And ya know what they're sayin' about you? That it's time ya moved onto another haltin' site.

HESTER. I was born on the Bog of Cats and on the Bog of Cats I'll end me days. I've as much right to this place as any of yees, more, for it holds me to it in ways it has never held yees. And as for me tinker blood, I'm proud of it. It gives me an edge over all of yees around here, allows me see yees for the inbred, underbred, bog-brained shower yees are. I'm warnin' ya now, Carthage, you go through with this sham weddin' and you'll never see Josie again.

CARTHAGE. If I have to mow ya down or have ya declared an unfit mother to see Josie I will, so for your own sake don't cause any trouble in that department. Look, Hetty, I want Josie to do well in the world, she'll get her share of everythin' I own and will own. I want her to have a chance in life, a chance you never had and so can never understand—

HESTER. Don't tell me what I can and can't understand!

CARTHAGE. Well understand this. Ya'll not separate me and Josie or I'll have her taken off of ya. I only have to mention your drinkin' or your night roamin' or the way ya sleep in that dirty auld caravan and lave Josie alone in the house.

HESTER. I always take Josie to the caravan when I sleep there.

CARTHAGE. Ya didn't take her last night.

HESTER. I wasn't in the caravan last night. I was walkin' the bog, but I checked on her three, four times.

CARTHAGE. Just don't cross me with Josie because I don't want to have to take her off of ya, I know she's attached to ya, and I'm not a monster. Just don't cross me over her or I'll come down on ya like a bull from heaven.

HESTER. So I'm meant to lie back and let Caroline Cassidy have her way in the rearin' of my child. I'm meant to lave her around Xavier Cassidy—sure he's capable of anythin'. If it's the last thing I do I'll find a way to keep her from ya.

CARTHAGE. I want you out of here before dusk! And I've put it to ya now about Josie. Think it over when ya've calmed down. And here. (*Producing envelope.*) There's your blood money. It's all there down to the last penny.

HESTER. No! I don't want it!

CARTHAGE. *(Throws it in the snow.)* Neither do I. I never should've took it in the first place. I owe ya nothin' now, Hester Swane. Nothin'. Ya've no hold over me now. *(Goes to exit.)*

HESTER. Carthage—ya can't just walk away like this.

CARTHAGE. I can and I am—ya know what amazes me, Hetty?

HESTER. What?

CARTHAGE. That I stayed with ya so long—I want peace, just peace—remember, before dusk.

And exit Carthage. Hester looks after him, Josie comes running on.

JOSIE. What's wrong of ya, Mam?

HESTER. Ah go 'way, would ya, and lave me alone.

JOSIE. Can I go down to Daly's and buy sweets?

HESTER. No, ya can't. Go on off and play, you're far too demandin'.

JOSIE. Yeah well, just because you're in a bad humour it's not my fault. I'm fed up playin' on me own.

HESTER. You'll get a clatter if you're not careful. I played on me own when I was your age. I never bothered me mother, you're spoilt rotten, that's what ya are. *(In a gentler tone.)* G'wan and play with your dolls, give them a bath, cut their hair.

JOSIE. Ya said I wasn't to cut their hair.

HESTER. Well now I'm sayin' ya can, alright.

JOSIE. But it won't grow back.

HESTER. So! There's worse things in this world than your dolls' hair not growin' back, believe me, Josie Swane.

JOSIE. Me name is Josie Kilbride.

HESTER. That's what I said.

JOSIE. Ya didn't, ya said Josie Swane. I'm not a Swane. I'm a Kilbride.

HESTER. I suppose you're ashamed of me too.

Enter Xavier Cassidy and Caroline, both in their wedding clothes.

JOSIE. Caroline, your dress, is that your weddin' dress? It's beautiful.

CAROLINE. Hello Josie.

Josie runs over to Caroline to touch her dress. Hester storms after her, picks her up roughly, carries her to corner of the house. Puts her down.

HESTER. Now stay around the back.

And exit Josie.

XAVIER. Was hopin' I wouldn't find ya still here, Swane.

HESTER. So ya came back with your daddy, ya know nothin', Caroline, nothin'. *(Sits at her garden table, produces a naggin of whiskey from her pocket, drinks.)*

XAVIER. Thought ya'd given up the drink.

HESTER. I had. Me first in months, but why should I try and explain meself to you?

XAVIER. Might interest Carthage to know you lashin' into a naggin of whiskey at this hour.

HESTER. Carthage. If it wasn't for you, me and Carthage'd be fine. Should've eradicated ya, Cassidy, when I could've. God's punishin' me now because I didn't take steps that were right and proper concernin' you. Aye. God's punishin' me but I won't take his blows lyin' down.

CAROLINE. What are ya talking about, Hester?

HESTER. What am I talkin' about? I'm talkin' about you, ya little fool, and I'm talkin' about James.

CAROLINE. Me brother James?

XAVIER. You keep a civil tongue, Swane, over things ya know nothin' about.

HESTER. Oh, but I do know things, and that's why ya want me out of here. It's only your land and money and people's fear of ya that has ya walkin' free. G'wan home and do whatever it is ya do with your daughter, but keep your sleazy eyes off of me and Josie. This is my property and I've a right to sit in me own yard without bein' ogled by the likes of you.

XAVIER. There's softer things on the eye, Swane, if it's oglin' I was after. This is no longer your property and well ya know it, ya signed it over six months ago, for a fine hefty sum, have the papers—here.

HESTER. I wasn't thinkin' right then, was bein' coerced and bullied from all sides, but I have regained me pride and it tells me I'm stayin'. Ya'll get your money back. *(Picks up envelope Carthage has thrown in the snow.)* Here's some of it.

XAVIER. I'm not takin' it. A deal's a deal.

HESTER. Take it! Take it! *(Stuffs it into his breast pocket.)* And it might interest ya to know, Caroline, that Carthage was just here in his weddin' clothes and he didn't look like no radiant groom and he axed me to take him back, but I said—

XAVIER. I'd say he did alright—

HESTER. He did! He did! Or as much as, but I said I couldn't be played with anymore, that I was made for things, he has lost the power to offer. And I was. I was made for somethin' different than these butchery lives yees all lead here on the Bog of Cats. Me mother taught me that.

XAVIER. Your mother. Your mother taught ya nothin', Swane, except maybe how to use a knife. Let me tell ya a thing or two about your mother, big Josie Swane. I used to see her outside her auld caravan on the bog and the fields covered over in stars and her half covered in an excuse for a dress and her croonin' towards Orion in a language I never heard before or since. We'd peace when she left.

HESTER. And what were you doin' watchin' her? Catwoman tould me ya were in a constant swoon over me mother, sniffin' round the caravan, lavin' little presents and Christmas dinners and money and drink, sure I remember the gatch of ya meself and ya scrapin' at the door.

XAVIER. Very presumptuous of ya, Swane, to think I'd have any interest in your mother beyond Christian compassion.

HESTER. Christian compassion! That what it's called these days!

XAVIER. Aye, Christian compassion, a thing that was never bet into you. Ya say ya remember lots of things, then maybe ya remember that that food and money I used to lave was left so ya wouldn't starve. Times I'd walk by that caravan and there'd be ne'er a sign of this mother of yours. She'd go off for days with anywan who'd buy her a drink. She'd be off in the bars of Pullagh and Mucklagh gettin' into fights. Wance she bit the nose off a woman who dared to look at her man, bit the nose clean off her face. And you, you'd be chained to the door of the caravan with maybe a dirty nappy on ya if ya were lucky. Oftentimes—

HESTER. Lies! All lies!

XAVIER. Oftentimes I brung ya home and gave ya over to me mother to put some clothes on ya and feed ya. More times than I can remember it'd be from our house your mother would collect ya, the brazen walk of her, and not a thank you or a flicker of guilt in her eye and her reekin' of drink. Times she wouldn't even bother to collect ya and meself or me mother would have to bring ya down to her and she'd hardly notice that we'd come and gone or that you'd returned.

HESTER. Ya expect me to believe anythin' that comes from your siled lips, Xavier Cassidy?

XAVIER. And wan other thing, Swane, for you to cast aspersions on me just because I'm an auld widower, that's cheap and low. Not everywan sees the world through your troubled eyes. There's such a thing as a father lovin' his daughter as a father should, no more, no less, somethin' you have never known, and I will—

HESTER. I had a father too! Ya'd swear I was dropped from the sky the way ya go on. Jack Swane of Bergit's Island, I never knew him— but I had a father. I'm as settled as any of yees—

XAVIER. Well, he wasn't much of a father, never claimin' ya when your mother ran off.

HESTER. He claimed me in the end—

XAVIER. Look, Swane, I don't care about your family or where ya came from. I care only about me own and all I've left is Caroline and if I have to plough through you to have the best for her, then that's what I'll do. I don't want to unless I have to. So do it the aisy way for all of us. Lave this place today. (*Takes envelope from breast pocket, puts it into her hand.*) This is yours. Come on, Caroline.

CAROLINE. Ya heard what Daddy says. Ya don't know his temper, Hester.

HESTER. And you don't know mine.

And exit Xavier followed by Caroline. Hester sits at her garden table, has a drink, looks up at the cold winter sky.

(*A whisper.*) Dear God on high, what have ya in store for me at all?

Enter Josie in her Communion dress, veil, buckled shoes, handbag, the works.

(*Looks at her a minute.*) What are ya doin' in your Communion dress?

JOSIE. For Daddy's weddin'. I'm grown out of all me other dresses.

HESTER. I don't think ya are.

JOSIE. I am. I can go, can't I, Mam?

HESTER. Ya have her eyes.

JOSIE. Whose eyes—whose eyes, Mam?

HESTER. Josie Swane's, me mother.

JOSIE. Granny said me real name is Josie Swane.

HESTER. Don't mind your granny.

JOSIE. Did ya like her, Josie Swane?

HESTER. More than anythin' in this cold white world.

JOSIE. More than me and Daddy?

HESTER. I'm talkin' about when I was your age. Ya weren't born then, Josie—ya know the last time I seen me mother I was wearin' me Communion dress too, down by the caravan, a beautiful summer's night and the bog like a furnace. I wouldn't go to bed though she kept tellin' me to. I don't know why I wouldn't, I always done what she tould me. I think now—maybe I knew. And she says, 'I' goin' walkin' the bog, you're to stay here, Hetty.' And I says, 'No,' I'd go along with her, and made to folly her. And she says, 'No, Hetty, you wait here, I'll be back in a while.' And again I made to folly her and again she stopped me. And I watched her walk away from me across the Bog of Cats. And across the Bog of Cats I'll watch her return.

Lights down.

END OF ACT I

ACT II

Interior of Xavier Cassidy's house. A long table covered in a white tablecloth, laid for the wedding feast. Music off, a band setting up. The Catwoman sits at centre table lapping wine from a saucer. A waiter, a lanky, gawky young fellow, hovers with a bottle of wine waiting to refill the saucer.

WAITER. You're sure now ya wouldn't like a glass, Catwoman?

CATWOMAN. No, no, I love the saucer, young man. What's your name? Do I know ya?

WAITER. I'm a Dunne.

CATWOMAN. Wan of the long Dunnes or wan of the scutty fat-legged Dunnes?

WAITER. Wan of the long Dunnes. Ya want a refill, Catwoman?

CATWOMAN. I will. Are ya still in school? Your voice sounds as if it's just breakin'.

WAITER. I am.

CATWOMAN. And what're ya goin' to be when ya grow up, young Long Dunne?

WAITER. I want to be an astronaut but me father wants me to work on the bog like him and like me grandfather. The Dunnes has always worked on the bog.

CATWOMAN. Oh go for the astronaut, young man.

WAITER. I will so, Catwoman. Have ya enough wine?

CATWOMAN. Plenty for now.

Exit young Dunne crossed by the ghost of Joseph Swane, entering; bloodstained shirt and trousers, a throat wound. He walks across the stage. Catwoman cocks her ear, starts sniffing.

JOSEPH. Hello. Hello.

CATWOMAN. Ah Christ, not another ghost.

JOSEPH. Who's there?

CATWOMAN. Go 'way and lave me alone. I'm on me day off.

JOSEPH. Who are ya? I can't see ya.

CATWOMAN. I can't see you aither. I'm the Catwoman but I tould ya I'm not talkin' to ghosts today, yees have me heart scalded, hardly got a wink's sleep last night.

JOSEPH. Please, I haven't spoken to anywan since the night I died.

CATWOMAN. Haven't ya? Who are ya anyway?

JOSEPH. I'm Joseph Swane of Bergit's Island. Is this Bergit's Island?

CATWOMAN. This is the Bog of Cats.

JOSEPH. The Bog of Cats. Me mother had a song about this place.

CATWOMAN. Josie Swane was your mother?

JOSEPH. Ya know her?

CATWOMAN. Oh aye, I knew her. Then Hester must be your sister?

JOSEPH. Hester, ya know Hester too?

CATWOMAN. She lives only down the lane. I never knew Hester had a brother.

JOSEPH. I doubt she'd be tellin' people about me.

CATWOMAN. I don't mean to be short with ya, Joseph Swane, but Saturday is me day off. I haven't a minute to meself with yees, so tell me what is it ya want and then be on your way.

JOSEPH. I want to be alive again. I want to stop walkin'. I want to rest, ate a steak, meet a girl. I want to fish for wild salmon and sow pike on Bergit's Lake again.

CATWOMAN. You'll never do them things again, Joseph Swane.

JOSEPH. Don't say that to me, Catwoman, I'm just turned eighteen.

CATWOMAN. Eighteen. That's young to die alright. But it could be worse. I've a two-year-old ghost who comes to visit, all she wants to do is play peep. Still eighteen's young enough. How come ya went so young? An accident, was it? Or by your own hand?

WAITER. (Going by.) Ya talkin' to me, Catwoman?

CATWOMAN. No, Long Dunne, just a ghost, a poor lost ghost.

WAITER. Oh. (Exits.)

JOSEPH. Are ya still there, Catwoman?

CATWOMAN. I am but there's nothin' I can do for ya, you're not comin' back.

JOSEPH. Is there no way?

CATWOMAN. None, none in this world anyway, and the sooner ya realize that the better for ya. Now be on your way, settle in to your new world, knock the best out of it ya can.

JOSEPH. It's fierce hard to knock the best out of nothin', fierce hard to enjoy darkness the whole time. Can't I just stay here with ya, talk to ya a while?

CATWOMAN. Ya could I suppose, only I'm at a weddin' and they might think I'm not the full shillin' if I have to be talkin' to you all day. Look, I'll take ya down to Hester Swane's house, ya can talk to her.

JOSEPH. Can she hear ghosts?

CATWOMAN. (Getting up.) Oh aye, though she lets on she can't.

JOSEPH. Alright so, I suppose I may as well since I'm here.

CATWOMAN. C'mon, folly me voice till I lead ya there.

JOSEPH. (Following her.) Keep talkin' so I don't take a wrong turnin'.

CATWOMAN. I will and hurry up now, I don't want to miss the weddin'. Ya still there?

JOSEPH. I am.

And they're off by now. Enter Caroline and Carthage as they exit.

CAROLINE. This is the tablecloth me mother had for her weddin' and it's the same silver too. I'd really like for her to have been here today—aye, I would.

CARTHAGE. A soft-boned lady, your mother. I used to see her in town shoppin' with you be the hand, ya wanted to bow when she walked by. She had class, and you have too, Caroline, like no wan else around here.

CAROLINE. I can't stop thinkin' about Hester.

CARTHAGE. *(Kisses her.)* Hester'll be fine, tough as an auld boot. Ya shouldn't concern yourself with her on your weddin' day. I've provided well for her, she isn't goin' to ever have to work a day in her life. Josie's the wan I worry about. The little sweetheart all done up in her Communion dress. Hetty should've got her a proper dress.

CAROLINE. But Hester didn't want her here, Carthage.

CARTHAGE. Ya know what I wish?

CAROLINE. What?

CARTHAGE. That she'd just give Josie to me and be done with it.

CAROLINE. You're still very tangled up with Hester, aren't ya?

CARTHAGE. I'm not wan bit tangled with her, if she'd just do what she's supposed to do which is fierce simple, clear out of the Bog of Cats for wance and for all.

CAROLINE. And I suppose ya'll talk about me as callously wan day too.

CARTHAGE. Of course I won't, why would I?

CAROLINE. It's all fierce messy, Carthage. I'd hoped ya'd have sourted it out by today. It laves me in a fierce awkward position. You're far more attached to her than ya'd led me to believe.

CARTHAGE. Attached to her? I'm not attached to her, I stopped lovin' her years ago!

CAROLINE. I'm not jealous as to whether ya love her or don't love her, I think maybe I'd prefer if ya still did.

CARTHAGE. Then what's botherin' ya?

CAROLINE. You and Hester has a whole history together, stretchin' back years that connects yees and that seems more important and real than anythin' we have. And I wonder have we done the wrong thing.

CARTHAGE. Ya should've said all this before ya took your vows at the altar.

CAROLINE. I've been tryin' to say it to ya for weeks.

CARTHAGE. So what do we do now?

CAROLINE. Get through today, I suppose, pretend it's the best day of our lives. I don't know about you but I've had better days, than today, far better.

CARTHAGE. Caroline, what's wrong of ya?

CAROLINE. Nothin', only I feel like I'm walkin' on somewan's grave.

Enter Mrs. Kilbride in what looks extremely like a wedding dress, white, a white hat, with a bit of a veil trailing off it, white shoes, tights, bag, etc.

MRS. KILBRIDE. *(Flushed, excited, neurotic.)* Oh the lovebirds! The lovebirds! There yees are, off hidin'. Carthage, I want a photo of yees. Would you take it, Caroline?

CARTHAGE. She means she wants wan of herself.

MRS. KILBRIDE. Shush now, Carthage, and stand up straight.

They pose like a bride and groom, Carthage glaring at Mrs. Kilbride.

That's it. Wan more, smile, Carthage, smile, I hate a glowery demeanour in a photograph. That's great, Caroline, did ya get me shoes in?

CAROLINE. I don't think I—

MRS. KILBRIDE. Doesn't matter, doesn't matter, thank ya, what a glorious day, what a glorious white winter's day, nothin' must spoil today for me, nothin'. *(Begins photographing her shoes, first one, then the other.)*

CARTHAGE. What in the name of God are ya at now?

MRS. KILBRIDE. I just want to get a photo of me shoes while they're new and clean. I've never had such a beautiful pair of shoes, look at the diamonds sparklin' on them. I saved like a Shylock for them, seen them in O'Brien's six months ago and I knew instantly them were to be me weddin' shoes. And I put by every week for them.

Guess how much they were, Carthage, g'wan guess, Caroline, guess, guess.

CAROLINE. I don't know, Mrs. Kilbride.

MRS. KILBRIDE. Elsie! Elsie! Call me Elsie, ah g'wan guess.

CAROLINE. Fifty pound.

MRS. KILBRIDE. *(Angrily.)* Fifty pound! Are ya mad! Are ya out of your tiny mind!

CARTHAGE. Tell us how much they were, Mother, before we die of the suspense.

MRS. KILBRIDE. *(Smug, can hardly believe it herself.)* A hundred and fifty pound. The Quane herself wouldn't pay more.

Monica and Xavier have entered. Monica has Josie by the hand.

MONICA. —And Father Willow seems to have lost the run of himself entirely.

XAVIER. They should put him down, he's eighty if he's a day.

MONICA. The state of him with his hat on all durin' the Mass and the vestments inside out and his pyjamas peepin' out from under his trousers.

XAVIER. Did you hear he's started keepin' a gun in the tabernacle?

MONICA. I did, aye.

XAVIER. For all them robbers, is it?

MONICA. No, apparently it's for any of us that's late for Mass. Ya know what I was thinkin' and I lookin' at Caroline up there on the altar, I was thinkin' about my young fella Brian and I decided not to think about him today at all.

XAVIER. Then don't, Monica. Don't.

MONICA. Don't you never think about your own young fella?

XAVIER. Never, I never think about him. Never. Children! If they were calves we'd have them fattened and sould in three weeks. I never think of James. Never.

MONICA. Or Olive aither?

XAVIER. Ah, Olive had no fight in her, wailed like a ewe in a storm after the young lad and then lay down with her face to the wall. Ya know what she died of, Monica? Spite. Spite again' me. Well, she's the wan who's dead. I've the last laugh on her.

MONICA. Strange what these weddin's drag up.

XAVIER. Aye, they cost a fortune. (*Takes two glasses of champagne from a passing waiter.*) Here, Monica, and cheers. (*To Josie.*) Child, a pound for your handbag.

MRS. KILBRIDE. What d'ya say, Josie?

XAVIER. Lave her. Two things in this world get ya nowhere, sayin' sorry and sayin' thanks—that right, Josie?

JOSIE. That's right, Mr. Cassidy.

MRS. KILBRIDE. (*Taking Josie a little aside.*) Here give me that pound till I mind it for ya.

JOSIE. First give me back me Communion money.

MRS. KILBRIDE. What Communion money?

CARTHAGE. Aye and ya can give me back mine while you're at it.

The Catwoman and Father Willow have entered, linking arms, both with their sticks. Father Willow has his snuff on hand, pyjamas showing from under his shirt and trousers, hat on, adores the Catwoman.

FATHER WILLOW. I'm tellin' ya now, Catwoman, ya'll have to cut back on the mice, they'll be the death of ya.

CATWOMAN. And you'll have to cut back on the snuff.

FATHER WILLOW. Try snails instead, far better for ya. The French ate them with garlic and tons of butter and Burgundy wine. I tried them wance meself and I in Avalon. Delicious.

CATWOMAN. We should go on a holiday, you and me, Father Willow.

FATHER WILLOW. Ah, ya say that every winter and come the summer I can't budge ya.

CATWOMAN. I'll go away with ya next summer and that's a promise.

FATHER WILLOW. Well, where do ya want to go and I'll book the tickets in the mornin'?

CATWOMAN. Anywhere at all away from this auld bog, somewhere with a big hot sun.

FATHER WILLOW. Burgundy's your man then.

MONICA. God help Burgundy is all I say.

CATWOMAN. Anywhere it's not rainin' because it's goin' to rain here all next summer, seen it writ in the sky.

MRS. KILBRIDE. Writ in the sky, me eye, sure she's blind as a bat.

Xavier, what did ya have to invite the Catwoman for? Brings down the tone of the whole weddin'.

MONICA. Hasn't she as much right to walk God's earth as you, partake of its pleasures too?

MRS. KILBRIDE. No, she hasn't! Not till she washes herself. The turf-smoke stink of her. Look at her moochin' up to Father Willow and her never inside the door of the church and me at seven Mass every mornin' watchin' that auld foot dribblin' into the chalice. And would he call to see me? Never. Spends all his time with the Catwoman in her dirty little hovel. I'd write to the archbishop if I thought he was capable of anythin'. Why did ya have to invite her?

XAVIER. Ya know as well as me it's bad luck not to invite the Catwoman.

Father Willow shoots Mrs. Kilbride in the back of the head with an imaginary pistol as he walks by or as she walks by.

MRS. KILBRIDE. I'd love to hose her down, fling her in onto the milkin' parlour floor, turn the water on full blast and hose her down to her kidneys.

CARTHAGE. (*With his arm around Caroline.*) Well, Catwoman, what do ya predict for us?

CATWOMAN. I predict nothin'.

CARTHAGE. Ah g'wan now, ya must have a blessin' or a vision or somethin'.

CAROLINE. Lave it, Carthage. You're welcome, Catwoman and Father Willow.

FATHER WILLOW. Thank you, Hester, thank you.

CARTHAGE. You mean, Caroline, Father Willow, this is Caroline.

FATHER WILLOW. Whatever.

CARTHAGE. Come on now, Catwoman, and give Caroline and me wan of your blessin's.

CATWOMAN. Seein' as ya insist. Separate tombstones. I'm sorry but I tould ya not to ax me.

JOSIE. Granny, will ya take a photo of just me and Daddy for to put in me scrapbook?

MRS. KILBRIDE. Don't be so rude, you, to Caroline. (*Hisses.*) And I tould ya to call me Grandmother!

JOSIE. (*Whispers boldly from the safety of her father's side.*) Granny, Granny, Granny.

CAROLINE. She's alright. Here, I'll take the photo of you and Carthage for your scrapbook. (*Does.*)

MRS. KILBRIDE. She's ruined, that's what she is, turnin' up in her Communion dress, makin' a holy show of us all.

CARTHAGE. It's you that's the holy show in that stupid dress.

MRS. KILBRIDE. What! I am not! There's gratitude for ya. Ya make an effort to look your best. (*Close to tears.*) I cut back on every-thin' to buy this dress. How was I supposed to know the bride'd be wearin' white as well?

CARTHAGE. Don't start whingin' now in front of everywan, sit down will ya, ya look fine, ya look great—alright, I'm sorry. Ya look stunnin'!

MRS. KILBRIDE. (*Beginning to smile.*) I don't, do I?

CARTHAGE. Christ! *Yes!*

They've all made their way to the table by now and are seated. Xavier tinkles his glass for silence.

XAVIER. Thank you. Now before we dig in I'd like to welcome yees all here on wan of the happiest days of me life. Yees have all long known that Caroline has been my greatest joy and reason for livin'. Her mother, if she was here today, would've been proud too at how she has grown into a lovely and graceful woman. I can take no credit for that, though I've taken the greatest pride these long years in watchin' her change from a motherless child to a gawky girl, to this apparition I see before me eyes today. We auld fathers would like to keep our daughters be our sides forever and enjoy their care and gen-tleness, but it seems the world does have a different plan entirely. We must rear them up for another man's benefit. Well if this is so, I can't think of a better man than Carthage Kilbride to take over the care of me only child. (*Raises his glass.*) I wish yees well and happiness and in-fants rompin' on the hearth.

ALL. Hear! Hear!

XAVIER. Father Willow, would ya do us the—

MRS. KILBRIDE. (*Standing up.*) I'd like to say a few words too—

XAVIER. Go ahead, Mrs. Kilbride.

MRS. KILBRIDE. As the proud mother of the groom—

CARTHAGE. Mother, would ya whisht up—

MRS. KILBRIDE. *(Posh public speaking voice.)* As the proud mother of the groom, I feel the need to answer Xavier's fine speech with a few words of me own. Never was a mother more blessed than me in havin' Carthage for a son. As a child he was uncommon good, never cried, never disobeyed, never raised his voice wance to me, never went about with a grumpy puss on him. Indeed he went to the greatest pains always to see that me spirits was good, that me heart was uplifted. When his father died he used to come into the bed to sleep beside me for fear I would be lonely. Often I woke from a deep slumber and his two arms would be around me, a small leg thrown over me in sleep—

CATWOMAN. The craythur—

MRS. KILBRIDE. He was also always aware of my abidin' love for Our Lord, unlike some here *(Glares at the Catwoman.)* and on wan occasion, me birthday it was, I looked out the back window and there he was up on the slope behind our house and what was he doin'? He was buildin' Calvary for me. He'd hammered three wooden crosses and was erectin' them on the slope Calvary-style. Wan for him, wan for me and wan for Our Lord. And we draped ourselves around them like the two thieves in the holy book, remember, Carthage?

CARTHAGE. I do not, would ya ever sit down.

MRS. KILBRIDE. Of course ya do, the three crosses ya made up on the slope and remember the wind was howlin' and the pair of us yellin' 'Calvary! Calvary!' to wan another. Of course ya remember. I'm only tellin' yees this story as wan of the countless examples of Carthage's kind nature and I only want to say that Caroline is very welcome into the Kilbride household. And that if Carthage will be as good a son to Caroline as he's been a husband to me then she'll have no complaints. *(Raises her glass.)* Cheers.

ALL. Hear! Hear!

XAVIER. And now, Father Willow, ya'll say grace for us?

FATHER WILLOW. It'd be an honour, Jack, thank you—

MRS. KILBRIDE. Who's Jack?

Father Willow gets up. All stand and bless themselves for the grace.

FATHER WILLOW. In the name of the Father and of the Son and of the Holy Ghost, it may or may not surprise yees all if I tould yees I was almost a groom meself wance. Her name was Elizabeth Kennedy, no that was me mother's name, her name was—it'll come to me, anyway it wasn't to be, in the end we fell out over a duck egg on a walkin' holiday by the Shannon, what was her name at all? Helen? No.

MRS. KILBRIDE. Would ya say the grace, Father Willow, and be—

FATHER WILLOW. The grace, yes, how does it go again?

MRS. KILBRIDE. Bless us, oh Lord, and these thy gifts which of—

FATHER WILLOW. Rowena. That was it. Rowena Phelan. I should never have ate that duck egg—no— (*Stands there lost in thought.*)

Enter Hester in her wedding dress, veil, shoes, the works.

MRS. KILBRIDE. Ya piebald knacker ya.

XAVIER. What's your business here, Swane, besides puttin' a curse on me daughter's weddin'?

MRS. KILBRIDE. The brazen nerve of her turnin' up in that garb.

HESTER. The kettle callin' the pot white. Remember this dress, Carthage? He bought it for me—

CAROLINE. Daddy, would ya do somethin'?

HESTER. Oh must be near nine year ago. We'd got to the stage where we should've parted and I said it to ya and ya convinced me otherwise and axed me to marry ya. Came home wan evenin' with this dress in a box and somehow it got put away. Ya only ever wanted me there until ya were strong enough to lave me.

CARTHAGE. Get outa here right now!

HESTER. You thought ya could come swaggerin' to me this mornin' in your weddin' clothes, well, here I am in mine. This is my weddin' day be rights and not wan of yees can deny it. And yees all just sit there glarin' as if I'm the guilty wan. (*Takes Carthage's glass of wine, drinks from it.*)

MRS. KILBRIDE. Run her off, Xavier! Run her off or I will. (*Gets up.*)

CARTHAGE. (*Pulls her back.*) Would you keep out of this!

MRS. KILBRIDE. And let her walk all over us?

MONICA. Hester, go home, g'wan.

MRS. KILBRIDE. (*Getting up again.*) I've had the measure of you this long time, the lazy shiftless blood in ya, that savage tinker eye ya turn on people to frighten them—

CARTHAGE. Would ya shut up! Ya haven't shut up all day! We're not havin' a brawl here.

MRS. KILBRIDE. There's a nice way to talk to your mother on your weddin' day. I'm not afraid of ya, Hester Swane, you're just a sad lost little woman—

HESTER. I still stole your son from ya, didn't I, Elsie? Your sissy boy that I tried to make a man of.

MRS. KILBRIDE. Ya took advantage of him, ya had to take advantage of a young boy for your perverted pleasures for no grown man would stomach ya.

HESTER. And weren't they great, Carthage, all them nights in the caravan I 'took advantage' of ya and you bangin' on the window and us stuffin' pillows in our mouths so ya wouldn't hear us laughin'—

MRS. KILBRIDE. You're absolutely disgustin', that's what ya are!

HESTER. Have you ever been discarded, Elsie Kilbride—the way I've been discarded? Do ya know what that feels like? To be flung on the ashpit and you still alive!

XAVIER. No wan's flingin' ya anywhere! We done everythin' proper by you—

HESTER. Proper! Yees have taken everythin' from me. I've done nothin' again' any of yees. I'm just bein' who I am. Carthage, I'm axin' ya the wance more, come away with me now, with me and—

MRS. KILBRIDE. Come away with her, she says—

HESTER. Yes! Come away with me and Josie and stop all this—

XAVIER. Come away with ya! Are ya mad! He's married to Caroline now—

CARTHAGE. Go home, Hester, and pack your things.

MONICA. C'mon, Hester, I'll take ya home.

HESTER. I have no home anymore for he's decided to take it from me.

MONICA. Then come and live with me, I've no wan—

HESTER. No, I want to stay in me own house. Just let me stay in the house, Carthage. I won't bother anywan if yees'd just lave me alone. I was born on the Bog of Cats, same as all of yees, though ya'd never think it the way yees shun me. I know every barrow and rivulet and bog hole of its nine square mile. I know where the best bog rosemary grows and the sweetest wild bog rue. I could lead yees around the Bog of Cats in me sleep.

CARTHAGE. There's a house, bought and furnished for ya in town as ya agreed to—

HESTER. I've never lived in a town. I won't know anywan there—

MONICA. Ah, let her stay in the house, the Bog of Cats is all she knows—

MRS. KILBRIDE. And since when do we need you stickin' your snout in, Monica Murray?

MONICA. Since you and your son have forgotten all dacency, Elsie Kilbride. Ya've always been too hard on her. Ya never gave her a chance—

MRS. KILBRIDE. A waste of time givin' chances to a tinker. All tinkers understands is the open road and where the next bottle of whiskey is comin' from.

MONICA. Well, you should know and your own grandfather wan!

MRS. KILBRIDE. My grandfather was a wanderin' tinsmith—

MONICA. And what's that but a tinker with notions!

HESTER. Carthage, ya could aisy afford another house for yourself and Caroline if ya wanted—

CARTHAGE. No! We're stickin' by what we agreed on—

HESTER. The truth is you want to eradicate me, make out I never existed—

CARTHAGE. If I wanted to eradicate ya, I could've, long ago. And I could've taken Josie off of ya. Facts are, I been more than generous with ya.

HESTER. You're plentiful with the guilt money alright, showerin' buckets of it on me. (*Flings envelope he had given her in Act I at him.*) There's your auld blood money back. Ya think you're gettin' away that aisy! Money won't take that guilt away, Carthage. We'll go to our grave with it!

CARTHAGE. I've not an ounce of guilt where you're concerned and whatever leftover feelin' I had for ya as the mother of me child is gone after this display of hatred towards me. Just go away, I can't bear the sight of ya!

HESTER. I can't lave the Bog of Cats—

MRS. KILBRIDE. We'll burn ya out if we have to—

HESTER. Ya see—

MRS. KILBRIDE. Won't we, Xavier?—

XAVIER. Ya can lave me out of any low-boy tactics. You're lavin' this place today, Swane, aren't ya?

HESTER. I can't lave—ya see me mother said she'd come back here. Father Willow, tell them what they're doin' is wrong. They'll listen to you.

FATHER WILLOW. They've never listened to me, sure they even lie in the confession box. Ya know what I do? I wear earplugs.

HESTER. *(Close to tears.)* I can't go till me mother comes. I'd hoped she'd have come before now and it wouldn't come to this. Don't make me lave or somethin' terrible'll happen. Don't.

XAVIER. We've had enough of your ravin', Swane, so take yourself elsewhere and let us try to recoup as best we can these marred celebrations.

JOSIE. I'll go with ya, Mam, and ya look gorgeous in that dress.

CARTHAGE. Stay where ya are, Josie.

JOSIE. No, I want to go with me mam.

CARTHAGE. *(Stopping her.)* Ya don't know what ya want. And reconsiderin', I think it'd be better all round if Josie stays with me till ya've moved. I'll bring her back to ya then.

HESTER. I've swallyed all me pride over you. You're lavin' me no choice but a vicious war against ya. *(Takes a bottle of wine from the table.)* Josie, I'll be back to collect ya later. And you just try keepin' her from me! *(Exits.)*

END OF ACT II

ACT III

Dusk. Hester, in her wedding dress, charred and muddied. Behind her, the house and sheds ablaze. Joseph Swane stands in the flames watching her.

HESTER. Well, Carthage, ya think them were only idle threats I made? Ya think I can be flung in a bog hole like a bag of newborn pups? Let's see how ya like this—ya hear that sound? Them's your cattle howlin'. Ya smell that smell? That's your forty calves roastin'. I tied them all in and flung diesel on them. And the house, I burnt the bed and the whole place went up in flames. I'd burn down the world if I'd enough diesel—will somewan not come and save me from meself before I go and do worse?

Joseph starts to sing.

JOSEPH. By the Bog of Cats I finally learned false from true,
Learned too late that it was you and only you
Left me sore, a heart brimful of rue
By the Bog of Cats in the darkling dew.

HESTER. Who's there? Who dares sing that song? That's my song
that me mother made up for me. Who's there?

JOSEPH. I think ya know me, Hester.

HESTER. It's not Joseph Swane, is it?

JOSEPH. It is alright.

HESTER. I thought I done away with you. Where are ya? I can't
see ya. Keep off! Keep away! I'm warnin' ya.

JOSEPH. I'm not here to harm ya.

HESTER. Ya should be. If you'd done to me what I done to you I'd
want your guts on a platter. Well come on! I'm ready for ya! Where
are ya?

JOSEPH. I don't know, somewhere near ya. I can't see you aither.

HESTER. Well, what do ya want, Joseph Swane, if you're not here
to harm me? Is it an apology you're after? Well, I've none for ya. I'd
slit your throat again if ya stood here in front of me in flesh and bone.

JOSEPH. Would ya? What're ya so angry about? I've been listenin'
to ya screamin' your head off this while.

HESTER. You've a nerve singin' that song. That song is mine! She
made it for me and only me. Can't yees lave me with anythin'!

JOSEPH. I didn't know it was yours. She used to sing it to me all
the time.

HESTER. You're lyin'! Faithless! All of yees! Faithless! If she
showed up now I'd spit in her face, I'd box the jaws off of her, I'd go
after her with a knife. *(Heartbroken wail.)* Where is she? She said she'd
return. I've waited so long. I've waited so long—have you come
across her where you are?

JOSEPH. Death's a big country, Hester. She could be anywhere in
it.

HESTER. No, she's alive. I can smell her. She's comin' towards me.
I know it. Why doesn't she come and be done with it! If ya see her tell
her I won't be hard on her, will ya?

JOSEPH. Aye, if I see her.

HESTER. Tell her there's just a couple of things I need to ax her,
will ya?

JOSEPH. I will.

HESTER. I just want to know why, that's all.

JOSEPH. What are ya on about, Hester?

HESTER. Was it somethin' I done on her? I was seven, same as me daughter Josie, seven, and there isn't anythin' in this wide world Josie could do that'd make me walk away from her.

JOSEPH. Ya have a daughter?

HESTER. Aye, they're tryin' to take her from me. Just let them try!

JOSEPH. Who's tryin'?

HESTER. If it wasn't for you, me and Carthage'd still be together!

JOSEPH. So it's my fault ya killed me, that what you're sayin'?

HESTER. He took your money after we killed ya—

JOSEPH. To my memory Carthage did nothin' only look on. I think he was as shocked as I was when ya came at me with the fishin' knife!

HESTER. He took your money! He helped me throw ya overboard! And now he wants to put it all on me.

JOSEPH. Ya came at me from behind, didn't ya? Wan minute I'm rowin' and the next I'm a ghost.

HESTER. If ya hadn't been such an arrogant git I may have left ya alone but ya just wouldn't shut up talkin' about her as if she wasn't my mother at all. The big smug neck of ya! It was axin' to be cut. And she even called ya after her. And calls me Hester. What sourt of a name is Hester? Hester's after no wan, And she saves her own name for you—didn't she ever tell ya about me?

JOSEPH. She never mentioned ya.

HESTER. She must've. It's a long time ago. Think, will ya? Didn't she ever say anythin' about me?

JOSEPH. Only what she tould me father. She never spoke to me about ya.

HESTER. Listen to ya! You're still goin' on as if she was yours and you only an auld ghost! You're still talkin' as if I never existed.

JOSEPH. I don't know what you're on about, Hester, but if it's any consolation to ya, she left me too and our father. Josie Swane hung around for no wan.

HESTER. What was she like, Joseph? Every day I forget more and more till I'm startin' to think I made her up out of the air. If it wasn't for this auld caravan I'd swear I only dreamt her. What was she like?

JOSEPH. Well, she was big for starters . . . and gentle.

HESTER. Gentle! She was a rancorous hulk with a vicious whiskey temper.

JOSEPH. You'd have liked the old man, Hester. All he wanted to do was go fishin'.

HESTER. Well, it wasn't me that shunned him.

JOSEPH. It wasn't his fault, Hester, she told him you were dead, that ya died at birth, it wasn't his fault. Ya would've liked the old man, but she told him ya died, that ya were born with your heart all wrong.

HESTER. Nothin' wrong of me heart till she set about banjaxin' it. The lyin' tongue of her. And he just believed her.

JOSEPH. Didn't he send me lookin' for ya in the end, see was there any trace of ya, told me to split the money with ya if I found ya? Hester, I was goin' to split the money with ya. I had it there in the boat. I was goin' to split it with ya when we reached the shore, ya didn't have to cut me throat for it.

HESTER. Ya think I slit your throat for the few auld pound me father left me?

JOSEPH. Then why?

HESTER. I should've been with her for always and would have only for you.

JOSEPH. If ya knew what it was like here ya'd never have done what ya done.

HESTER. Oh I think I know, Joseph, for a long time now I been thinkin' I'm already a ghost.

JOSEPH. I'll be off, Hester, I just wanted to say hello.

HESTER. Where are ya goin'?

JOSEPH. Stravagin' the shadows. (*And he's gone.*)

HESTER. Joseph?

Hester sits on the steps of the caravan, drinks some wine from the bottle she took from the wedding, lights a cigar. Monica shouts offstage.

MONICA. Hester! Hester! Your house! It's on fire! Hester! (*Runs on.*) Come quick, I'll get the others!

HESTER. Don't bother.

MONICA. But your house—ya set it yourself?

HESTER. I did.

MONICA. Christ almighty woman, are ya gone mad?

HESTER. Ya want a drink?

MONICA. A drink, she says! I better go and get Carthage, the livestock, the calves—

HESTER. Would ya calm down, Monica, only an auld house, it should never have been built in the first place. Let the bog have it back. Never liked that house anyway.

MONICA. That's what the tinkers do, isn't it, burn everythin' after them?

HESTER. Aye.

MONICA. They'll skin ya alive, Hester, I'm tellin' ya, they'll kill ya.

HESTER. And you with them.

MONICA. I stood up for ya as best I could, I've to live round here, Hester. I had to pay me respects to the Cassidys. Sure Xavier and meself used to walk to school together.

HESTER. Wan of these days you'll die of niceness, Monica Murray.

MONICA. A quality you've never had any time for.

HESTER. No, I'm just wan big lump of maneness and bad thoughts. Sit down, have a drink with me, I'll get ya a glass. *(Goes into the caravan, gets one.)* Sit down before ya fall.

MONICA. *(Sitting on steps, tipsily.)* We'll go off in this yoke, you and me.

HESTER. Will we?

MONICA. Flee off from this place, flee off to Eden.

HESTER. Eden—I left Eden, Monica, at the age of seven. It was on account of a look be this caravan at dusk.

MONICA. And who was it gave ya this look, your mother, was it? Josie Swane?

HESTER. Oh aye, Monica, she was the wan alright who looked at me so askance and strangely—who'd believe an auld look could do away with ya? I never would've 'cept it happened to me.

MONICA. She was a harsh auld yoke, Hester, came and went like the moon. Ya'd wake wan mornin' and look out over the bog and ya'd see a fire and know she had returned. And I'd bring her down a sup of milk or a few eggs and she'd be here sittin' on the step just like you are, with her big head of black hair and eyes glamin' like a cat and long arms and a powerful neck all knotted that she'd stretch like a swan in a yawn and me with ne'er a neck at all. But I was never comfortable with her, riddled by her, though, and I wasn't the only wan. There was lots spent evenin's tryin' to figure Josie Swane, somethin' cold and dead about her except when she sang and then I declare ya'd fall in love with her.

HESTER. Would ya now?

MONICA. There was a time round here when no celebration was complete without Josie Swane. She'd be invited everywhere to sing, funerals, weddin's, christenin's, birthdays of the bigger farmers, the harvest. And she'd make up songs for each occasion. And it wasn't so much they wanted her there, more they were afraid not to have her.

HESTER. I used go with her on some of them singin' sprees before she ran off. And she'd make up the song as we walked to wherever we were goin'. Sometimes she'd sing somethin' completely different than the song she'd been makin' on the road. Them were her 'Blast from God' songs as opposed to her 'Workaday' songs, or so she called them. And they never axed us to stay, these people, to sit down and ate with them, just lapped up her songs, gave her a bag of food and a half a crown and walked us off the premises, for fear we'd steal somethin', I suppose. I don't think it bothered her, it did me—and still rankles after all these years. But not Josie Swane, she'd be off to the shop to buy cigars and beer and sweets for me.

MONICA. Is there another sup of wine there?

HESTER. (Pours for her.) I'm all the time wonderin' whatever happened to her.

MONICA. You're still waitin' on her, aren't ya?

HESTER. It's still like she only walked away yesterday.

MONICA. Hester, I know what it's like to wait for somewan who's never walkin' through the door again. But this waitin' is only a fancy of yours. Now I don't make out to know anythin' about the workin's of this world but I know this much, it don't yield aisy to mortal wishes. And maybe that's the way it has to be. You up on forty, Hester, and still dreamin' of storybook endin's, still whingin' for your mam.

HESTER. I made a promise, Monica, a promise to meself a long while back. All them years I was in the Industrial School I swore to meself that wan day I'm comin' back to the Bog of Cats to wait for her there and I'm never lavin' again.

MONICA. Well, I don't know how ya'll swing to stay now, your house in ashes, ya after appearin' in that dress. They're sayin' it's a black art thing ya picked up somewhere.

HESTER. A black art thing. (*Laughs.*) If I knew any black art things, by Christ, I'd use them now. The only way I'm lavin' this place is in a box and if it comes to that I'm not lavin' alone. I'll take yees all with me. And, yes, there's things about me yees never understood and makes yees afraid and yees are right for other things goes through my veins besides blood that I've fought so hard to keep wraps on.

MONICA. And what things are they?

HESTER. I don't understand them meself.

MONICA. Stop this wild talk then, I don't like it.

HESTER. Carthage still at the weddin'?

MONICA. And where else would he be?

HESTER. And what sourt of mood is he in?

MONICA. I wasn't mindin'. Don't waste your time over a man like him, faithless as an acorn on a high wind—wine all gone?

HESTER. Aye.

MONICA. I'll go up to the feast and bring us back a bottle unless you've any objections.

HESTER. I'll drink the enemy's wine. Not the wine's fault it fell into the paws of cutthroats and gargiyles.

MONICA. Be back in a while, so.

HESTER. And check see Josie's alright, will ya?

MONICA. She's dancin' her little heart out.

Exit Monica. Hester looks around, up at the winter sky of stars, shivers.

HESTER. Well, it's dusk now and long after and where are ya, Mr. Ghost Fancier? I'm here waitin' for ya, though I've been tould to flee. Maybe you're not comin' after all, maybe I only imagined ya.

Enter Josie running, excited.

JOSIE. Mam!—Mam! I'm goin' on the honeymoon with Daddy and Caroline.

HESTER. You're goin' no such where.

JOSIE. Ah, Mam, they're goin' drivin' to the sea. I never seen the sea.

HESTER. It's just wan big bog hole, Josie, and blue, that's all, nothin' remarkable about it.

JOSIE. Well, Daddy says I'm goin'.

HESTER. Don't mind your daddy.

JOSIE. No, I want to go with them. It's only for five days, Mam.

HESTER. There's a couple of things you should know about your precious daddy. You should know how he has treated me!

JOSIE. I'm not listenin' to ya givin' out about him. (*Covers her ears with her hands.*)

HESTER. That's right, stand up for him and see how far it'll get ya. He swore to me that after you'd be born he'd marry me and now he plans to take ya off of me. I suppose ya'd like that too.

JOSIE. (*Still with ears covered.*) I said I'm not listenin'!

HESTER. (*Pulls Josie's hands from her ears.*) You'll listen to me, Josie Swane, and you listen well. Another that had your name walked away from me. Your perfect daddy walked away from me. And you'll walk from me too. All me life people have walked away without a word of explanation. Well, I want to tell ya somethin', Josie, if you lave me ya'll die.

JOSIE. I will not.

HESTER. Ya will! Ya will! It's a sourt of curse was put on ya be the Catwoman and the black swan. Remember the black swan?

JOSIE. (*Frightened.*) Aye.

HESTER. So ya have to stay with me, d'ya see, and if your daddy or anywan else axes ya who ya'd prefer to live with, ya have to say me.

JOSIE. Mam, I would've said you anyway.

HESTER. Would ya?—Oh, I'm sorry, Josie, I'm sorry, sweetheart. It's not true what I said about a curse bein' put on ya, it's not true at all. If I'm let go tonight I swear I'll make it up to ya for them awful things I'm after sayin'.

JOSIE. It's alright, Mam, I know ya didn't mean it—can I go back to the weddin'? The dancin's not over yet.

HESTER. Dance with me.

Begins waltzing with Josie. Music.

Come on, we'll have our own weddin'.

Picks her up, they swirl and twirl to the music of the song 'By the Bog of Cats.' They sing it together.

Ya beautiful, beautiful child, I could ate ya.

JOSIE. I could ate ya too—can I go back to the weddin' for a while?

HESTER. Ya can do anythin' ya want 'cept lave me. *(Puts her down.)* G'wan then, for half an hour.

JOSIE. I brung ya a big lump of weddin' cake in me handbag. Here. Why wasn't it your weddin', Mam?

HESTER. It sourt of was. G'wan and enjoy yourself.

And exit Josie running. Hester looks after her eating the wedding cake. Xavier Cassidy comes up behind her from the shadows, demonic, red-faced, drink taken, carrying a gun.

XAVIER. Ya enjoyin' that, are ya, Swane, me daughter's weddin' cake?

HESTER. Oh. It's yourself, Xavier, with your auld gun. I was wonderin' when I'd see ya in your true colours. Must've been an awful strain on ya behavin' so well all day.

XAVIER. Ya burnt the bloody house to the ground.

HESTER. Did ya really think I was gain' to have your daughter livin' there?

XAVIER. Ya won't best me, Swane, ya know that. I ran your mother out of here and I'll run you too like a frightened hare.

HESTER. It's got nothin' to do with ya, Cassidy, it's between me and Carthage.

XAVIER. Got everythin' to do with me and ya after makin' a mockery of me and me daughter in front of the whole parish.

HESTER. No more than yees deserve for wheedlin' and cajolin' Carthage away from me with your promises of land and money.

XAVIER. He was aisy wheedled.

HESTER. He was always a feckless fool.

XAVIER. Aye, in all respects bar wan. He loves the land and like me he'd rather die than part with it wance he gets his greedy hands on it. With him Cassidy's farm'll be safe, the name'll be gone, but never the farm. And who's to say but maybe your little bastard and her offspring won't be farmin' my land in years to come.

HESTER. Josie'll have nothin' to do with anythin' that's yours. I'll see to that. And if ya'd looked after your own son better ya wouldn't be covetin' Josie nor any that belongs to me.

XAVIER. Don't you talk about my young fella.

HESTER. Wasn't it me that found him, strychnined to the eye-balls, howlin' 'long the bog and his dog in his arms?

XAVIER. My son died in a tragic accident of no wan's makin'. That's what the inquest said. My conscience is clear.

HESTER. Is it now? You're not a farmer for nothin', somethin' about that young lad bothered ya, he wasn't tough enough far ya probably, so ya strychnined his dog, knowin' full well the child'd be goin' lookin' for him. And ya know what strychnine does, a tayspoon-ful is all it takes, and ya'd the dog showered in it. Burnt his hands clean away. Ya knew what ya were at, Cassidy, and ya know I know. I can tell the darkness in you, ya know how? Because it mirrors me own.

XAVIER. Fabrications! Fabrications of a mind unhinged! If ya could just hear the mad talk of yourself, Swane, and the cut of ya. You're mad as your mother and she was a lunatic.

HESTER. Nothin' lunatic about her 'cept she couldn't breathe the same air as yees all here by the Bog of Cats.

XAVIER. We often breathed the same air, me and Josie Swane, she was a loose wan, loose and lazy and aisy, a five-shillin' hoor, like you.

HESTER. If you're tryin' to destroy some high idea I have of her you're wastin' your time. I've spent long hours of all the long years thinkin' about her. I've lived through every mood there is to live con-cernin' her. Sure there was a time I hated her and wished the worst for her, but I've taught meself to rise above all that is cruel and unworthy in me thinkin' about her. So don't you think your five-shillin' hoor stories will ever change me opinion of her. I have memories your cheap talk can never alter.

XAVIER. And what memories are they, Swane? I'd like to know if they exist at all.

HESTER. Oh they exist alright and ya'd like to rob them from me along with everythin' else. But ya won't because I'm stronger than ya and ya'll take nothin' from me I don't choose to give ya.

XAVIER. (*Puts gun to her throat.*) Won't I now? Think ya'll outwit me with your tinker ways and—

HESTER. Let go of me!

XAVIER. (*A tighter grip.*) Now let's see the leftovers of Carthage Kilbride.

Uses gun to look down her dress.

HESTER. I'm warnin' ya, let go!

A struggle, a few blows, he wins this bout.

XAVIER. Now are ya stronger than me? I could do what I wanted with ya right here and now and no wan would believe ya. Now what I'd really like to know is when are ya plannin' on lavin'?
HESTER. What're ya goin' to do, Cassidy? Blow me head off?
XAVIER. Ya see, I married me daughter today! Now I don't care for the whiny little rip that much, but she's all I've got, and I don't want Carthage changin' his mind after a while. So when are ya lavin', Swane? When?
HESTER. Ya think I'm afraid of you and your auld gun. *(Puts her mouth over the barrel.)* G'wan shoot! Blow me away! Save me the bother meself. *(Goes for the trigger.)* Ya want me to do it for ya?

Another struggle, this time Xavier trying to get away from her.

XAVIER. You're a dangerous witch, Swane.
HESTER. *(Laughs at him.)* You're sweatin'. Always knew ya were yella to the bone. Don't worry, I'll be lavin' this place tonight, though not the way you or anywan else expects. Ya call me a witch, Cassidy? This is nothin', you just wait and see the real—

Enter Carthage running, enraged, shakes her violently.

CARTHAGE. The cattle! The calves! Ya burnt them all, they're roarin' in the flames! The house in ashes! A' ya gone mad altogether? The calves! A' ya gone mad?
HESTER. *(Shakes him off.)* No, I only meant what I said. I warned ya, Carthage, ya drove me to it.
XAVIER. A hundred year ago we'd strap ya to a stake and roast ya till your guts exploded.
CARTHAGE. That's it! I'm takin' Josie off of ya! I don't care if I've to drag ya through the courts. I'll have ya put away! I'll tell all about your brother! I don't care!
HESTER. Tell them! And tell them your own part in it too while you're at it! Don't you threaten me with Josie! This pervert has just been gropin' me with his gun and you want Josie round him—

XAVIER. The filthy lies of her—

HESTER. Bringin' a child on a honeymoon, what are ya at, Carthage? Well, I won't let ya use Josie to fill in the silences between yourself and Caroline Cassidy—

XAVIER. She's beyond reasonin' with, if she was mine I'd cut that tinker tongue from her mouth, I'd brand her lips, I'd—

CARTHAGE. (*Exploding at Xavier.*) Would you just go back to the weddin' and lave us alone, stop interferin'? If ya'd only let me handle it all the way I wanted to, but, no, ya had to push and bring the weddin' forward to avoid your taxes, just lave us alone, will ya!

XAVIER. I will and gladly. You're a fiasco, Kilbride, like all the Kilbrides before ya, ya can't control a mere woman, ya'll control nothin'. I'm havin' serious doubts about signin' over me farm—

CARTHAGE. Keep your bloody farm, Cassidy. I have me own. I'm not your scrubber boy. There's other things besides land.

XAVIER. There's nothin' besides land, boy, nothin'! And a real farmer would never think otherwise.

CARTHAGE. Just go back to the weddin', I'll follow ya in a while and we can try hammerin' out our differences.

XAVIER. Can we? (*Exits.*)

HESTER. All's not well in paradise.

CARTHAGE. All'd be fine if I could do away with you.

HESTER. If ya just let me stay I'll cause no more trouble. I'll move into the caravan with Josie. In time ya may be glad to have me around. I've been your greatest friend around here, Carthage, doesn't that count for nothin' now?

CARTHAGE. I'm not havin' me daughter livin' in a caravan!

HESTER. There was a time you loved this caravan.

CARTHAGE. Will ya just stop tryin to drag up them years! It won't work!

HESTER. Ya promised me things! Ya built that house for me. Ya wanted me to see how normal people lived. And I went along with ya again' me better judgement. All I ever wanted was to be by the Bog of Cats. A modest want when compared with the wants of others. Just let me stay here in the caravan.

CARTHAGE. And have the whole neighbourhood makin' a laughin'stock of me?

HESTER. That's not why ya won't let me stay. You're ashamed of your part in me brother's death, aren't ya?

CARTHAGE. I had no part in it!

HESTER. You're afraid I'll tell everywan what ya done. I won't. I wouldn't ever, Carthage.

CARTHAGE. I done nothin' except watch!

HESTER. Ya helped me tie a stone around his waist!

CARTHAGE. He was dead by then!

HESTER. He wasn't! His pulse was still goin'!

CARTHAGE. You're only sayin' that now to torture me! Why did ya do it, Hetty? We were doin' fine till then.

HESTER. How does anywan know why they done anythin'? Somethin' evil moved in on me blood—and the fishin' knife was there in the bottom of the boat—and Bergit's Lake was wide—and I looked across the lake to me father's house and it went through me like a spear that she had a whole other life there—how could she have and I a part of her?

CARTHAGE. Ya never said any of this before—I always thought ya killed your brother for the money.

HESTER. I met his ghost tonight, ya know—

CARTHAGE. His ghost?

HESTER. Aye, a gentle ghost and so lost, and he spoke so softly to me, I didn't deserve such softness—

CARTHAGE. Ah, would you stop this talk!

HESTER. You rose in the world on his ashes! And that's what haunts ya. You look at me and all you see is Joseph Swane slidin' into Bergit's Lake again. You think doin' away with me will do away with that. It won't, Carthage. It won't. You'll remember me, Carthage, when the dust settles, when ya grow tired scourin' acres and bank balances. Ya'll remember me when ya walk them big, empty, childless rooms in Cassidy's house. Ya think now ya won't, but ya will.

CARTHAGE. Ya always had a high opinion of yourself. Aye, I'll remember ya from time to time. I'll remember ya sittin' at the kitchen table drinkin' till all hours and I'll remember the sound of the back door closin' as ya escaped for another night roamin' the bog.

HESTER. The drinkin' came after, long after you put it into your mind to lave me. If I had somewan to talk to I mightn't have drunk so hard, somewan to roam the bog with me, somewan to take away a tiny piece of this guilt I carry with me, but ya never would.

CARTHAGE. Seems I done nothin' right. Did I not?

HESTER. You want to glane lessons for your new bride. No,

Carthage, ya done nothin' right, your bullheaded pride and economy and painful advancement never moved me. What I wanted was some-wan to look me in the eye and know I was understood and not judged. You thought I had no right to ax for that. Maybe I hadn't, but the way ya used to judge me—didn't it ever occur to ya that however harshly ya judged me, I judged meself harsher? Couldn't ya ever see that?

CARTHAGE. I'm takin' Josie, Hester. I'm takin' her off of ya. It's plain as day to everywan 'cept yourself ya can't look after her. If you're wise ya'll lave it at that and not have us muckin' through the courts. I'll let ya see her from time to time.

HESTER. Take her then, take her, ya've taken everythin' else. In me stupidity I thought ya'd lave me Josie. I should've known ya always meant to take her too.

Enter Caroline with a bottle of wine.

CAROLINE. *(To Carthage.)* Oh, this is where ya are.

CARTHAGE. She's after burnin' all the livestock, the house, the sheds in ruins. I'm away up there now to see what can be salvaged. G'wan back home, I'll be there in a while. *(Exits.)*

CAROLINE. Monica said ya wanted wine, I opened it for ya.

HESTER. Take more than wine to free me from this place. Take some kind of dark sprung miracle. *(Takes the wine.)*

CARTHAGE. *(Coming back.)* Caroline, come on, come on, I don't want ya around her.

HESTER. G'wan back to your weddin' like Carthage says.

Caroline goes to exit, stops.

CAROLINE. I just wanted to say—

HESTER. What? Ya just wanted to say what?

CAROLINE. Nothin'—only I'll be very good to Josie whenever she stays with us.

HESTER. Ya better be!

CAROLINE. I won't let her out of me sight—I'll go everywhere with her—protect her from things. That's all. *(Goes to exit.)*

HESTER. Didn't ya enjoy your big weddin' day, Caroline?

CAROLINE. No, I didn't—everywan too loud and frantic—and when ya turned up in that weddin' dress, knew it should've been you—and Daddy drinkin' too much and shoutin', and Carthage gone away in himself, just watchin' it all like it had nothin' to do with him, and everywan laughin' behind me back and pityin' me. When me mother was alive, I used go into the sickroom to talk to her and she used take me into the bed beside her and she'd describe for me me weddin' day. Of how she'd be there with a big hat on her and so proud. And the weddin' was goin' to be in this big ballroom with a fountain of mermaids in the middle, instead of Daddy's idea of havin' the do at home to save money—none of it was how it was meant to be, none of it.

HESTER. Nothin' ever is, Caroline. Nothin'. I've been a long time wishin' over me mother too. For too long now I've imagined her comin' towards me across the Bog of Cats, and she would find me here standin' strong. She would see me life was complete, that I had Carthage and Josie and me own house. I so much wanted her to see that I had flourished without her and maybe then I could forgive her—Caroline, he's takin' Josie from me.

CAROLINE. He's not, he wouldn't do that, Hester.

HESTER. He's just been here tellin' me.

CAROLINE. I won't let him, I'll talk to him, I'll stand up for ya on that account.

HESTER. Ya never stood up for nothin' yet, I doubt ya'll stand up for me. Anyway, they won't listen to ya. You're only a little china bit of a girl. I could break ya aisy as a taycup or a wineglass. But I won't. Ya know why? Because I knew ya when ya were Josie's age, a scrawky little thing that hung on the scraps of my affection. Anyway, no need to break ya, you were broke a long while back.

CAROLINE. There's somethin' wrong of me, isn't there? *(Stands there, lost-looking.)*

HESTER. G'wan back to your weddin' and lave me be.

CAROLINE. I promise ya I'll do everythin' I can about Josie.

HESTER. *(Softly.)* G'wan. G'wan.

Exit Caroline. Hester stands there alone, takes a drink, goes into the caravan, comes out with a knife. She tests it for sharpness, teases it across her throat, shivers.

Come on, ya done it aisy enough to another, now it's your own turn.

Bares her throat, ready to do it. Enter Josie running, stops, sees Hester with the knife poised.

JOSIE. Mam—what's that ya've got there?

HESTER. *(Stops.)* Just an auld fishin' knife, Josie, I've had this years.

JOSIE. And what are ya doin' with it?

HESTER. Nothin', Josie, nothin'.

JOSIE. I came to say good-bye, we'll be goin' soon. *(Kisses Hester.)*

HESTER. Good-bye, sweetheart—Josie, ya won't see me again now.

JOSIE. I will so. I'm only goin' on a honeymoon.

HESTER. No, Josie, ya won't see me again because I'm goin' away too.

JOSIE. Where?

HESTER. Somewhere ya can never return from.

JOSIE. And where's that?

HESTER. Never mind. I only wanted to tell ya good-bye, that's all.

JOSIE. Well, can I go with ya?

HESTER. No ya can't.

JOSIE. Ah, Mam, I want to be where you'll be.

HESTER. Well, ya can't, because wance ya go there ya can never come back.

JOSIE. I wouldn't want to if you're not here, Mam.

HESTER. You're just bein' contrary now. Don't ya want to be with your daddy and grow up big and lovely and full of advantages I have not the power to give ya?

JOSIE. Mam, I'd be watchin' for ya all the time 'long the Bog of Cats. I'd be hopin' and waitin' and prayin' for ya to return.

HESTER. Don't be sayin' them things to me now.

JOSIE. Just take me with ya, Mam. *(Puts her arms around Hester.)*

HESTER. *(Pushing her away.)* No, ya don't understand. Go away, get away from me, g'wan now, run away from me quickly now.

JOSIE. *(Struggling to stay in contact with Hester.)* No, Mam, stop! I'm goin' with ya!

HESTER. Would ya let go!

JOSIE. *(Frantic.)* No, Mam. Please!

HESTER. Alright, alright! Shhh! *(Picks her up.)* It's alright, I'll take ya with me, I won't have ya as I was, waitin' a lifetime for some-wan to return, because they don't, Josie, they don't. It's alright. Close your eyes.

Josie closes her eyes.

Are they closed tight?
    JOSIE. Yeah.

Hester cuts Josie's throat in one savage movement.

(Softly.) Mam—Mam— *(And Josie dies in Hester's arms.)*
    HESTER. *(Whispers.)* It's because ya wanted to come, Josie.

Begins to wail, a terrible animal wail. Enter the Catwoman.

    CATWOMAN. Hester, what is it? What is it?
    HESTER. Oh, Catwoman, I knew somethin' terrible'd happen, I never thought it'd be this. *(Continues this terrible sound, barely recognizable as something human.)*
    CATWOMAN. What have ya done, Hester? Have ya harmed yourself?
    HESTER. No, not meself and yes meself.
    CATWOMAN. *(Comes over, feels around Hester, feels Josie.)* Not Josie, Hester? Not Josie? Lord on high, Hester, not the child. I thought yourself, maybe, or Carthage, but never the child. *(Runs to the edge of the stage shouting.)* Help, somewan, help! Hester Swane's after butcherin' the child! Help!

Hester walks around demented with Josie. Enter Carthage running.

    CARTHAGE. What is it, Catwoman? Hester? What's wrong with Josie? There's blood all over her.
    HESTER. *(Brandishing knife.)* Lave off, you. Lave off. I warned ya and I tould ya, would ya listen, what've I done, what've I done?

Enter Monica.

    CARTHAGE. Give her to me!
    MONICA. Sweet Jesus, Hester—
    CARTHAGE. Give her to me! You've killed her, she's killed her.
    HESTER. Yees all thought I was just goin' to walk away and lave her at yeer mercy. I almost did. But she's mine and I wouldn't have

Joan O'Hara and Olwen Fouéré in *By the Bog of Cats*
Courtesy Amelia Carr.

her waste her life dreamin' about me and yees thwartin' her with black stories against me.

CARTHAGE. You're a savage!

Enter the Ghost Fancier. Hester sees him, the others don't. He picks up the fishing knife.

HESTER. You're late, ya came too late.

CARTHAGE. What's she sayin'? What? Give her to me, come on now. *(Takes Josie off Hester.)*

HESTER. Ya won't forget me now, Carthage, and when all of this is over or half remembered and you think you've almost forgotten me again, take a walk along the Bog of Cats and wait for a purlin' wind through your hair or a soft breath be your ear or a rustle behind ya. That'll be me and Josie ghostin' ya. *(She walks towards the Ghost Fancier.)* Take me away, take me away from here.

GHOST FANCIER. Alright, my lovely.

They go into a death dance with the fishing knife, which ends plunged into Hester's heart. She falls to the ground. Exit Ghost Fancier with knife.

HESTER. *(Whispers as she dies.)* Mam—Mam—

Monica goes over to her after a while.

MONICA. Hester—she's gone—Hester—she's cut her heart out— it's lyin' there on top of her chest like some dark feathered bird.

Music. Lights.

END OF PLAY